ROUTLEDGE LIBRARY EDITIONS
DEVELOPME

AID AND INEQUALITY IN KENYA

AID AND INEQUALITY IN KENYA

British Development Assistance to Kenya

GERALD HOLTHAM

and

ARTHUR HAZLEWOOD

Volume 9

Routledge
Taylor & Francis Group
LONDON AND NEW YORK

First published in 1976

This edition first published in 2011
by Routledge
2 Park Square, Milton Park, Abingdon, Oxon, OX14 4RN

Simultaneously published in the USA and Canada
by Routledge
711 Third Avenue, New York, NY 10017

Routledge is an imprint of the Taylor & Francis Group, an informa business

First issued in paperback 2013

British Library Cataloguing in Publication Data
A catalogue record for this book is available from the British Library

ISBN 13: 978-0-415-58414-2 (Set)
eISBN 13: 978-0-203-84035-1 (Set)
ISBN 13: 978-0-415-59273-4 (Volume 9)
eISBN 13: 978-0-203-84016-0 (Volume 9)
ISBN 13: 978-0-415-84598-4 (Pbk)

Publisher's Note
The publisher has gone to great lengths to ensure the quality of this reprint but points out that some imperfections in the original copies may be apparent.

Disclaimer
The publisher has made every effort to trace copyright holders and welcomes correspondence from those they have been unable to contact.

AID AND INEQUALITY IN KENYA

BRITISH DEVELOPMENT ASSISTANCE TO KENYA

GERALD HOLTHAM and ARTHUR HAZLEWOOD

CROOM HELM LONDON
in association with
THE OVERSEAS DEVELOPMENT INSTITUTE

First published 1976

Croom Helm Ltd, 2-10 St John's Road, London SW11

ISBN 0–85664–344–0

CONTENTS

LIST OF TABLES

ACKNOWLEDGEMENTS

Our thanks must first go to the Social Science Research Council which has financed the research for this book, as it did the companion studies on British aid to Malawi and to Botswana, Lesotho and Swaziland. We are indebted to the Director of the Oxford University Institute of Economics and Statistics for permission for one of us to devote his time to the study, and to the Director of the Institute for Development Studies, University of Nairobi, for providing accommodation and a congenial working atmosphere during our stay in Nairobi.

Our other acknowledgements for help we have received in carrying out the study must be brief, not because we have few debts of gratitude but because we have so many. A large number of civil servants of various nationalities in Kenya and others at the Ministry of Overseas Development, UK, gave of their time and experience and we have had the benefit of conversations and correspondence with academic colleagues in both countries. We should like to thank them all. The research also had the benefit of an Advisory Committee of eminent academics, administrators and businessmen chaired by Professor Ian Little, and colleagues at the Overseas Development Institute, headed by the Director, Robert Wood, took a lively interest throughout. We should like to thank them. Gratitude is also due to the secretarial staff at ODI who typed, reproduced, collated and despatched numerous drafts. For errors of fact and judgement that remain the authors are solely responsible, having only the refuge of co-authorship, that they can unhesitatingly blame each other.

INTRODUCTION

Our task has been to describe and assess the implications of aid for the economic development of independent Kenya and to suggest conclusions for policy, particularly British policy. Economic development cannot be assessed without making value judgements. Even after these have been made it is necessary to remember that there is no such thing as an economy. Movements in variables commonly regarded as economic have effects that are commonly classified as political or social; these in turn will certainly affect economic developments. To take a narrowly economistic view is often to misunderstand patterns of causation. So in saying something about the influence of aid on the economic face of Kenyan society we have tried to keep the administrative and political faces in focus. Even so, we despair of taking everything properly into account.

We can think of four ways in which we might have proceeded: firstly we could have analysed economic, political, social and aid statistics and attempted to infer causation; secondly, we could have made case studies and attempted to generalise; thirdly, we could have talked to lots of people, studied statements of policy and administrative procedures, collected theories, impressions, anecdotes, opinions with supporting facts and attempted to form a coherent view – a sort of judicial approach; fourthly we could have prejudged the issue and collected selected facts to support our predetermined conclusion.

In writings on aid and development, the last is quite a popular technique. Indeed, it has been claimed to be the only respectable technique on the grounds that no one can really be disinterested and objective and an approach that claims to be so can only be sinister ideological apologetics. We are reluctant to descend into this abyss of relativism. Through the mists of conditioning and (after all – distant) self-interest it is sometimes possible to identify a spade as a spade for all practical purposes and to secure agreement in calling it such. One can then say whether one likes it or not. In any case, we had (and in some cases still have) insufficient self-confidence in the correctness of our judgements, to make this fourth a sustainable approach.

The difficulties with the first approach in studying aid to Kenya are more than the usual ones of sparse and unreliable data and the compatibility of tests of statistical significance with more than one theory of causation. In Kenya the size of aid flows in money terms has not been great relative to many other economic aggregates which are subject to other influences. It is, therefore, impossible to study the latter and infer anything, even probabilistically, about the effects of the former without a properly specified model of the whole political economy. Furthermore, statistical aggregates disguise components of considerable heterogeneity and this is particularly true of aid statistics. One senior adviser's salary may be insignificant macroeconomically but his influence conceivably could be out of all proportion to it. Parameters will therefore be unstable and hypothesis-testing likely to yield consistently negative conclusions. That probably just reflects the impossibility of making valid high-level generalisations about aid. Data, however, are certainly inadequate for more refined statistical analysis of less general propositions. Statistical analysis can in our view be no more than a check on conclusions arrived at by other means.

We have relied therefore largely on the second and third approaches. These methods are, of course, far from ideal. Case studies can be of special cases that do not generalise and anyway it may not be possible to get an impression of the characteristics of a wood from a study of single trees. Neither is the truth always anything like a correctly weighted summary of people's perceptions, even if one could weight accurately and people related their perceptions with unvarying truthfulness.

Other methodological problems confront any approach. Many of the propositions in this study must be based on 'counterfactual hypotheses' that, by their nature, cannot be tested. A lot of argument about aid is possible even if people agree in some minimal sense about what it did, because they can fall out over what would have happened without it. Often those most vociferous in accusing others of disguised value judgements are guilty here; they do not distinguish between the most probable outcome in the absence of aid and their preferred outcome. Hence aid to the same country can be said by the radical left to have reinforced dependency and postponed socialism, by a radical liberal to have pre-empted indigenous capitalism causing centralisation and pauperism, and by an aid-employed bureaucrat to have prevented economic stagnation and political chaos. We have heard all these views expressed about Kenya, the first and third more than the second.

We shall now admit a bias in our perception: we are sceptical of any cataclysmic view. Societies are organisms not usually given to violent changes of course as a result of relatively minor stimuli. Looking at aid in a 'partial equilibrium' framework, our money would be on the proposition that not one of these views correctly describes the workings of aid to Kenya although aid has had effects described, and exaggerated, in each one of them. We can only hope that this bias has not blinded us to the truth on occasions when aid was critical. The perception is, of course, partly the result of our strictly limited approach. We really have been concerned with the aid relationship and the influence of aid rather than with the whole complex of relations between Britain and Kenya. Other elements of the relationship have been considered only intermittently where they seemed to impinge directly on aid. This, we believe, is justifiable. Whatever the genesis of aid it is now administered in Britain and elsewhere by a distinct government department that in important day-to-day decisions enjoys considerable autonomy. It is possible therefore to study the effects of these decisions separately within the larger framework. Even those people, for example, who are satisfied that Britain's relationship with Kenya is one of steady exploitation may like to know whether aid is merely part of the medicine, or the sugar around the pill.

At this point we shall not define our terms – on the grounds that there is a considerable consensus about the denotation of 'aid' even if people cannot agree about a statement of its connotation. We have dealt mainly with the 'aid' programme to Kenya administered by the Ministry of Overseas Development, ignoring both non-governmental aid by voluntary agencies and some general ODM activities like financing research, and students visiting Britain, which benefit Kenya along with other less developed countries (ldcs). 'Development' is, admittedly, more difficult than 'aid' and we have sometimes used this piece of shorthand. Where serious ambiguity was possible we have tried to circumvent it by discussing positivistically the effects of aid and then saying whether we like them, rather than disputing whether aid has been conducive to 'development'.

In pursuit of the approach outlined the book has the following plan: the first two chapters provide a background to the remainder of the study. Chapter One gives a description of the main features of the Kenyan economy at the time of independence; Chapter Two relates and discusses the progress of the economy since independence and describes and interprets Kenya government policy. The next four chapters contain the bulk of the study's findings. Chapter Three gives the main facts of British capital aid and technical assistance, and brief summaries of the aid of some other donors and attempts to refine official statistics. Chapter Four is an historical discussion of British aid policy and a description of the current British policy stance and administrative arrangements, with some comparison with other donors. Chapter Five contains a detailed account and analysis of the Land Transfer Programme, quantitatively and historically the most important part of British aid, and case studies of two other aided projects. Chapter Six analyses the concept of fungibility and its implications for aid evaluation and then discusses in turn aid's effects on Kenyan public finance, development policy, the Kenyan administration and the Kenyan political scene. It concludes with judgements of aid's effects on income levels and income equality in Kenya. The last two chapters are concerned with the implications of the study's findings. Chapter Seven suggests the policy implications for donors, particularly Britain. Chapter Eight reviews some academic controversies about aid in the light of the study.

1 THE BACKGROUND[1]

Kenya is no longer *White Man's Country*[2] but its economic structure, its economic and social policies, and the form and function of the international aid it has received and is receiving are deeply affected by its history as a land of European and Asian settlement. Before Kenya achieved national independence in December 1963, a fundamental determinant of the nature of its economy and of the policies of its government was the existence of wealthy and – by tropical African standards – relatively large non-African communities.

By the time of independence, changes had been in progress for several years, and 1959 and 1960 were the last years in which the situation had not been deeply influenced by the approach of majority rule.[3] In 1960 the total population was estimated to be 8.1m. of which 7.8m. were Africans and 169,000 Asians. The European population numbered 61,000. There are no adequate data of the racial distribution of money income, but from all the evidence it is clear that, despite the overwhelming numerical preponderance of Africans, non-Africans received a high proportion of the total. Tax returns show 92 per cent of Europeans receiving incomes of over £400 p.a. while only 0.5 per cent of Africans were in this income group.[4] Eighty per cent of the value of the marketed produce of agriculture came from the European-owned farms and estates; 55 per cent of the total wage-bill accrued to non-Africans, though they amounted to only 10 per cent of the labour force; profits from manufacturing and trade were received almost entirely by non-African individuals or companies.

Pre-independence agriculture was characterised above all by the division of the land between Europeans and Africans. Asians were largely excluded from the ownership of agricultural land, and Africans were prohibited from acquiring land in the 'White Highlands', which by the Agricultural Ordinance of 1955 became officially invested with the more neutral title of the Scheduled Areas. These European-owned Scheduled Areas occupied some 7½m. acres, about half of which was suitable for arable farming, the remainder being limited to pastoral use by lack of rainfall. The African lands – the Reserves, or Native Trust Lands – totalled about 130m. acres, but only about 18m. were suitable for agriculture. Low rainfall restricted the use of the remainder of the non-scheduled areas to grazing, nine-tenths of it being classed as 'suited only to poor quality ranching or wild life exploitation'.[5]

Farming in the Scheduled Areas included estate production of permanent crops for export – coffee, tea, sisal – and livestock ranching, as well as mixed farming. European mixed farming had at one time concentrated on cereals, but by 1960 efforts made after the Second World War to develop and diversify mixed farming had achieved considerable success. Farming in the African areas was overwhelmingly for the household consumption of the farmers, not for sale, and although cash-cropping was increasing in importance, perhaps only about 15 per cent of total output was marketed. In consequence, some 80 per cent of the total marketed output of agriculture came from the European areas. Livestock and dairy produce accounted, roughly equally, for about one-quarter of total sales from the scheduled areas; coffee, tea and sisal contributed 45 per cent; cereals, mainly wheat, and to a lesser extent maize, provided another 15 per cent of the total, and the remainder of total sales was made up of a number of crops, including cotton, tobacco, pyrethrum, sugar and oilseeds.

Livestock, together with a very small value of dairy produce, also accounted for about one-quarter of sales from the non-scheduled areas, and coffee, a crop which Africans had only recently been permitted to cultivate on any scale,[6] accounted for another one-quarter; 14 per cent was produced by cereals, mainly maize, and a number of minor crops accounted for the remainder of sales, of which the most important was cotton.

The limited extent of the shift that had taken place in African agriculture towards cash-cropping by 1960 was to an important degree caused by the administrative and legal restraints on such development, notably those on the cultivation of coffee. It was also partly the result of the limited development of transport in the African areas, and of the fact that Kenya's highly developed and controlled structure of marketing and credit focused on the Scheduled Areas, as did the research and other agricultural services. Although the government agricultural service dealt with both African and European farmers, the statutory boards, committees and organisations concerned with marketing, mainly administered by the farmers themselves, were primarily concerned with the Scheduled Areas. It was natural for European settlers to establish European-type institutions to serve European settler interests. Until late in the colonial period, the possibility of radical developments in African agriculture and of African participation in the modern economy, except as employees of Europeans, cannot have seemed to most Europeans to be matters of any practical importance. A great divide between the European and African economies was an inevitable consequence of settlement by Europeans concerned to create and maintain their own particular standards and way of life.

Substantial changes in land tenure and in the occupation of land began towards the end of the colonial period. They were a response to a belief in the inability of the African reserves under existing tenure systems and agricultural practices to accommodate the expanding African population. There were two kinds of change. One was the transfer of land from European ownership and the settlement of African farmers on it. The other was the 'commercialisation' of African-occupied lands by means of consolidation and adjudication and registration of title. Both kinds of change were advocated in 1955 by the East Africa Royal Commission, the analysis and recommendations of which were described as 'Adam Smith in East Africa' and had already become government policy. The Royal Commission proposed the abandonment of the 'tribal approach' to land, including the 'racial approach to the Highlands question', and prescribed 'individualisation of land ownership and mobility in the transfer of land'.

The commercialisation of land had been a feature of the Swynnerton Plan[7] of 1954, which argued that the reform of African land tenure was a prerequisite of agricultural improvement. Consolidation, enclosure and registration of title, it was argued, would make credit obtainable for improvements and enable progressive farmers to acquire more land. The African lands would be enabled to move away from being overwhelmingly devoted to production for subsistence towards a commercial agriculture:

> able, energetic or rich Africans will be able to acquire more land and bad or poor farmers less, creating a landed and a landless class. This is a normal step in the evolution of a country.

There had already been some individualisation of land-holding in different parts of the country, even in the absence of machinery to adjudicate and register titles, and landlessness was not unknown in traditional society. The already existing pressures on the African lands in Central Province had been raised by the forced return of Kikuyu to their home areas from other parts of the country (and from elsewhere in East Africa) under the Emergency Regulations introduced in 1952 to combat the Mau Mau rebellion. In the White Highlands a class of landless Africans had become established in the form of squatters on European farms, who provided wage-labour and were allowed to cultivate some land for their own subsistence. The political circumstances were favourable for government action. Under the Emergency Regulations many African politicians who might have used the changes in tenure as a stick to beat the government were in detention; in parts of the country people who had formerly lived scattered on their holdings had been gathered together in villages, making consolidation and redistribution of the land easier; money was available to support policies which might help to defeat and to remove the causes of the rebellion; and the authorities were able, if necessary, to exert force to make people conform.

Consolidation of land and registration of title began in 1955 and by the year before independence about half the land of high potential had been consolidated and enclosed, and about half of that had been registered. Registration had, in fact, been completed in Central Province, but had not proceeded significantly elsewhere, where the pressures from the rebellion were less severe. The land tenure changes were supported by credit and extension services and by the final removal of restrictions on the growth of cash crops. It is probable that the removal of these restrictions, particularly those on the cultivation of coffee, was by far the most important cause of the increase in marketed production by small farmers. The value of produce sold from small holdings increased from £5.1m. in 1955 to £9.5m. in 1960 and to £11.6m. in 1963. The contribution of coffee to total sales increased from 6 per cent to 27 per cent,[8] as the large-scale investment in coffee in the late 1950s came into full production. However, the large farms retained their dominant position in production for the market. In 1963, the large farms still accounted for as much as 78 per cent of total sales, compared with 86 per cent in 1955. The large farms also remained the source of the bulk of agricultural exports. Nevertheless, by the end of the colonial period Kenya had made decisive progress towards the establishment of a peasant cash-crop agriculture in what had been the African Trust Lands.

In 1959 it was decided by the colonial Kenya government that the racial allocation of land should be abandoned, and this decision paved the way for African ownership of land in the White Highlands. Schemes for transferring European farms to Africans began to be devised in 1960. The new policy marked a sharp change of direction, and seems all the more radical in the light of the fact that the settlement of new European immigrants in the Highlands was among the most important projects of the first post-war development plan. The fundamental principle of the land transfer schemes was that farms were to be purchased from Europeans and sold to Africans. They were not schemes for expropriation – there is a view that farms were over-priced[9] – and were designed as much to reassure the Europeans who remained as to transfer the land of those who departed to African small holders. At the time, the vital importanceof large-scale farming to the economy of Kenya was accepted doctrine,[10] and the preservation of large-scale farming as a major economic sector was a fundamental consideration in the design of the Land Transfer Programme.

External aid was sought for land purchase and settlement. Funds were raised from the World Bank (IBRD) and the Commonwealth Development Corporation (CDC – Colonial Development Corporation, as it then was) for the purchase of farms and their settlement at a 'low density' to provide annual incomes, in addition to subsistence and loan charges, of £100 and more. The following year the UK government agreed to provide funds on loan terms for land purchase, and this programme was expanded at the end of 1962 into what became known as the Million Acre Scheme. 'High density' settlement was planned under this scheme with the intention that settlers should be able to obtain a net annual income of between £25 and £70. By the time of independence, 236,000 hectares had been purchased and ten thousand families settled under the Million Acre Scheme, and a further thousand or so families had been settled on low-density schemes. Small-scale African farming had been firmly established in the Highlands.

The influx of Africans into large farming had begun, but remained unimportant until after independence.

The existence of the non-African population, both as producers and consumers, provided the initial stimulus for the development of manufacturing and processing in Kenya. The constraints on African monetary agriculture limited the possibility of a manufacturing industry to serve a largely African market. The earliest developments were in the processing of the products of European agriculture, but as the size of the market expanded, particularly during and after the Second World War, and with the increased use of tariff protection, the manufacturing sector of the economy became more diversified. It was not only the European and Asian communities of Kenya which provided a market for Kenya manufactures. Kenya had for long been associated in a common market with Tanganyika and Uganda, and the early impetus to the development of industry in Kenya resulting from its relatively large non-African population put it in a strong position to capture the markets of its common market partners. By the late 1950s Kenya had become the manufacturing centre for the whole of East Africa, and something like 20 per cent of the output of its manufacturing industry was sold to Tanganyika and Uganda. Whatever the origin of the market for Kenya manufactures, by the time of independence the African market was of great importance. A number of products had a widespread market among Africans – shoes, cigarettes, beer and grain-milling products, for instance.

In the middle 1950s manufacturing and construction accounted for about 20 per cent of GDP in the monetary economy (as large, in fact, as that of agriculture and livestock production), and manufacturing alone for 13 per cent. Industry was still heavily oriented towards agricultural processing. Food, beverages and tobacco industries together produced one-half of the gross production of manufacturing industry.[11] Repairing transport equipment was an important activity (11 per cent of gross production) fostered by the growth in the number of motor vehicles and by the location in Kenya of the railways and harbours and airways headquarters for the whole of East Africa. The ownership of industry was divided between Kenyan Europeans (grain milling, dairy produce, pig products, sisal products, canning), East African Asians (sugar milling, bakery products), and what are now known as 'multinationals' (tobacco, footwear, pharmaceuticals, cement, paints, soap), but with expansion and a scarcity of capital in the locally-owned firms the participation of the multinationals was increasing.

The construction industry had received a great stimulus during the war. The stimulus continued into the post-war years with the demands of development plans, which were heavily oriented towards public works, continued military expenditure, construction arising from the Emergency, and the expansion of facilities for the East African common services. Much of the industry was in the hands of Kenyan Asian firms, but international construction companies were becoming of increasing importance by the time of independence.

Wholesale and retail trade accounted for 17 per cent of gross domestic product recorded in the monetary economy in 1960. Large-scale domestic commerce in exporting, importing and in the distribution of domestic production was divided between European firms, some of them branches of international companies, and Asians. Asians were widely engaged also in small-scale retailing, and they were to be found in the smallest and remotest centres. Africans had hardly begun to enter large-scale commerce and their trading activities were carried on in a very small way and largely in the rural areas.

The existence of the non-African communities, particularly the Europeans, was responsible for the development of technical, financial and government services to a much greater extent than might have been expected from the low average level of income in the population as a whole. European residents demanded public and private services appropriate to their own level of income. European agriculture was associated with a highly developed structure of marketing and advisory services. The position of Kenya at the centre of the common arrangements in East Africa substantially increased the activities of government. These factors account for the remarkable development of the city of Nairobi. Its attractions were cumulative. Originally a railway construction encampment, it became the seat of government for Kenya and for those activities (notably in transport and communications) administered in common for the whole of East Africa. It developed as the centre for the provision of services to agriculture and manufacturing, and as the location of most manufacturing activity, and became the natural location for the headquarters of international firms entering the East African market. By the time of independence it had long been established as a centre relevant to a level of income and way of life totally different from that of the vast majority of the population of Kenya.

The part played by Africans – except as wage-earners – in manufacturing, construction and trade was of little importance. Of course, the smallest enterprises escape the statistical net (surveys of manufacturing, for instance, were confined to firms with five or more employees) and so understate the role of African business activity. But African participation and initiative in any but the smallest manufacturing, construction and trading activities remained negligible until the end of the colonial period.

The inheritance of independent Kenya was, therefore, an economy the modern sector of which had been fashioned largely in response to the existence of a non-African population. Change had already gone some way in agriculture, although not far enough to destroy the central position of the former White Highlands. In other sectors of the economy change had hardly begun. In the few years preceding independence the economic growth of the post-war period was halted by the uncertainties of the future. There was a sharp downturn in construction; employment declined; capital flowed out; the government's finances deteriorated and Britain had to provide grants-in-aid. In the event, many of the fears proved groundless.[12]

Jomo Kenyatta had declared that:

> The Government of an independent Kenya will not be a gangster government. Those who have been panicky . . . can now rest assured that the future African government . . . will not deprive them of their property or rights of ownership. We will encourage investors . . . to come to Kenya . . . to bring prosperity to this country.[13]

When economic growth began again it was firmly within the structure established in the colonial period. The years since independence have seen many changes, but equally noteworthy has been the continuity with the past.

NOTES

1. In writing this chapter we had the advantage of seeing in advance the contribution of Michael McWilliam, 'The Kenya Economy, 1945 to 1963', to Volume 3 of the *Oxford History of East Africa*, which has subsequently been published.

   London, Chatto and Windus, 1968.

3. The European population reached its peak in 1960. It had increased from less than 30,000 in 1945, and by 1961 it had already fallen to 59,000. In valuing European farms under the Land Transfer Programme (see Chapter Five) land prices in 1959 were taken as a basis.
4. See *Development Plan 1966-1970*, Government Printer, Nairobi, 1966, p. 29.
5. *Kenya African Agricultural Sample Census, 1960/61*, Part I, pp. 1-2. In 1960 there were only 3,609 holdings in the Scheduled Areas. 278,000 Africans were employed on these holdings as wage-earners, as were 1,905 Europeans and 866 Asians. The vast majority of Kenya's nearly 8m. Africans lived in the non-scheduled areas.
6. In 1954 coffee accounted for less than 4 per cent of the value of sales of produce from small farms.
7. *A Plan to Intensify the Development of African Agriculture in Kenya*, Nairobi, Government Printer, 1955.
8. The increase in coffee production was the major reason for the growth in the value of small holders' total sales:

   Coffee production in non-scheduled areas ('000 tons)

1955/56	0.8
1960/61	7.9
1963/64	15.3

9. It is said that some farmers sold out, bought another farm and sold out again, which suggests that they got a good bargain.
10. The view is still held today, though it may receive a jolt from the need to provide funds for the rehabilitation of certain large farms. A loan has been provided for this purpose by the IBRD. (See *The Standard*, 19 August 1975.)
11. *Survey of Industrial Production*, 1957.

12. Though not those of the Asian population, particularly of Asians who did not acquire Kenya citizenship.
13. Reprinted in Jomo Kenyatta, *Suffering without Bitterness*, Nairobi, East African Publishing House, 1968, p. 157.

2 AIMS AND ACHIEVEMENTS SINCE INDEPENDENCE

The economic policies of independent Kenya have been essentially pragmatic, unencumbered by much in the way of overt ideology. To foster the entrepreneurial society and to increase the role of Africans within it is, perhaps, the most summary form in which the general aims of policy can be expressed. Formally, the policy is labelled African Socialism. *Sessional Paper No. 10 of 1965, On African Socialism and its Application to Planning in Kenya* defined the social and economic objectives of the Kenya government and outlined the policies through which these objectives were to be pursued. The policies set out there have been repeated and elaborated in the various Development Plans and in other documents.

African Socialism is not a programme for public ownership on ideological grounds. Nationalisation, the Sessional Paper declared,

> will be used only where the national security is threatened, higher social benefits can be obtained, or productive resources are seriously and clearly being misused, when other means of control are ineffective and financial resources permit, or where a service is vital to the people and must be provided by the Government as a part of its responsibility to the nation.[1]

It has been suggested, in fact, that Kenya is committed not to Socialism but to a capitalist mode of production, and that African Socialism is a 'verbal pretence'. The idea of African Socialism is best seen as that of softening the impact of the market economy by bringing into play the 'mutual social responsibility' which operated in traditional African society. However, there is little evidence that there has been any serious attempt to elaborate this line of thought or to give it practical application. Certainly, the policy of African Socialism has involved no revolutionary break with the past; great changes there have been, but the thread of continuity has been strong.

The Agricultural Sector

It is in agriculture that change has been the most dramatic, while continuity has, nevertheless, been marked. The changes in the ownership of land and in the nature of land tenure during the decade after independence resulted from the application and intensification of the policies adopted before independence had been achieved. Agricultural marketing arrangements and price-fixing policies betray the strong influence of the past.

The policies initiated in 1960 under which European farms were to be transferred to African farmers continued to operate. There was to be no expropriation and no free land.[2] The programme for the purchase of European mixed farms suitable for subdivision into small holdings was the subject of a series of aid agreements between the Kenya and British governments. The transfer of land under the Million Acre Scheme and the low-density scheme, begun before independence, was completed by 1970. A minor additional programme (the so-called *Harambee* scheme) of relatively low-density settlement was carried out on land transferred under the 1965 and subsequent aid agreements. A new form of settlement was important for a time when the Kenya government recognised the need to make some provision for squatters. In the Development Plan for 1970-74 squatter settlement, renamed *Haraka*, had a substantial place. The intention to establish further *Haraka* settlements was abandoned in 1971, though it is proposed in the Development Plan for 1974-78 to put more money into the existing settlements. They had been designed to yield little more than subsistence for the settlers, who had been provided with few facilities and resources. No additional land was purchased for *Haraka* settlements as the squatters were mainly on farms which had been abandoned or from which the owners had been evicted for neglecting them.[3] The *Haraka* schemes were seen by the government as a political necessity rather than as a desirable form of economic development, though there is a view that they soon became indistinguishable from high-density settlements under the more elaborate and costly schemes.

There have been problems with the settlement schemes, particularly in obtaining loan repayments from settlers. Little more than half the amount due in loan repayments has been collected, and most settlers are in arrears. To alleviate the problem it is proposed to offer settlers the option of converting their freehold title into a leasehold title from the government.[4] During the process of settlement under the Million Acre and *Harambee* schemes there was some disruption of production, but production recovered and considerably greater outputs per acre are being obtained from the settlement areas than before settlement. There remains a need to improve credit facilities, extension services, and roads and water supplies, despite the fact that settlers are much better supplied with these services than small farmers in other areas.

In 1971, in fact, it was decided to abandon the old form of high-density settlement, undertaken by the subdivision of large farms. Its place was taken by co-operative or *Shirika* settlement in which it is hoped that the avoidance of subdivision into individual holdings will bring greater efficiency. However, it cannot be assumed that there will no further settlement on subdivided farms because the Development Plan 1974-78 declares that 'most farm products can be produced very successfully on small-scale farms. In the long run, therefore, a considerable amount of land used for large-scale farms will be subdivided.'[5]

Not all the transfer of land from Europeans to Africans has taken place through official settlement schemes. There has been substantial direct purchase by African individuals, partnerships and companies. The funds for these purchases have come from private institutions, from the Agricultural Finance Corporation, and to a significant extent from private accumulations of wealth, often acquired outside agriculture. The purchasers have often had their primary interest elsewhere, in business, politics, and the civil service.[6] Some of these new large-scale farmers lacked both experience and capital, and a programme of rehabilitation is being embarked upon, with the aid of funds from the World Bank. The Development Plan says that 'where appropriate the Ministry will encourage subdivision of these farms into smaller more manageable units'.[7]

The statistics confirm the success of the programmes for the transfer of land from Europeans to Africans. Some 3.5m. acres of the Scheduled Areas were under mixed farming before land transfer got under way; rather more than one-third of this area has been transferred under settlement schemes. Something over two million acres of mixed farming land remain in 1,540 large farms (1972 figures). Of these large farms, 1,234 embracing about half of the land area of the remaining large farms, are in African ownership, either individuals, partnerships or companies; a few more, where special circumstances prevailed, have been taken into state ownership.[8] More than two-thirds of the European mixed farming area had, therefore, passed into African hands by the end of the first decade of independence. There had in addition been some African purchases of estates and ranches.

There remained outside African ownership nearly 300 mixed farms, covering an area of about one million acres, large commercial ranches, and some 1,500 tea, coffee and sugar estates, mostly owned by companies. Commercial agriculture by non-African companies has not proved to be incompatible with the development of African agriculture, however, and the two have been linked by associating small holders with company estates, in particular where access to a factory is essential to producers, as in the cultivation of sugar-cane.[9] Small-holder and estate production have also been associated, though less successfully and perhaps with less concern for success, in the production of pineapples for canning.

In addition to the settlement schemes, the other leg of the land reform programme, the adjudication, consolidation, and registration of land so as to replace communal by individual tenure in the former African areas, proceeded rapidly after independence. In 1963 only 5 per cent of the registrable land had been adjudicated; at the end of 1973 adjudication and registration had been completed on 20 per cent of the land and the process was under way on a further 20 per cent. Indeed, there is a view that the procedures are being applied indiscriminately, so as to include areas where they are inappropriate, as in areas devoted to migratory pastoralism.

No simple comparison is possible between the quantitative importance of settlement on the one hand, and development of the former African

Trust Lands on the other, by which the significance of settlement can be judged. In terms of population, of course, the contribution of settlement seems tiny. It has been estimated that there are about 1.7m. rural households and 1.2m. settled agricultural holdings in Kenya. About 60,000 families have been settled on former European farms. However, despite the difficulty of statistical comparisons, it is evident that development of the traditional African lands is fundamental to any progress. Indeed, by 1965 there was official disillusionment with settlement, and *Sessional Paper No. 10* declared, stating a view that had already received some consideration, that:

> We have to consider what emphasis should be given in future to settlement as against development in African areas.
>
> The same money spent on land consolidation, survey, registration and development in the African areas would increase productivity and output on four to six times as many acres and benefit four to six times as many Africans. It therefore follows that if our resources must be used to achieve maximum growth we must give priority in the future to development in the former African areas.[10]

Settlement can be a safety-valve, relieving the pressures exerted by the landless, but it is doubtful if it can take place on a sufficient scale to be more than a safety-valve, and to make a serious contribution towards solving the problem of landlessness. Nevertheless, the political necessity of further settlement as an obvious aid to the landless remains, and indeed is strengthened by the 'individualisation' of land in place of customary tenure in the former African lands.

Although the land reform in the African areas has been a major change, it would be wrong to see it as the fundamental cause of progress in small-scale agriculture. Progress has not been confined to areas where the land reform has been carried furthest. In any case, the fragmentation of holdings was not a serious problem in many areas, so that substantial benefits could not be expected from consolidation, and in areas where consolidation was carried out at an early date an informal fragmentation has subsequently taken place. Much of the benefit of the tenure changes was expected to arise from their effect on the availability of credit to the farmers. 'The need to develop and invest requires credit,' *Sessional Paper No. 10* argued, 'and a credit economy rests heavily on a system of land titles and registration. The ownership of land must, therefore, be made more definite and explicit.'[11] The political difficulty of dispossessing small farmers[12] must cast doubt on the value of title to land as a security for credit and, in fact, there has not been a large influx of capital into small-scale farming. The Agricultural Finance Corporation provides credit to virtually all large-scale farmers but to little more than one per cent of small farmers, and only about one-fifth of its total lending is to the small-farm sector.[13] The progress in small-scale agriculture has occurred through the expansion of cash crops, particularly coffee, which followed the relaxation and eventual abolition of the restrictions that had existed on their cultivation by African farmers.

That there has been greatly increased participation of Africans in monetary agriculture cannot be doubted. The output of the large-farm sector has increased and the African share has become substantial.[14] The marketed output from small farms has increased five-fold in value in the decade since independence, and the share of small farms in marketed agricultural output has risen from a quarter to a half of the total.

It would not be universally accepted that the increase in African participation and African money income in the aggregate is sufficient evidence on which to pronounce the policy towards agriculture and land tenure a success. It can be argued, as it was argued in the report of the ILO mission in 1972,[15] that the changes have perpetuated and, indeed, increased the inequalities in the distribution of income and wealth which were characteristic of colonial Kenya, merely eliminating – or at least reducing – the racial dimension in the inequality. The broad distribution of population has not been fundamentally affected by the removal of the racial barriers to land ownership and by settlement on European farms. The African population is still densely settled in what were the African reserves, and the ratio of population to land is still much higher in those areas than in the former Scheduled Areas. When the agriculture of the White Highlands was the overwhelmingly important component of monetary agriculture, it is not surprising that the arrangements for marketing, credit, price-fixing, extension services and transport were focused on its needs. It has been argued that these services are still focused on the large farms, and will continue to be agents of inequality until there is a major reorientation of their activities.

The commercialisation of land might have been expected – as it clearly was expected in the Swynnerton Plan – to lead to the accumulation of large holdings by some farmers and the loss of land by others through the operation of the market, once the original consolidation and adjudication had been made. There is no statistical evidence by which it can be determined whether or not such a process is taking place. It is reasonable to expect that the growth of population would lead to an increase in the number of landless even without the changes in tenure in the African areas; indeed, it had already done so before land adjudication and registration were far advanced. Although the extent to which the operation of the market has displaced people from the land is not known, it is clear that a trend towards differentiation within the African population accelerated in the years following independence. This is clear, if for no other reason, from the fact that some large African farmers have become established by succeeding, in effect, in stepping into the shoes of departing Europeans, and, as was remarked above, these farmers often have outside interests in business, politics, or the civil service.

Among the small holders, the impressionistic conclusion of the ILO Mission was that about 225,000, or one-fifth of all small holders, have been able to benefit sufficiently from settlement and land registration to achieve rapidly rising incomes; they have become significant employers of labour so as to give themselves more leisure and more time to engage in business and salaried employment. The report of the ILO Mission suggests that a further quarter million small holders have been able to commercialise their activities enough to achieve incomes of between £60 and £110 a year, but have been unable to do more because they cultivate too little land or too poor land or lack knowledge or capital. The majority of farming families – some 620,000 – have, according to the ILO Mission, benefited from the developments since independence only marginally, if at all. These families have an income from farming of less than £60 p.a. Some have income from other sources – remittances from relatives working in the towns, for example – but some can have no additional income; some are squatters on land they do not own, and some are landless. But this is only one view, and other observers would say that the great majority of Kenya's rural population has become significantly better-off since independence. On this view, the growth of economic differentiation and inequality within the African population has not proved incompatible with an improvement in the absolute standards of the mass of rural families.

Whatever the truth about the absolute living standards of the population, the growth of economic differentiation should be no surprise. The policies enunciated in the Swynnerton Plan and by the East Africa Royal Commission were designed to give the 'progressive farmer' scope to exercise his talents, and to help those most able to help themselves, rather than those most in need. The application of these policies is a major example of the continuity which has been a feature of the post-independence years. It is easy to believe that they have fostered the growth of inequality of income and wealth within the African population. They do not necessarily stand condemned by that fact; greater inequality may be accompanied by, and indeed be a condition of, a general rise in living standards. It would be a more serious reflection on the success of the policies if the improvement had been confined to a few, and if the position of the masses had not improved or had worsened. But even if that had been the case, it would not follow that the policies which offered opportunities to be grasped by the successful were themselves responsible for the failure of others to advance. Given the pressures on the land that had already built up,[16] and the frightening rate of population growth, a failure to change land tenure in the African areas and to regulate and plan the influx into the Highlands may simply have made more difficult the path to improvement for all. Certainly it should be the aim to extend the benefits of economic growth more widely, and this is official policy. The

Development Plan for 1974-78 proclaims a fundamental goal to be 'an improvement in the distribution of the national income', but this is not a change of heart – it was also the declared aim in the Plan for 1966-70.[17] If this aim is to be achieved, one requirement is a more equitable distribution of agricultural services. According to the 1974-78 Development Plan, an important instrument for greater equality is to be the subdivision of a considerable amount of land still farmed on a large scale. Where large-scale farming is necessary for efficiency an important role is proposed for the Agricultural Development Corporation, and 'Where private farmland is retained as large-scale units, the Government will encourage the occupation of these farms by groups of people or co-operative societies rather than by a few privileged individuals'.[18] That would involve a very considerable shift in the trend of development, in the face of vested interests, and one wonders about its compatibility with the possibilities for private accumulation resulting from the commercialisation of land.

The process of differentiation within the African population has not only a personal, but also a tribal and – to a large degree the same thing – a regional dimension. The opportunities opened by the changes in land policy and by the removal of restrictions on cash-crop production were more eagerly grasped in some areas than in others, and by some peoples than by others. The distribution of high-potential land favoured some and not others, and the widely recognised relative expansion in the wealth and strength of the Kikuyu is in part the result of the natural advantage of the land in Central Province. Nyanza Province and Central Province had roughly the same value of marketed agricultural output until 1957, after which date Central Province drew rapidly ahead, so that at the time of independence its marketed output from small farms was roughly twice that of Nyanza Province. Central Province has retained its lead in independent Kenya.[19] The advance of Central Province was based to a large degree on coffee production, which expanded rapidly once the restrictions on its cultivation had disappeared. The exploitation of the opportunities offered by the removal of these restrictions – in coffee and other products – was facilitated by the high level of infrastructure and of extension services that had been established in the Province as a consequence of the Emergency. In contrast to the progress of Central Province, money income may even have declined in some areas during the 1960s, as in South Nyanza and Busia, where disease and poor quality led to the uprooting of robusta coffee, and in some marginal and drought-stricken areas where production has not kept pace with the growth of population. That the growth of regional and tribal inequality results in part from such natural and historical circumstances does not, however, diminish the political tensions it creates. And it is therefore all the more important that policy-makers – including aid donors – should be alive to the dangers of fostering the cumulative growth of inequality.

Manufacturing

The process of import substitution through the establishment of domestic manufacturing gained speed after independence. It was fostered by policies to attract foreign capital and at the same time to promote a greater participation by Africans in ownership and management. During the 1950s there had begun to be a sizeable inflow of Kenyan-Asian (and other East African)-owned capital from trade into manufacturing. In the years after independence capital from abroad became relatively more important.

The first step to stimulate the inflow of capital was to create an appropriate 'investment climate'. In 1961 and 1962 foreigners had been withdrawing capital, and a reversal of this flow required a reversal of the expectations that had stimulated the outflow. Even before independence it had become clear that – in the words of Jomo Kenyatta already quoted – the British were not to be succeeded by 'a gangster Government' and that the new government would 'encourage investors in various projects to come to Kenya'; in 1963 capital was already flowing in again. With independence, new legislation reinforced and codified the favourable attitude towards foreign capital.

Under the Foreign Investment Protection Act (No. 35 of 1964) an undertaking can be granted an Approved Enterprise Certificate which entitles the holder to transfer profits and capital out of Kenya. A constraint on foreign enterprises as a channel for the export of local capital is provided by restrictions on local borrowing. Policies concerning taxation, protection, and the provision of finance have been designed to encourage private investment, including investment from abroad. Company profits are taxable at a rate of 45 per cent, though the rate is 52½ per cent for branches of foreign companies. There is an initial investment allowance of 20 per cent of the cost of industrial building, plant and machinery. Wear-and-tear deductions are allowed at the rate of 2½ per cent on buildings, 12½ per cent on plant and machinery, and 25 per cent on certain vehicles. The government advertises that the effect of all allowances is that 'an industrialist can write off 120 per cent of his investment against taxable income over a period of a few years'.[20] However, the tax rates are relatively high, and the allowances not conspicuously generous. It is to be noted that there is no provision for tax holidays. Foreign capital has been encouraged, therefore, rather by the attempt to establish a reputation for stability and order than by the offer of excessively generous financial terms.

Protection of industry is given by the common external tariff of the East African Community.[21] It is also given by import licensing and quantitative restrictions. In addition, a system of import-duty refunds and remissions operates to assist producers to compete with imports and in foreign markets, though it is intended to dispense with these concessions in the course of a general revision of the tariff. A 'Manufactures Export

Compensation Scheme' provides a subsidy of 10 per cent of the f.o.b. value or of the foreign currency proceeds of exported local manufactures. After independence tariff and other instruments became increasingly protective, though 'not as part of a coherent strategy, but piece by piece in response to pressures and temptations of various kinds'.[22]

Despite the measures designed to attract capital into manufacturing, the growth of output did not accelerate notably in the decade after independence. The official quantity index of manufacturing output increased from 60 to 120 between 1954 and 1964 (1960 = 100); between 1964 and 1974 it rose from 70 to 149 (1969 = 100). In value terms, at current prices, output rose from K£34m. in 1964 to K£105m. in 1973, and increased its contribution to GDP in the monetary economy from 14 per cent to 18 per cent, though measured at constant 1964 prices its contribution increased only to 15 per cent.[23] Nevertheless, the growth was substantial. Value added in manufacturing increased at an annual rate of 7.9 per cent between 1964 and 1972, while employment in manufacturing rose over the same period at a rate of 6.6 per cent.[24] The number of manufacturing establishments employing five or more persons increased from 676 in 1963 to 1,298 in 1971, and with that increase industry became more diversified. The market remained primarily within Kenya, but its export component became less tied to East African markets.

The Kenya market changed less than might have been expected in the years following independence. The non-African population remained large, though its composition altered. The European population had numbered 31,000 in 1948, and had increased to a peak of 61,000 in 1960. Thereafter it declined, but in 1969, six years after independence, it was still as large as 41,000.[25] Employment of Europeans (another indicator of the size of the market provided by the European community) had been 23,000 at its maximum in 1960, and had fallen to 18,200 by 1963. In 1972 it was still more than 13,000, though it declined to 9,500 in the following year. The Asian population continued to increase to a maximum of 192,000 in 1967, and had fallen to 139,000 in 1969. But the demand for manufactures from the high-income non-African population had come to be supplemented by a growing African demand. As the Development Plan predicted:

> In the Kenya domestic market the main change will be the shift that is taking place from production for a market largely composed of non-citizens to a market where these are being replaced or added to by a rising African middle-class.

The import substitution of non-durable consumer goods had been carried a long way by the end of the first decade of independence. Production of intermediate products and capital goods had already developed and the greatest scope for future growth was in these sectors. One difficulty was the greater limitation imposed by the size of the market in these industries than in many consumer goods industries. Despite the preferential access to the markets of Tanzania and Uganda under the terms of the 1967 Treaty for East African Co-operation,[26] and despite some successes in other export markets,[27] the smallness of the Kenya market seemed likely to be a greater constraint on industrial development in the future than in the past.

It has been argued that the reliance of industrialisation in Kenya on foreign capital, and particularly on international firms and imported technology, has resulted in the establishment of an industrial structure in which inappropriate goods are produced by inappropriate methods.[28] Multinational firms, it is said, have adopted the capital-intensive methods they use in the developed countries to manufacture the products they manufacture in those countries. Industrialisation has, in consequence, become not just a matter of import substitution but of 'import reproduction' in which the identical goods, previously imported, are produced domestically. These products are designed for the markets of the developed countries and are often not relevant to the needs of a poor society, but a demand for them among the better-off is created by advertising. These products, it is claimed, are socially divisive. They are the medium for a 'transfer of tastes' from the developed countries to the better-off in the poor countries, whose pattern of consumption is made to conform to that of the developed countries, and to diverge from that of the mass of the population in their own country. The activities of the international firms increase the inequality of income because the firms pay their employees (labour costs are not an important component of total costs when capital-intensive methods are used), particularly in management, at rates greatly above the level prevailing in the economy generally. Methods of production are not designed to use locally available materials, so that the demand for imports grows despite import substitution. Products which are not themselves inappropriate to the needs of the mass of the population are often produced – because of the need to maintain the quality of the internationally-marketed brand – to an inappropriately high standard of quality, which can only be achieved at a price which confines demand to the rich. Finally, the argument runs, there are strict limits on the growth possible in an industrialisation pattern directed at the needs of the better-off, because in Kenya the market is too small for the efficient production of many goods demanded by high-income consumers.

There is a good deal of truth in this analysis of the nature of industrialisation in Kenya. After all, its initial proposition is simply that production is established to serve a market that exists, and when the great majority of the population has very small money incomes, that market will be provided by the better-off minority. That is, of course, why import substitution is a basis for industrialisation, to satisfy by domestic production an existing demand previously satisfied by imports.

However, for all its truth, this criticism of the nature of Kenyan industrialisation can easily be carried too far. It is not a fact that Kenyan manufacturing is concerned solely with the demands of the rich. In reality, a wide range of goods is produced for consumption by people who cannot in any absolute sense be considered wealthy. The statistics of industrial production do not provide a sufficiently fine classification of products for their nature to be clearly identified, but they do provide some indication. In the first place, the *Census of Industrial Production* showed that, in 1963, 16 per cent of total production by private industry was of food, and another 15 per cent of drink and tobacco. The largest output among food industries was from grain-milling, which accounted for nearly one-third of their total output. Clothing, textiles and footwear contributed 8 per cent of industrial production.[29] These industries did not produce only for the rich: maize meal, cheap cigarettes, plastic sandals and cooking fat are among their products. It is true that even these products are not available to the very poor. But the very poor, in the rural areas particularly, provide virtually no market for manufactures. Even in the urban areas the purchases of the poor are very restricted. In the budget used for computing the low-income urban price index,[30] three-quarters of expenditure on goods is accounted for by food, and another 6 per cent by drink and tobacco. With 8 per cent on clothing and footwear, and 4 per cent on fuel, there is very little left to constitute a demand for a wide range of manufactures.

It must be accepted as a fact that when the money incomes of most people are extremely small, manufacturing will inevitably be largely directed at a minority market. Policies might reasonably aim at a widening of the market, but hardly at production only for majority markets. A more equal distribution of money income would doubtless result in a different pattern of demand – an *equal* distribution of the present aggregate of consumer's expenditure might eliminate altogether the demand for all but a few manufactures. Growth must depend on a further expansion of aggregate money income. Changes in industrial structure and in the pattern of demand will come about only in response to an expansion of rural incomes, and this may be achieved by the further development of small-scale agriculture. The policies of multinational companies can have no more than a marginal effect in this respect.

The 'transfer of tastes' is the familiar 'demonstration effect', the disadvantages of which have long been recognised. It is not clear that the disadvantages of the 'rising expectations' created by the demonstration of higher standards of consumption inevitably outweigh the beneficial incentive effects, and it is even less clear that policies to deal with the disadvantages are available in which the cure is not worse than the disease. Kenya's development policy, after all, aims at least in some respects to emulate the rich countries, and the move to the consumption of superior goods is part of the process of development. Other patterns of change are conceivable; in Kenya they are 'non-agenda'. And just as it is easy to exaggerate the extent to which Kenyan manufacturing is concerned to serve the rich, so is it easy to exaggerate the disadvantages of the transfer of tastes. It might readily be agreed that a transfer of tastes from maize meal to corn flakes would not be an important ingredient of development. But could the same be said for a shift from thatch to iron for roofing, or the stimulation of a demand for plastic sandals? It has, in fact, been argued that local materials are potentially available that would provide improved roofing without the high import content and high capital intensity of the manufacture of corrugated iron, and that plastic sandals are an 'inappropriate' product because the alternative exists of sandals made from old motor tyres. If consumers believed themselves to be as well-off or better-off using some other roofing material, and if they preferred motor-tyre sandals, then it would be reasonable to declare corrugated iron and plastic sandals to be inappropriate products. There is a case here for research into improvements of the alternative products and for the advertising of their benefits. But unless such activity persuades consumers – and with the consumers of these two products, and of many others, we are not dealing with a small, wealthy minority – that the alternative products are to be preferred, it cannot reasonably be maintained that the transfer of tastes is detrimental – not to consumers' welfare, at any rate. It is not as if the availability of corrugated iron and of plastic sandals precludes the availability of alternative products. By definition, 'appropriate' products are not capital-intensive, so that there are no significant economies of scale in their manufacture. The demand for plastic sandals does not, therefore, raise the cost of motor-tyre sandals by limiting the size of their market. They are available for those who wish to buy them, and their availability is not affected by the availability of plastic sandals. It is simply that, for many people, for many uses, plastic sandals are a superior product for which they are prepared to pay. The buyer's standard of living is higher with plastic sandals than without them. Of course, distortion of factor prices may make plastic sandals too cheap relative to motor-tyre sandals, but that is another question. It does not alter the fact that higher standards of living are often associated with the consumption of so-called 'inappropriate' products, the taste for which has been created by their being made available by modern-sector manufacturers and by imports.

Doubtless there can be a transfer of tastes to products the social utility of which (one's judgement may suggest) is small.[31] This is hardly a problem confined to poor countries, and it provides an argument for intervention (if one's judgement is shared by those who make policy and those for whom it is made!). It is not an easy matter to know how to intervene. It is not a question of regulating the behaviour of domestic producers. The demonstration effect is exercised by imports,[32] by the cinema, by tourists and returning travellers. To insulate the population from the disease would not be easy, and the draconian measures that would be required do not seem to be practical politics in present-day Kenya, even where it is judged that the welfare loss would be outweighed by other benefits. There is a role for fiscal policy and for research and promotion of alternative products. It can also be argued that there is a case for a tougher and more sceptical attitude on the part of the Kenya government to overseas manufacturers than has, perhaps, been the case in the past, and that 'stricter scrutiny of investment proposals and a more critical appraisal of applications for protection are necessary to achieve appropriate import substitution'.[33] In fact, the intention to modify policies towards industrialisation had already been announced in 1972. The government had become more aware of the disadvantages of a rather indiscriminate and excessive encouragement of industrialisation through the attraction of foreign capital, and of the costs of highly protected import substitution, which are familiar from the experience of other countries. The 1972 budget speech gave:

> due warning to our manufacturers that the Government proposes to lower the protective barriers around domestic industry and require our manufacturers to compete on more equal terms with producers from overseas.[34]

Tariff changes require the agreement of Tanzania and Uganda, the other members of the East African Community, but subject to that agreement the Kenya government's policy, as set out in the Development Plan for 1974-78, is to establish a more uniform tariff by raising the lowest rates, reducing the highest rates, introducing duties on items, mainly capital and intermediate goods, that now enter free, and eliminating refunds and remissions of duty.[35] These changes in the tariff would reduce the opportunity for very high rates of effective protection of domestic processing to emerge. It was said that the changes were intended 'to render Kenyan industry more competitive, more employment creating, and more development oriented', and that it was 'envisaged that these measures will have a substantial impact upon the composition of industries which will be established over the next Plan period'.[36]

However, in response to the economic situation which arose out of the increase in oil prices and other adverse developments, it was decided to impose tighter quantitative controls on imports. It was announced in 1974 that 'imports of luxury consumer goods will be banned, and other items now subject to import quota will be cut back in order to reduce the overall import bill'.[37] These quantitative restrictions could result in a very high degree of protection for domestic manufactures and encourage the domestic production of luxury goods the import of which is prohibited. Price controls exist which might limit the effect of the increase in protection accorded by quantitative restrictions, and the government is aware of the encouragement to the domestic production of inessentials given by import restrictions.[38] It is also intended to improve project appraisal and to impose a 'stricter scrutiny of investment proposals and a more critical appraisal of applications for protection'.[39] 'The Government will specify where and under what conditions foreign investment will be welcomed. Investment in industries with an export potential will be given priority. Technological and organisational expertise, with long-run benefits to Kenya, and improvement in ability to compete internationally will also be considerations.'[40]

African Participation

The desirability of and, indeed, the likelihood of the adoption of policies adversely affecting the interests of the foreign-owned sector of the economy is in part determined by the extent to which Kenyan participation in and association with the foreign-owned sector has already become substantial. There is no doubt that industrial development since independence has been predominantly financed from abroad. The government has taken an equity interest in a number of enterprises (including oil-refining and banking) and has provided loan finance through different institutions. There has been some private participation in the equity of overseas firms, as well as a growth of holdings by Africans in non-African-owned local companies. But so far as ownership is concerned, the intention of *African Socialism in Kenya* that 'a large share of the planned new expansion is African owned and managed' has not been fulfilled, although a few Africans have very large stakes in economic enterprise of all kinds.

It is a different matter with respect to management. Restrictions on the issue of work permits for non-citizens, and a realisation by international firms of the advantages of localisation have resulted in a considerable degree of Africanisation of management, particularly in large companies. There has also been an inflow of Africans into local directorships, though the degree of ultimate control exercised by Kenyans may not be great, because of the control exercised by overseas headquarters. But the process of Kenyanisation has gone far enough to ensure that the interests of the foreign companies and of many Kenyans are not in conflict.

Kenyanisation – in practice Africanisation[41] – has, in fact, gone far in all spheres of activity. Within a year or two of independence most of the heads of government departments were Africans. But there was no desire to Africanise regardless of cost and efficiency. Many senior executive positions continued and continue to be occupied by expatriates supported by the British government through OSAS (Overseas Service Aid Scheme) and in the University and other institutions there are many expatriates supported by BESS (British Expatriate Supplementation Scheme). There has been an inflow of technical assistance personnel into advisory positions (though in practice some carry out executive functions), and there is a large contingent of expatriate teachers. Expatriates, therefore, continue to be important, particularly in some activities. Nevertheless, citizens of Kenya occupied three-quarters of all the posts in high- and middle-level occupations in 1972, compared with 59 per cent five years earlier.[42]

The Kenyanisation of trade was pursued through a Trade Licensing Act, under which progressively more areas of trade have been confined to Kenya citizens. Manufacturers have been encouraged or required to distribute their products through citizen traders, and the Kenya National Trading Corporation (KNTC), which has a monopoly in the distribution of certain products, has fostered Kenyanisation by awarding agencies to citizens. The Kenyanisation of existing businesses owned by non-citizens has been pursued, almost to completion for small businesses, through compulsory sales to Kenya citizens. Credit has been made available to finance Kenyans in the purchase and operation of the businesses. Trade had been largely in the hands of Asians, some of whom became Kenyan citizens, but many did not, either because they were not qualified for citizenship, did not apply for it, or were not granted it. The Kenyanisation of trade has therefore been essentially a process of Africanisation.[43] By the middle of 1975 it had gone very far, particularly in the rural areas and small towns and was being pushed ahead in Nairobi and Mombasa.

Advantage has not been taken in the past of the possibilities for increasing African participation in the money economy through the encouragement of what has become known as the 'informal sector'. This term refers to a wide range of economic activities which are outside the scope both of normal statistical assessment and of government recognition. Those who operate in the informal sector do so without licences – in an economy where so many activities require licensing – without what would officially be recognised as proper premises, and doubtless infringing certain standards of safety and health and, perhaps on occasions, of business probity and reliability. But the informal sector is not an unproductive and parasitic growth, though some of its activities may be so. The ILO Mission took the view that the informal sector employs:

> a variety of carpenters, masons, tailors and other tradesmen, as well as cooks and taxi-drivers, offering virtually the full range of basic skills needed to provide goods and services for a large though often poor section of the population . . . [It] provides income-earning opportunities for a large number of people. Though it is often regarded as unproductive and stagnant, we see it as providing a wide range of low-cost, labour-intensive, competitive goods and services.[44]

Far from receiving encouragement and assistance from the authorities, the informal sector is more the subject of neglect and even of positive harassment. Although the ILO Mission perhaps took a somewhat romantic view of the character of the informal sector, it can without doubt be a source of goods and services of a kind and quality in demand by the poorer sections of the population. The official attitude to informal sector activities has reflected the implicit assumption, which was common in the colonial administration, that only 'modern', large-scale activities deserved attention. The assumption is nicely illustrated by the story[45] of the official in Uganda who, when asked about Kampala's industrial area, replied, 'There are no industries there – only a lot of furniture works, bakeries, maize mills and soda water factories.' The attitude also reflects an attachment to 'standards' and 'quality' appropriate to a wealthy society. The relevance of this consideration to the structure of manufacturing industry has already been discussed. It is found in the regulation of public transport, where safety requirements are the ostensible reason for restricting the provision to expensive, relatively high-quality services. The harassment by the police of unlicensed *matatu*[46] taxis in Nairobi limits the availability of a cheap service. It has been a common feature of the control of markets and of housing, where an appeal to public health requirements is used to prevent the provision of services which the poor could afford. The destruction from time to time of 'squatters' ' housing and of unlicensed market stalls by *askaris* of the Nairobi City Council has been a distasteful consequence of this insistence on the standards of a wealthy society. Some actions by the authorities – the periodic clearing of beggars from the streets, for instance – have perhaps also been stimulated by a desire to present a modern and respectable image to the tourist.

There are indications, however, that official attitudes are changing. The government now recognises the potential for development that exists within the informal sector. It is proposed to stop the demolition of slum housing when no specific benefit results, to liberalise transport licensing and traders' licensing, and to encourage the informal sector in various ways.[47] The government paper issued in response to the recommendations of the ILO Mission says:

> The Government acknowledges that there is much counter-productive harassment of the so-called informal sector. This harassment will cease and more realistic standards and controls will be applied. The Government has already taken initial steps to ensure that the informal sector is provided with sufficient credit and management and technical services.[48]

A change in policy towards the informal sector may take some time to penetrate down from those who make policy to those who execute it.[49] The authorities continue to be reluctant to allow 'site and services' housing development, and the harassment of *matatus* and the demolition of unauthorised dwellings may not quickly be halted.[50] If a change in policy towards the informal sector is fully implemented, it may assist the declared aim of 'a more equitable distribution of resources and income'.[51] The same cannot be said for the increase in the salaries of the higher civil service which followed the recommendations of the Ndegwa Commission on public service structure and remuneration in 1971.[52] Although the general level of salary increase recommended was extraordinarily modest – a mere 4 per cent – very substantial percentage increases were proposed for the higher grades (many of whose salaries had not been increased for ten years), that for the Head of the Civil Service being 24 per cent. It was further recommended – doubtless to formalise what had become common practice – that there should be no objection to public servants owning property or businesses. The position of the higher ranks of the civil service was greatly improved as a result of the Ndegwa Commission's recommendations, but a sense of proportion is necessary in judging them. The ratio of the highest to the lowest public service salaries is certainly much greater than is to be found in developed countries. Even wider is the gap between the salary of the senior civil servant and that of the wage-earner in agriculture.[53] The average wage paid by the Kenya government in 1969 was £293 p.a. Wages (including housing allowance) were less than Shs 300/- per month for 45 per cent of all central government employees. In agriculture the average wage was Shs 121/- per month and 97 per cent of all wage-earners in modern agriculture received less than Shs 300/- per month. The salary of the Head of the Civil Service was K£3,200 p.a.[54] and the Commission recommended that it should be increased to K£3,960 p.a. Compared with the salaries of corresponding officials in the developed countries[55] that is little enough in a country where it is not notably cheaper to pursue a similar way of life. Of course, the senior civil servant of a poor country should not follow the same mode of life as his counterpart in a rich country, and some levels of the civil service may be overpaid, but there is a certain way of life which is necessary for the efficient pursuit of the activities required of such an official, and it would be entirely unrealistic to suppose that these activities could be efficiently carried out by an official whose income was, say, equal to that of the average paid in the civil service.[56] It is also relevant that the civil service has to compete with the private sector for scarce personnel. Despite the increase in civil service salaries there is a high turnover in senior posts. Efficiency might, indeed, be increased by the payment of even higher salaries, if it were coupled with effective restrictions on private business activity. It is often said that some officials devote more time and effort to their businesses and farms than is compatible with the most efficient discharge of their official duties.

The ILO Mission recommended a five-year freeze on salaries above £700 p.a., and the Kenya government has expressed its general support for the Mission's recommendations on wages policy.[57] A freeze on higher salaries seemed to be foreshadowed in the 1972 budget speech, when the Minister said:

> We must define a minimum poverty line. We must then go all out with total commitment to ensure that everyone below such a minimum line is brought up to at least that minimum standard. If you agree with me in this objective, has not the time come to freeze all incomes above, say, K£700 per annum to enable us to achieve it?

Although no freeze has, in fact, been instituted, new guidelines on wages issued to the Industrial Court favour the lower-paid, and the minimum wage has been increased.[58] There may, therefore, be a narrowing of the gap between rich and poor in wage employment. But this will do nothing to improve, absolutely or relatively, the lot of the poorest, who do not receive wages.

The Role of Government

The Constitution of the Republic of Kenya was of fundamental importance in defining the direction of subsequent policy, and particularly the attitude to nationalisation. It provided for prompt payment of full compensation when property was compulsorily acquired and that 'every person having an interest or right in property which is compulsorily taken possession of shall have a right of direct access to the Court'. Policy statements from the beginning indicate the absence of any ideological commitment to public ownership. The President declared in 1964 that 'nationalization will not serve to advance the cause of African Socialism', and *Sessional Paper No. 10 of 1965* stated that 'African Socialism in Kenya does not imply a commitment to indiscriminate nationalization'. The approach in practice is illustrated by the nationalisation of the East African Power and Lighting Company, which was acquired by the open market purchase of shares. Government participation in some other industries – banking, insurance, oil refining, for example – has also taken the form of the acquisition of shares by government ministries, particularly the Treasury.

In addition to the direct acquisition of shares by ministries, government financial participation in industrial development has taken place through a number of institutions. There is, however, no development corporation, such as exists in some other countries, through which foreign capital is channelled, and which takes responsibility for the management of enterprises.

Projects which qualify for government financial participation through one of the development finance institutions have been classed[59] as follows:

(a) profitable but needing encouragement;
(b) profitable but risky;
(c) only marginally profitable, but involving external economies;
(d) too big for individual private domestic investors and entrepreneurs;

(e) projects in which there is a strong public interest and in which financial participation is desirable to establish public control, promote Africanisation, prevent abuse of monopoly power, and generally to ensure operation for the public interest.

The first of the financial institutions to be established was the ICDC (Industrial and Commercial Development Corporation), which was established in 1954. The ICDC is concerned with the promotion of African enterprise, although it was not until 1960 that it initiated a scheme of small industrial loans to assist African businessmen. The concern of ICDC with the promotion of African enterprise does not prevent its participating with foreign investors. On the contrary, that has been a major activity and it has a financial interest in, for example, the Firestone tyre plant, textile factories, a metal-forging plant, and a pencil factory. But its bias is towards smaller projects, which it deals with partly through a subsidiary, Kenya Industrial Estates. Some of the Corporation's holdings in foreign enterprises have been transferred to Kenyans, as in the transfer of shares to the ICDC Investment Company, the equity of which is held by Kenya citizens. One analysis of ICDC activities in the field of small business concluded that, although ICDC had had its successes, it had primarily helped successful businessmen to consolidate their success; it had not played an initiating and creative role, and would have been more effective if it had taken equity participation instead of offering fixed-interest loans.

A second institution, the Development Finance Company of Kenya (DFCK), is particularly concerned with large-scale projects. It is a privately incorporated company and operates with finance obtained from the Kenya government, through ICDC, and from agencies of the British, Dutch and German Governments. It can participate in a project through loans or equity holdings, and it is the intention that it should raise some of its funds by selling from its equity portfolio to the general public.

A new institution appeared on the scene in 1973 with the establishment of an Industrial Development Bank, under separate management from the ICDC though owned jointly by ICDC (51 per cent) and the Kenya Treasury. The ICDC, with its Kenyanisation aims, and its use in the implementation of trade licensing and the transfer of businesses to Kenyans, was not considered by the World Bank as an appropriate vehicle for the investment of its funds. The Industrial Development Bank will raise external loans, including loans from the World Bank, to finance major industrial development projects.

Despite the absence of any ideological inclination towards the expansion of government economic activity, there is a widespread impression that the role of government in the economy has greatly expanded. In absolute terms the contribution of government to monetary GDP (at constant prices) increased by 140 per cent between 1964 and 1974.[60] However, as a proportion of monetary GDP the contribution of government increased only modestly, from 18 per cent to 21 per cent. Nor is the position significantly different for the public sector as a whole, the contribution of which to monetary GDP rose only from 33 per cent to 35 per cent between 1964 and 1973.[61]

Within the public sector, and within the narrower government sector, there have been large changes. The share of East African Community institutions has declined and that of Kenya parastatal bodies more than doubled. Administration has declined and social services increased in importance. However, between sectors, it is the constancy of the shares which is striking.

Table 1: Sector shares of monetary GDP (constant 1964 prices)

(percentages of monetary GDP)

	1964	*1974*
Agriculture	22	19
Manufacturing	14	16
Construction	3	3
Trade	14	10
Transport	10	10
Banking etc.	4	5
Government	18	21
Other	15	16

Source: Economic Survey 1975.

It is a different matter with respect to the distribution of resources (monetary GDP *plus* the import surplus) between consumption and investment. Gross investment took 32 per cent of available resources in the monetary economy in 1974 compared with 16 per cent in 1964. The relative decline in consumption which was the counterpart of this increase was concentrated on private consumption. The share of public consumption was constant, taking approximately one-fifth of total resources; the share of private consumption declined from 64 per cent in 1964 to 48 per cent in 1974.[62]

The share of the private sector in monetary capital formation also declined from nearly three-quarters of the total in 1964 to barely more than one-half in 1974. The increased role of the public sector is therefore reflected not so much in the sectoral contribution to GDP as in the increasing proportion of resources devoted to investment and the increasing part of investment being carried out by the public sector.

Table 2: Use of resources (current prices)

	1964 K£m.	%	*1974* K£m.	%
Monetary GDP at market prices	267.7		791.2	
Import surplus of goods and services	– 17.4		– 81.1	
Total resources available	250.3	100	872.3	100
Gross investment	41.4	16	283.1	32
Consumption: Total	208.9	84	589.2	68
Public	49.4	20	169.0	19
Private	159.5	64	420.2	48

Source: Economic Survey 1975, Tables 2.5 and 2.8A.

A review of the policies pursued by the Kenya government would be misleading if it contained no reference to the 'style' of government in Kenya. To an important extent it is government by the civil service. The initiative of the civil service in policies, particularly economic policies, is far-reaching, but it reaches only so far, and cannot be exercised without thought for the possibility of presidential intervention. Major policy changes have been made from time to time by presidential announcement, without apparently much foreknowledge by civil servants, or even ministers. The desirability of careful preparation and planning of major innovations is not allowed to stand in the way of 'the felt necessities of the times' – the President's feel for the political realities. In this manner the price of milk was increased, creating financial problems for Kenya Cooperative Creameries, which had to buy at the higher price, and making it necessary to raise other produce prices to prevent an excessive switch to grazing; so the prices paid to maize, wheat and pyrethrum farmers were raised, although a policy of reducing producer-prices was embodied in the Development Plan.[63] Similarly, free primary education in certain grades was introduced, and in a different field of policy *Kiswahili* was declared to be the national language.

The attitude to aid

This chapter has been concerned to set the scene in which the provision of external aid and technical assistance to Kenya takes place. Kenya's policy towards aid has been consistent with its other economic policies. Aid and technical assistance are welcome because they mean that 'development here need not be limited quite so severely by the shortage of domestic savings and education'; but aid will not be welcomed 'if it is designed to promote the economic or political dominance of the aiding country'.[64]

An elaboration of policy towards aid is contained in *Sessional Paper No. 10* in connection with the terms of bilateral aid, particularly with reference to aid in inconvertible currencies, the financing of local costs, and the repayment of loans. Aid offers, the paper states, must be examined in the light of foreign exchange policies:

> We must avoid, for example, aid which requires us merely to advance credit to a developed country or to mortgage our future production to any given country or which makes us a mere dumping ground for products of a donor country. Aid terms must be related to the productivity of the project and its positive contribution to our economy. These are matters which must not be decided upon just on political or emotional considerations.[65]

The need to develop expertise in the assessment of aid offers was, therefore, recognised early. By 1969 the Minister of Finance in his budget speech was able to remark:

> We are now experienced in the negotiation of overseas aid, and have been much encouraged by indications that the World Bank, which is already our largest overseas source, will be prepared to increase the rate of its lendings to Kenya. The strings attached to World Bank loans are, in fact, no more than the sort of guide lines which we would, in any case, wish to use . . .

A less totally optimistic assessment of Kenya's aid policy was given by a former economic adviser to the Treasury. The tendency to expand aid for its own sake has, he suggested, been resisted:

> The pressures from abroad (and within for that matter) to build clearly distinguishable plaque-hanging projects to high specifications have in general been resisted. Moreover, many of the opportunities to finance turnkey projects have been rejected following cost-benefit analysis. Nevertheless, the tendency exists to tailor projects to donor requirements, to accept aid for imported goods which could be produced domestically, to finance imports through aid even though the true aid element may be dissipated through higher prices, and to reduce or eliminate in the Plan projects and programmes essential for development which do not, however, appear to be attractive to donors. It requires vigilance and perseverance to avoid these pitfalls and Kenya's record, while not perfect, is certainly good.[66]

The temptations have not, however, always been resisted. In fact, a Treasury circular to the spending departments informs them that projects have a chance of acceptance only if foreign aid for them has already been arranged, though this does not mean, of course, that projects inconsistent with the Development Plan would be accepted simply because they had the support of a potential aid donor. (These and other issues of policy towards aid are taken up in detail in later chapters.)

The Current Situation

The background to an analysis of economic aid – to bring together the various arguments of this chapter – is a decade of substantial progress in Kenya as measured by the conventional indicators. The Minister of Finance was able to say in 1974:

> Since independence, our economy has grown at an average rate of 6.8 per cent per year. Moreover, such a statistic does not reveal the great extent to which the economy has been modernised by employing more efficient methods of production. Manufacturing output (price adjusted) has grown by 8.1 per cent per year since 1963, while agriculture has grown at 6.5 per cent. Before independence, most high- and middle-level occupations were manned by expatriates; by 1972, 74 per cent of them were in the hands of Kenyans. The number of pupils enrolled in primary schools has almost doubled since independence, while those in secondary schools and the university have increased by more than fivefold. The major targets of the second Five-Year Plan (1970-74) were all realised.[67]

In addition, among other achievements, including a rise in exports by 140 per cent,[68] there has been the achievement in agriculture of a large-scale and orderly transfer of land into African ownership, and a great expansion in the contribution of small holders.

All this was success, indeed. Nevertheless, in the middle of the 1970s strong doubts remain about the effects and the future of the pattern of development pursued since independence. Despite the growth of productive capacity, the progress of import substitution, and the expansion of exports, the potential balance of payments position remained serious, even before the effects of the oil crisis began to be experienced. The current account deficit had fluctuated from year to year, and had been tending to increase, but except for two years (1967 and 1971) had been adequately covered by the inflow of long-term capital and aid. However, the projections of the economy made at the beginning of the 1970s assumed an inflow of capital at a much higher level than had been achieved in the past, and even at the time seemed unrealistic.[69] In 1974, the current account deficit jumped to K£116.1m. from the 1973 figure of K£47.5m. and as a proportion of GDP increased from less than 6 to more than 12 per cent.

Despite the progress that has been made, the absolute number of the poor may not have diminished. Unemployment and underemployment have become worse. Migration to the towns, often into a poverty-stricken and unproductive way of life, has increased, indicating perhaps that the opportunities offered in the rural areas are even worse. This state of affairs in the rural areas persists despite the commitment to 'direct an increasing share of the total resources available to the nation towards the rural areas',[70] and a policy of redistributing income through increased expenditure on education and health combined with widespread remissions of charges for these services.[71] Population growth continues at an accelerating rate,[72] adding to the intensity of these problems. This darker side of success has stimulated the recent emphasis on inequality within Kenyan society, though the concern about inequality might not be so great if the absolute level of the poorest sections of the population were seen clearly to be improving.

The government is committed to a policy of greater equality, but it has been committed to such a policy from the beginning.[73] It is acknowledged that:

> In spite of the rapid growth of the economy, in the first ten years of independence, the problems associated with a rapidly growing population – unemployment and income disparities – have become more apparent than they were in 1963.[74]

And the President has declared that economic growth

> can no longer be regarded as the only objective of our nation. Rather, it is a means of attaining other goals . . . these include full participation of our people in the economy, greater employment opportunities, and a more equitable distribution of resources and income.[75]

The commitment is clear. Unfortunately, the middle 1970s is the least auspicious time since independence for achieving a substantially more egalitarian distribution of income and wealth. The days of relatively easy growth and redistribution are over. The major transfers of land have been completed. The high-potential lands are approaching full utilisation with existing techniques, and with the informal constraints that operate on the use of land by people from other areas. Obvious import substitution has been carried out. Commerce has been Africanised. In general, the easy options have been taken up and the way to further progress is a more difficult one.

On top of that change in the opportunities for growth and redistribution came the increase in oil prices, which was a major blow to the economy, seriously affecting the balance of payments, in which structural difficulties were already evident, and boosting the inflationary forces that were already active. A *Sessional Paper* of early 1975 said that 'Kenya's impressive record of economic growth – 6.8 per cent per annum during the first decade of independence – is currently in danger of erosion'.[76] The Paper forecast that over the Development Plan period the annual increase in GDP in the monetary economy would amount to 6.7 per cent, compared with the Development Plan target of 8.4 per cent, and that real income per head would rise by only 1.3 per cent, compared with the target of 3.7 per cent.

The strategy of the ILO Report was 'redistribution from growth'. There were those who thought that, despite the commitment of policy, it was optimistic to expect substantial redistribution in the face of powerful vested interests in the economic structure that had been created. If there was truth in this view it must indeed be Utopian to expect redistribution in the absence of growth. With a low rate of growth, no major improvements in the situation of the poor, and with the spectre of the population explosion standing over all, the prospect would be uncertain, but menacing.

The remainder of this book analyses the part played by external aid, particularly British aid, in the developments in Kenya that have been outlined, and suggests its future role. One point concerning the role of aid has, we believe, already emerged from this summary examination of developments in Kenya. Whatever may have been the alternatives at an earlier stage, decisions made during the transition to independence and changes initiated at that time have had an enormous influence on later events. The structure of the economy and the policies pursued in independent Kenya have been deeply rooted in the past. Equally they are now firmly rooted in the interests of influential sections of Kenyan society. It would be a serious misreading of the situation to see Kenya as a reluctant practitioner of policies forced on it by the 'leverage' of foreign aid donors.

Notes

1. *Sessional Paper No. 10 of 1965*, p. 51.
2. The fact that most settlers are in arrears with loan repayments qualifies in practice the principle that they had to pay for the land. (See below, pp. 110, 122-3.)
3. This was as near as Kenya came to expropriation for settlement. There was dispute between the UK and Kenya governments over the treatment of farmers excluded from their farms for mismanagement. The legislation provided for the compensation of farmers, and this was not done. Eventually the courts ruled that compensation should be paid.
4. *Development Plan 1974-1978*, Part I, Government Printer, Nairobi, p. 199.
5. Ibid.
6. The phrase 'telephone farmers' has been coined to describe the activities of some of these buyers of farms.
7. *Development Plan 1974-1978*, Part I, p. 200.

8. ILO, *Employment, Incomes and Equality: A Strategy for Increasing Productive Employment in Kenya*, Geneva, 1972, pp. 34-5.
9. The Mumias development of sugar production is examined in Chapter Five.
10. *Sessional Paper No. 10 of 1965*, para. 82.
11. Ibid., pp. 10-11.
12. A senior official of the Ministry of Agriculture 'dismissed as lies the talk by some people that the Government would auction their farm if they failed to repay the loans'. (*The Standard*, 19 August 1975.)
13. *Development Plan 1974-1978*, Part I, p. 212.
14. Gross marketed production from large farms was £37m. in 1963, £72m. in 1974 (*Economic Survey 1967*, p. 33, and *Economic Survey 1975*, p. 89). The changes in producer prices over the period indicate that the increase in value is not simply the result of rising prices:

Producer Prices, 1974 (1963 = 100)

Wheat	Maize	Coffee	Pyrethrum	Sisal	Tea	Seed Cotton
125	140	172	153	115	92	149

Coffee accounted for only 17 per cent of total sales from large farms in 1967 (the last year for which data are available of the value of output of particular crops from large and small farms separately). Output from large farms has been under a number of influences, including the reduction in area as a result of settlement and the use of improved seeds.

15. ILO, op. cit., Chapter 6, especially pp. 83, 95-8.
16. See below, p. 106.
17. *Development Plan 1966-1970*, Government Printer, Nairobi, 1966, p. 56.
18. *Development Plan 1974-1978*, Part I, p. 199.
19. Judith Heyer, IDS Working Paper No. 194, p. 26.
20. Ministry of Commerce and Industry, *A Guide to Industrial Investment in Kenya*, 2nd ed., 1972, p. 3.
21. See A, Hazlewood, *Economic Integration: The East African Experience*, London, Heinemann, 1975.
22. ILO, op. cit., p. 286.
23. *Statistical Abstract* and *Economic Survey 1975*, p. 129. Value of output = manufacturing and repairs component of GDP.
24. *Development Plan 1974-1978*, Part I, p. 278.
25. No later figures have been published.
26. Hazlewood, op. cit.
27. The allocation of markets to their different plants by multinationals could either benefit or limit Kenyan exports, as compared with a more competitive situation. A product-by-product analysis would be necessary to determine the total effect.
28. See Frances Stewart, 'Kenya: Strategies for Development' in Ukandi Danaachi *et al.* (eds), *Development Paths in Africa and China*, London, Macmillan, 1976.
29. *Census of Industrial Production, 1967*.
30. See 'Lower Income Index of Consumer Prices – Nairobi: New Weights', *Kenya Statistical Digest* (quarterly). Roughly 70 per cent of total expenditure is on goods and 30 per cent on services, mainly rent (20 per cent) and school fees (nearly 5 per cent).
31. Products can also be positively deleterious. The British government believes this to be so for milk-based baby foods and feeding bottles. A letter from the Parliamentary Under-Secretary of State for Overseas Development, of July 1975, says:

> There are strong reasons for arguing that these foods are not appropriate for

use by mothers in developing countries, who often do not understand how they should be administered or lack the facilities for preparing and sterilising feeding bottles in hygienic conditions. In the MOD we share this concern, and have no doubt that promotion of the sales of milk-based baby foods in developing countries is contributing to infant mortality and malnutrition.

32. Imports were the vehicle in the original exposition of the effect.
33. *Development Plan 1974-1978*, Part I, p. 280. See also I. M. D. Little, T. Scitovsky and M. F. Scott, *Industry and Trade in Some Developing Countries: A Comparative Study*, London, OUP for the OECD Development Centre, 1970.
34. Paradoxically, later in the speech the Minister announced that import duties were to be raised in order 'to restrict the growth of demand for a number of import items in the luxury or semi-luxury class', some of which are produced domestically.
35. *Development Plan 1974-1978*, Part I, p. 280.
36. *Sessional Paper on Employment* (No. 10 of 1973), para. 279.
37. *Sessional Paper No. 1 of 1974: On the Current Economic Situation in Kenya*, p. 6.
38. It is proposed increasingly to replace tariffs and import controls by excise and sales taxes so as to discourage the consumption of inessentials, whether imported or home-produced. See *Development Plan 1974-1978*, Part I, p. 281.
39. Ibid., p. 280. See also *Sessional Paper on Employment* (No. 10 of 1973), p. 31, para. 112, and p. 38, para. 138.
40. *Development Plan 1974-1978*, Part I, p. 284.
41. Employment: percentages of total

	Citizens	Non-citizens	Africans
1967	92	8	91
1972	96	4	95

(Calculated from Table 2.2, *Development Plan 1974-1978*, Part I, p. 39.)

42. 83 per cent of the total in public employment and 68 per cent of the total in private employment. See *Development Plan 1974-1978*, Part I, p. 38.
43. One cannot but be impressed by the different attitude adopted to British farmers of United Kingdom origin, and British traders of Asian origin. The latter had to dispose of their businesses, when required to do so by the Kenya government, in the market context of such forced disposal. There was no finnance from Britain to buy out the traders at a free market price, though it is believed that the Kenya government at one time suggested that the UK should make funds available for this purpose on the lines of the Land Transfer Programme.
44. ILO, op. cit., pp. 5 and 21.
45. See Walter Elkan, 'Criteria for Industrial Development in Uganda', *East African Economic Review*, Vol. 5, No. 2, January 1959.
46. From 30 cents, the fare at one time charged. *Tatu* is 'three' in Kiswahili.
47. See *Sessional Paper on Employment* (No. 10 of 1973), paras. 154 and 170, and *Development Plan 1974-1978*, Part I, p. 11.
48. *Sessional Paper on Employment*, para. 99.
49. At lower levels of the administration the degree of understanding may remain abysmal, as perhaps is illustrated by the newspaper report that the authorities in Kisumu were taking action against shoe-shine boys who, because there were so many of them, were exploiting the public.
50. Despite the new policy it could be reported in August 1975 that 'Nairobi City Council's "wrecking squad" yesterday moved into swift action and pulled down several shanties at Mathare Valley leaving 100 families homeless.' (*Daily*

Nation, 15 August 1975.)

51. Introduction by the President to *Development Plan 1974-1978*.
52. See *Report* of the Commission of Inquiry (Public Service Structure and Remuneration Commission) 1970-71, May 1971 (Ndegwa Report).
53. See Ndegwa Report, op. cit., Chapter VI for the figures.
54. There must be added a housing allowance which for the higher salaries varied according to circumstances between 13 and 30 per cent of salary. Ibid., pp. 246-8.
55. The salary of the Head of the UK civil service at the time was £16,750.
56. It might be argued that it is possible if political and ideological commitment is sufficiently strong, and some might point to China and Tanzania as examples. There is no such commitment in Kenya.
57. *Sessional Paper on Employment* (No. 10 of 1973), para. 212.
58. *Sessional Paper No. 4 of 1975*, p. 14.
59. Ministry of Commerce and Industry, *A Guide to Industrial Investment*, 2nd edition, 1972.
60. A greater increase in the relative importance of the government sector is indicated when the government sector is compared with total GDP, monetary and non-monetary, because the official figures of non-monetary production show its share declining from 27 per cent to 21 per cent. Measured in this way the government share increased from 13 per cent to 17 per cent. Given the difficulties associated with the measurement and the meaning of the statistics of non-monetary production, the reality of the sector shares is best expressed in terms of monetary production alone.

GDP monetary economy (1964 prices)

	1964		1974	
	K£m.	%	K£m.	%
General government	42.5	18	102.5	21
Other sectors	198.6	82	377.4	79
Total	241.1	100	479.9	100

Source: Economic Survey 1975, Table 2.1.

61. *Economic Survey 1974*. Figures for 1974 are not available.
62. Figures for the contribution of education to GDP are not available for 1974. But education has been a growth sector, partly as the result of deliberate policy – primary school fees have been abolished in Standards I to IV – and partly, one suspects, because the government is unable to control the growth.
63. See C. Leys, *Underdevelopment in Kenya: the Political Economy of Neo-Colonialism 1964-1971*, London, Heinemann, 1975, pp. 110 and 112.
64. *Sessional Paper No. 10 of 1965*, para. 25.
65. Ibid., p. 24.
66. E. O. Edwards, 'Development Planning in Kenya since Independence', *East African Economic Review*, Vol. 4, No. 2, December 1968.
67. Preface to *Development Plan for 1974-1978*. The growth rate stated is in real terms, i.e. at constant prices.
68. Exports by Kenya

	1963	1973
To outside E. Africa	43.8	122.6
Re-exports	7.1	6.3
To Tanzania and Uganda	19.8	38.8
Total	70.7	167.7

69. See ILO, op. cit., p. 280.
70. *Development Plan 1970-1974.*
71. *Development Plan 1974-1978*, Part I, pp. 42-3. Expenditure on social services accounted for 17 per cent of total government expenditure in 1965/6 and for 32 per cent in 1974/5.
72. 'The 1962 census suggested that the rate of growth was 3 per cent per annum; that of 1969 indicated that it had risen to 3.3 per cent.' (*Development Plan 1974-1978*, Part I, p. 43.) It is now said that the figure is 3.5 per cent.
73. Compare *Sessional Paper No. 10 of 1965* and *Sessional Paper No. 10 of 1973.*
74. *Development Plan 1974-1978*, Part I, p. 1.
75. Introduction to *Development Plan 1974-1978.*
76. *Sessional Paper No. 4 of 1975.*

3 THE FACTS OF AID

Many different states and international bodies give aid to Kenya. The UK's relative importance as a donor has quite naturally declined since independence. In 1964 well over 80 per cent of all Kenya's official aid receipts came from the UK, compared with under a half of aid gross and 22.6 per cent of aid net of amortisation in 1972. West Germany and the United States have remained significant donors for much of the independence period and a development has been the emergence of the Scandinavians and the Dutch as important donors. The World Bank group has been a very important donor of financial aid with a tendency in recent years for credits by the International Development Association (IDA) to decline in importance compared to IBRD lending, so hardening the terms of multilateral aid to Kenya.

Table 3 shows these trends. As it relates to aid net of amortisation, however, it overestimates the decline in Britain's contribution because, as a longer-standing donor, Britain receives more repayments than the others.

Technical assistance remains a considerable part of total aid. There does not seem to be any marked trend one way or the other in the number of technical assistance personnel in Kenya since independence. The rundown in operational personnel whose emoluments are partly financed by Britain has been balanced by increases in the numbers of advisers from other countries.

Compared with the total number of people employed by the Kenya government, the number of technical assistance personnel is small. Wage employment by the central government was 135,000 in 1973[1] and there were fewer than 3,000 expatriates. There are, however, some remarkable concentrations. J. R. Nellis[2] calculated that in 1971 the Ministry of Finance and Planning had 111 Nairobi-based upper-level posts and a number were vacant (around 19). At that time there were 34 expatriate technical assistance personnel working there altogether, 22 being technical advisers. By the not-foolproof technique of studying names and looking at the number of established posts in different ministries in 1969 and 1972, Nellis compiled percentages of expatriates in senior positions in all ministries. In 1972 they varied from nil in the Ministries of Foreign Affairs, Co-operatives, and Defence to 31.76 in Agriculture (38.23 in 1969). The average figure for all ministries was 15.68 per cent (23.15 per cent in 1969). Those ministries with over 20 per cent senior expatriate workers in 1972 were (1969 figures in brackets): Agriculture – 31.76 per cent (38.23); Finance and Planning – 30.43 per cent (28.37); Works – 29.62 per cent (37.93); Education – 20.56 per cent (18.03).

Table 3: Source of aid disbursements to Kenya

(percentages)

	1964	1965	1966	1967	1968	1969		1970		1971		1972	
	B	B	B	B	B	A	B	A	B	A	B	A	B
Canada	0.6	1.0	1.9	2.7	2.4	6.2	2.5	6.3	3.0	7.5	3.0	5.5	2.2
Denmark	–	0.3	0.2	0.5	1.3	3.6	1.8	3.0	2.0	6.8	3.8	9.0	5.2
W. Germany	8.1	2.1	6.3	3.9	6.2	8.2	3.3	8.0	7.3	1.4	6.6	11.0	4.7
Netherlands	–	0.2	–	2.8	0.1	–	0.3	6.6	2.7	8.1	4.1	11.6	5.3
Norway	–	0.2	0.7	1.7	2.9	5.3	5.4	4.7	3.9	5.0	3.5	4.9	3.5
Sweden	0.2	0.5	2.2	5.2	6.2	10.6	5.9	8.1	4.1	8.3	4.1	7.9	7.3
UK	87.3	74.8	47.4	40.1	40.9	26.8	36.9	28.8	34.9	21.6	22.3	27.4	22.6
US	3.6	17.7	24.3	3.9	8.7	20.4	9.5	14.7	8.9	12.3	11.7	7.3	4.7
Other bilateral	0.5	0.5	1.1	1.9	1.1	4.9	2.3	3.9	2.5	3.5	8.7	2.9	1.5
IBRD	–0.7	–1.3	9.9	28.0	8.8	–	9.4	–	13.3	–	19.5	–	29.6
IDA	–33.0	1.0	4.3	7.2	14.3	–	15.3	–	9.8	–	3.6	–	5.5
UNDP	...	...	...	...	...	10.8	4.1	12.3	4.9	12.7	4.7	9.0	3.5
Other multilateral	3.4	2.9	1.7	2.5	7.2	3.1	3.4	3.6	2.8	2.8	4.4	3.3	4.3
	100	100	100	100	100	100	100	100	100	100	100	100	100

Source: OECD, *Development Co-operation:* various issues.

Key: A: percentage of total technical assistance received by Kenya.
B: percentage of total aid (financial + TA) net of amortisation but *gross* of interest payments.

Table 4: Technical assistance to Kenya and EAC by country of origin: September 1973

	Operational posts		Advisers		Volunteers		Total
	A	B	A	B	A	B	
Australia	5	5	–	–	–	–	5
UK	987	1377	62	78	107	112	1565
Canada	–	–	54	56	–	–	56
Denmark	30	32	63	65	106	106	208
Finland	–	–	10	10	–	–	10
France	19	19	10	10	–	–	29
Ford Foundation	–	–	4	4	–	–	4
West Germany	–	–	74	75	34	34	109
India	–	–	1	1	–	–	1
Italy	–	–	8	8	24	24	32
Japan	–	–	28	28	44	44	72
Netherlands	2	2	63	64	73	73	139
Norway	30	32	39	42	33	33	107
Rockefeller Foundation	–	–	6	6	–	–	6
Sweden	43	43	5	5	25	25	73
Switzerland	2	3	12	12	–	–	15
UNDP	5	5	91	97	–	–	102
USA	11	11	12	20	180	181	212
USSR	8	8	–	–	–	–	8
WHO	–	–	33	33	–	–	33
Yugoslavia	3	3	–	–	–	–	3

Totals:	Overseas Service Aid Scheme (OSAS)*	1134
	British Expatriates Supplementation Scheme (BESS)*	160
	Operational personnel, not from UK	246
	Advisers	614
	Volunteers	637
	Grand total:	2,791

A: numbers working for the Kenya government only.
B: numbers working for the Kenya government plus East African Community.

Source: Kenya government.

* See below, p. 63.

Two ministries, Finance and Planning and Education, were the only ones to show absolute and percentage increases in the number of expatriates employed between 1969 and 1972. Since 1974, however, there has been a reduction – from 20 to 11 – of British expatriates in the Ministry of Finance and most of the survivors are in technical rather than policy positions, in the Tax Department and Bureau of Statistics. It is interesting that the ministries on Nellis's list are by-and-large those whose efficiency is most criticised by donor agencies except for the Ministry of Finance, which is, however, the major link with donors. The conjunction suggests that technical assistance may be a response to the felt needs of donor agencies as much as of the Kenyan government.[3]

Table 4 gives a breakdown of technical assistance in Kenya in 1973 by type of personnel and country of origin.

British Capital Aid

British aid to Kenya has not been typical either of the programmes of other donors there, or of British aid in general. About 45 per cent of British capital aid since independence has been for purposes other than general development. Most of this money has gone into the Land Transfer Programme (LTP) or into land adjudication and registration. Excluding the independence settlement (see Table 5) and considering only commitments made since 1964, over half of British aid has been for land transfer, settlement or adjudication. Despite the bias towards LTP, British aid was very important in financing the Kenya government's development budget in the early years of independence. In 1963/64, gross financial aid accounted for 87 per cent of development revenue, and 77 per cent of that revenue came from Britain.[4]

Aid, net of loan repayments and interest, was equivalent to 5.9 per cent of Kenya's GDP in 1964, and the proportion has changed little since. In 1970 it was 4.3 per cent and in 1972 5.4 per cent. Owing to the expansion of public sector development spending, however, financial aid has declined in importance as a means of financing the development budget. In recent years it has averaged around 50 per cent of development revenue, and Britain's contribution has fallen to around 10-15 per cent. Britain also contributed to Kenya's recurrent budget expenditure with technical assistance grants but aid is now an insignificant proportion of the recurrent budget.

For some years aid has been around 12-15 per cent of total government expenditure, but despite this relatively modest proportion the Kenyans have difficulty in spending the aid on offer. This certainly applies to British aid. In 1974, three-quarters of the loan agreed in 1973 had not been definitely allocated to any project; nearly £1m., one-fifth, of the 1970 loan was unallocated, and there were even small sums outstanding from the 1966 loan and the pre-independence Colonial Development and Welfare grant. Other donors have had similar experiences. One reason

Table 5: British official capital aid commitments to Kenya since Independence

		£m.
1964	Independence settlement	
	Land Transfer Programme[a]:	
	Unissued balance of commitment of £21.3m. as grant and loan	11.0
	Further loan for Land Bank	1.0
	Development grants and loans: unissued balances	4.3
	Development grant 1964/5	1.0
	Development loan 1964/5	2.0
	Pension loans	13.6
	Budgetary grant	1.25
	Special land purchase scheme loan	1.275
		34.475
1965/6		
	General development loan (interest-free, 42% import content)	3.0
	Land Bank loan	1.0
		4.0
1966/70		
	Land Transfer Programme (interest-free loan)	6.3
	General development loan (interest-free, 60% import content)	8.7
	Land adjudication loan (previously classified under general development)	3.0
		18.0
1970		
	Land Transfer Programme:	
	Settlement (grant)	2.5
	Agricultural Development Corporation and Agricultural Finance Corporation loan (2% interest)	1.0
	Special scheme grant	0.25
	General development loan (2% interest, 75% import content)	5.0
	Land adjudication/Rural development loan (2% interest)	2.75
		11.5
1973		
	Land Transfer Programme:	
	Settlement grant	6.0
	Agricultural Finance Corporation loan (2% interest)	2.0
	General development loan (2% interest, 50% import content)	10.0
		17.0
TOTAL		85.975

[a] In addition between 1963 and 1969 about £1m. was provided specially for the purchase of farms of compassionate cases outside the settlement areas.

is the procurement-tying of funds, whereby Kenya is obliged to spend part or all of an aid commitment in the donor country. That is not the main reason, however. Of the £1m. of British aid outstanding from 1970, only some £103,000 had to be spent on British goods, showing that most of the tied aid had been spent and much of the untied portion of aid loans had not.[5]

Up to 1970, British financial aid for general development was spent in a large number of mainly small packets. Having a Development Plan including many small projects, the Kenyans approached HMG with a 'shopping list' of aid requirements, mainly for capital equipment. The only projects carried out before 1970 where the British aid contribution was over a quarter of a million Sterling were: construction of the Nairobi-Mombasa road, which was financed by money from more than one loan (£2.2m.); the Chemelil sugar factory (£405,000), which also received much German aid; afforestation schemes (£715,000); and provision of road-building equipment for the North-East Region (£320,000). Of the five projects financed by the 1970 loan, however, four received aid of over £250,000. They were: Mumias sugar factory (£2.9m.); Mombasa TV (£260,000); Naivasha-Suswa pipeline (£465,000); livestock marketing scheme (£288,000). The fifth project, provision of large hermetically-sealed bins for grain storage, received aid of £170,000. That was still more than the average loan disbursement of £150,000 before 1970. This pattern for larger discrete disbursements continued with the 1973 loan. Apart from continuing land adjudication expenditures (now classed with general development) costing £1.8m., the other projects where aid was settled by end-1975 were the second phase of a livestock marketing scheme receiving over £1m., and a pilot scheme for rural access roads receiving £250,000. Other projects under consideration included construction of a Polytechnic and University colleges, grain storage, and a scheme for rural access roads. All were likely to receive over £1m. each.

Over the whole post-independence period the sectoral breakdown by value of British general development aid disbursements was:[6] agriculture, 17 per cent; processing agricultural products, 23 per cent; physical infrastructure, 32 per cent; social services, 25 per cent; other, 3 per cent. If the Land Transfer Programme and land adjudication programmes are counted as assistance for agriculture, however, total aid to that sector is 59 per cent of gross capital aid.

The trend in the real value of British capital aid to Kenya has been steadily downwards since independence. Table 6, which includes disbursements by the Commonwealth Development Corporation[7] and technical assistance (covered separately in Table 8), gives disbursements at current prices. As Britain has been a donor for some years, amortisation and interest repayments on earlier British loans are now quite considerable. In 1972, for example, Britain's total net aid flow was barely more than technical assistance disbursements; new financial flows were practically wiped out by repayments and interest on earlier loans. For the period 1963-72 Britain received some £50m. from Kenya in amortisation and interest payments. Net and gross aid figures therefore diverge substantially and it is necessary to consider which are appropriate when examining the British aid effort.

The concept of 'net aid' suggests that, if new aid flows are balanced by amortisation and interest payments, Britain is not aiding Kenya. That is an odd formulation because earlier flows ought to have engendered investments leading to a social return exceeding loan charges. If current and future disbursements do not do so, aid should not be accepted. If it was right to accept the aid, the subsequent netting of flows for any particular year is quite arbitrary, although it has the useful effect of emphasising the budgetary and balance of payments difficulties which may be encountered by a developing country. It also goes some way to offset the crudeness of statistical series that show total aid flows without discriminating between loan and grant or loans on different terms. Rather than netting aid figures, however, a better procedure is to take account of terms directly and to compute the 'grant equivalent' of each aid disbursement showing its net value at disbursement when the present value of future charges has been deducted.[8]

British net aid disbursement to Kenya 1963-73 was some 60 per cent of gross disbursements. Grants accounted for a third of the latter and the loans have a grant equivalent of at least 80 per cent, depending on discount rate. Net British aid in the superior sense of grant equivalent would thus be over 87 per cent of gross aid. For many purposes, therefore, the gross aid figures give a better picture of the transfer than the net figures.

We now attempt to refine the figures for aid disbursements given in official statistics by taking account of important developments that they ignore. We shall adjust the figures for inflation in Britain, parity changes of the pound Sterling and the extent of procurement-tying. All figures in Table 6 are in current prices. If they are deflated for changes in the British price level[9] they reveal that aid has been falling in real terms, even ignoring the 1967 devaluation, and the float of the pound from 1972.

The accumulating burden of Kenya's repayments to the UK is shown by the rate of decline of the net aid disbursement figure of nearly 20 per cent a year.

These figures take account of the changing purchasing power in the UK of aid flows to Kenya but take no account of the changing purchasing power of UK aid in Kenya and elsewhere in the world. Two factors affect that: the extent of the procurement-tying of aid and the value of the pound relative to other currencies. Procurement-tying is an important feature of aid and we consider it in some detail.

British aid is tied entirely to the purchase of British goods or goods produced in Kenya (so-called local costs). If the Kenyans wish to spend

Table 6: Total British aid disbursements to Kenya and the East African Community

					(£'000)						Total
	1964	*1965*	*1966*	*1967*	*1968*	*1969*	*1970*	*1971*	*1972*	*1973*	*1964-73*
To Kenya											
gross disbursements	14391	16692	12095	9583	10965	10756	11099	9820	24434	11668	131503
net of amortisation	13989	16142	11096	7751	9968	9706	9804	7870	8437	8793	103556
net of amortisation and interest	12739	14736	8481	4842	7016	6485	6357	4465	4895	5009	75025
To the East African Community[b]											
gross disbursements	6039	5451	5355	4166	3001	2394	2535	3587	7787[c]	2977	43292
net of amortisation	5679	4986	4875	3673	2496	1804	1669	2829	1209	2177	31397
net of amortisation and interest	5024	4447	4198	2938	1686	1003	897	2093	520	1537	24343

a Includes £13,797m. to write off loans for civil servants' compensation and pensions. This does not appear in Table 5.
b Owing to the establishment of the headquarters of many EAC services in Kenya, much of this aid was actually spent in Kenya.
c Includes some £5.8m. write-off of pension loans.

Sources: British Aid Statistics 1964-68 to *1968-72*.

Table 7: British aid disbursements at 1964 prices

	£m.									
	1964	*1965*	*1966*	*1967*	*1968*	*1969*	*1970*	*1971*	*1972*	*1973*
Gross disbursements	14.4	16.3	11.3	8.6	9.2	8.8	8.5	6.6	7.0[a]	8.7
Net transfer (gross disbursements less amortisation and interest payments)	12.7	14.3	7.9	4.4	5.9	5.3	4.7	3.0	3.0	3.7

a Excluding pension payments.

British aid directly on goods from third countries, they have to secure the approval of ODM which in turn approaches the Department of Trade. Both ministries have to be satisfied that no equivalent British good is available before any special dispensation is given. Such requests and dispensations are rare. The proportion of general development loans that has been tied to purchases of British goods as opposed to local costs has varied between aid agreements.[10] A weighted average proportion for all general development loans after 1964 is 51.7 per cent. The proportion of all British capital aid to Kenya tied formally to procurement in the UK is 24.6 per cent, as LTP and land adjudication funds are untied. In addition, all technical assistance is tied to acquisition of personnel in the UK. This was carried to derisory lengths. A British passport holder, for example, if educated and resident in Kenya, might not be eligible for employment by the Kenya government under UK technical assistance. There has been some liberalisation of these conventions owing to the personal intervention of the former Minister for Overseas Development, Judith Hart. Special authority can now be obtained from 'higher channels' within ODM for non-British residents to be designated technical assistance personnel. It remains rare.

Formal procurement-tying is not the only sort. Much British money has been tied to its use in the purchase of land under the Land Transfer Programme where there is no question of the acquisition of British goods, but some 60 per cent of the money paid to British farmers for their landholdings is brought back from Kenya to Britain, as Kenyan Exchange Control allows, so it too is effectively procurement-tied. The practice of procurement-tying clearly involves costs for the recipient country which should be deducted from the nominal value of aid.[11] The most obvious cost is the prevention of competitive international tendering for contracts, so the price the Kenyans have to pay British suppliers for goods may consequently be well above the world market price. This is particularly likely where the supplier is in a monopolistic position in the British market. Empirical studies of these effects in many ldcs have produced widely differing estimates of the additional costs. An UNCTAD publication cites a figure of 20 per cent as being quite a reasonable estimate of the higher prices tying entails on average for ldcs.[12]

There are other costs, however, when procurement-tying is combined with project-tying (making aid conditional on the execution of approved projects) which may well be even more considerable. The commitment of aid funds to specific projects might well be delayed and there is a drain of administrative resources. As Clive Gray puts it:

> The additional costs of tied project aid in terms of administrative resources and delays in project execution are headaches familiar to anyone who has ever been involved in aid administration, on the side of either a donor or a recipient. To begin with, the aid administrators must identify and measure those components of a project which can reasonably be imported from the aid source, rather than leaving it to the more efficient procurement staff of a contractor, or simply to the workings of the free market. One should not under-estimate the drain on aid, and host government staff resources, involved in deciding questions such as what types of the myriads of standard components that go into a building can be purchased out of local distributors stocks as opposed to being ordered and shipped specially from the aid source country. Next, if the local economy is presently importing its requirements of the goods and services in question from sources with are ineligible for purposes of the project, new procurement channels must be developed, and the procurement must be supervised by aid administrators in both the source and recipient countries. The writer has repeatedly been struck by the high opportunity cost of the government staff time required to manipulate commercial trade channels and procedures in order to satisfy tied-aid requirements – staff time that, from an economic point of view would be far better spent evaluating projects more closely and administering their substantive aspects more intensively.[13]

Tying slows the commitment of funds, while high-import projects are found, then it slows disbursement of funds and the execution of projects. British goods are notoriously subject to long delays in delivery and the Kenyans may have to wait months for British equipment to be supplied when comparable goods are available immediately from the local agents of third-country suppliers. The tradition in Kenya of trading with Britain may mean, however, that some of the difficulties which Gray describes are less severe for tied British aid than for that of other donors.

While the agreement to provide a proportion of local costs of any project represents an advance on simply providing the import content of projects, it is still a form of tying, although one that is applied with some flexibility. Local-cost provisions are usually used to finance labour costs and costs of construction. Where they include locally supplied goods it may be that the proportion of Kenyan value-added in the price of the goods is low and the third-country import content consequently high. In addition, paying a local agent for goods off the shelf can count as part of the costs of a project tied to British procurement if the agent agrees to re-stock with British goods, but it is clearly hard to check this. Fortunately, ODM realises the difficulties which source-tying creates for recipients. Its maintenance is the result of British Treasury and, to a lesser extent, Department of Trade pressure.

Clearly, in valuing British aid, the existence of, and changes in, the intensity of tying have to be considered. Some of the costs mentioned do not necessitate any modification of the figures of Table 7. Delays in disbursement, for example, simply mean that in the absence of tying, the figures would be higher. The important administrative costs are impossible to quantify. The extra paid for British goods over world market prices as a result of tying ought, however, to be deducted.[14]

Although an average of around half of British aid for general development has been tied to procurement in Britain, this cannot always have been a problem. Kenya naturally takes a high proportion of its merchandise imports from Britain – an average of around 30 per cent in the period we are considering. If British aid had not been project-tied, the procurement-tying might have been no problem at all. The money could perhaps have been used entirely for goods that would have been imported from the UK anyway, as it is hard to enforce stipulations that aid should lead to 'additional' imports. When aid is also project-tied, however, it may not be possible to spend all British aid on projects where British imports would have been used. Some might have to be spent on projects where other countries' products would have been first choice, in which case the combination of project-tying and procurement-tying succeeds in raising British exports to Kenya. If the Kenya government would have imported for projects in a similar way to the economy as a whole – a very strong assumption – tying might result in a surcharge on a proportion of the imports for British-aided projects equal to the difference between the marginal propensity to import from Britain and the proportion of British loans that is procurement-tied. It will be less of a problem in so far as Britain can be allocated projects for which its exports are competitive. On the other hand, that ignores the possibility that British firms may tender one price when competing freely with foreigners for an order, but offer quite another when they know they are faced with a captive market owing to aid-tying.

With these qualifications in mind, we can guess that tying might be a real constraint for about 15 per cent of gross British general development aid and the goods it buys are about 20 per cent overpriced (the UNCTAD estimate). That would mean the value of the 50 per cent of British capital aid that has been for general development is overstated by some 3 per cent. The overstatement of total gross aid including LTP and land adjudication funds is therefore less still. The overstatement of net aid for the period is greater as reverse flows of interest and amortisation to Britain consist of free foreign exchange. Although technical assistance is tied, this is unlikely to be so much of a problem. It is unlikely that Kenya could get suitable people more cheaply by hiring on the world market. It may well be that people work in Kenya for less when they feel the job has the backing of their own government than they would if hired directly by the Kenya government.[15] However, some jobs, especially consultancies, could probably be done more cheaply and efficiently if technical assistance were not tied, and the donor hired anyone qualified.

The cost of British aid-tying to Kenya therefore appears very modest – perhaps as low as 1 per cent and very unlikely to be more than a 5 per cent overstatement of the value of the aid. This, however, is not counting the inevitable administrative costs and delays which are probably more important.

The effect of the parity of Sterling on the value of British aid cannot be separated from the problem of tying. That proportion of aid that is for local costs is in effect free foreign exchange. The Kenyan government is committed to making payments to residents in Kenyan shillings but it then receives an equivalent amount in Sterling to add to its foreign exchange reserves. The injection of money into the domestic economy gives rise to extra import demand which is financed by the additional foreign reserves. That proportion of local-cost aid (denoted in Sterling) which would finally finance non-Sterling imports is reduced in value by the full amount of the devaluation, but the proportion itself might be altered by any relative price movements caused by the devaluation. The value of that proportion of local-cost aid that is eventually spent on British goods is, however, not affected by the devaluation. (Clearly devaluation is bound to affect the internal British price level and the cost of exports, but this effect is covered by deflating aid flows by a price index.) Similarly, the value of tied aid is not reduced by the devaluation *per se*. Indeed it should be increased. The reason is that if a devaluation of Sterling makes Kenya want to import more goods from Britain, any given degree of tying of aid may become less onerous following a devaluation. There is, however, no evidence that the Sterling devaluation of 1967 did much to affect the proportion by value of Kenya's imports coming from Britain,[16] and as the direct pecuniary costs of tying (as opposed to the costs of administrative demands and delayed disbursements) are modest anyway in relation to total aid flows, it is doubtful if this beneficial effect of a devaluation is significant. The effect of the devaluation for practical purposes is therefore confined to that proportion of local-cost aid that would eventually have been used to import non-British goods, i.e., we should subtract from British aid flows for 1968 and subsequent years a proportion of the total equal to 1 X 0.143 (devaluation) X 0.45 (approximate proportion of aid that is untied) X 0.70 (approximate proportion of imports not from Britain). This is a mere 4.5 per cent. So if capital aid flows are written down by up to 5 per cent to allow for the effect of procurement-tying, it is only necessary to deflate the 1968-73 figures by some four and a half per cent in allowing for devaluation. And for net aid the adjustment should be even less because the devaluation reduces the debt burden of repayments in Sterling. Consideration of devaluation, therefore, fortifies the conclusion that aid has been falling in real terms, but hardly makes a dramatic difference.

In 1975, there were two departures in UK aid policy towards Kenya, representing a softening in terms. Owing to Kenya's balance of payments difficulties following the oil crisis, Britain made a balance of payments support grant of £2.5m. This was nominally for British goods but was untied to any project. Later in the year, ODM announced that future aid to countries with an annual income per head of $ 200 or under would be entirely in the form of grants. Kenya is among those countries.

British Technical Assistance

Table 8: British technical assistance disbursements to Kenya and the East African Community

	(£'000)					
	1963	*1964*	*1965*	*1966*	*1967*	*1968*
To Kenya	3887	2323	4849	2604	3815	4075
To East African Community	2823	3123	3527	3329	2205	2355
	1969	*1970*	*1971*	*1972*	*1973*	Total *1963-73*
To Kenya	2733	3271	2891	4499	4741	39688
To East African Community	2390	2340	2603	1972	2972	29639

Sources: British Aid Statistics 1963-67 to *1968-72.*

Table 9: British technical assistance to Kenya[a]: by recipient ministry at 31 March 1974

	OSAS	Advisers[b]	% of total
Agriculture	54	18[c]	8.2
Commerce and industry	1	1	0.5
Finance & Planning	17	3	2.3
Education	559	4	63.8
Natural Resources	5	–	0.3
Health	25	1	2.9
Home Affairs (Police, etc.)	42	2	5.0
Information and Broadcasting	4	–	0.5
Labour	2	–	0.2
Attorney General's Office	8	–	0.9
Judicial Department	14	–	1.6
Power & Communications	4	3	0.8
Office of the President	23	–	2.6
Land and Settlement	13	1	1.6
Tourism & Wildlife	1	1	0.2
Works	74	–	8.6
TOTAL	846	34	100.0

Source: Ministry of Overseas Development.

a Excluding EAC. There are 362 additional OSAS personnel with EAC, most of them serving in Kenya (Harbours 46, Railways 149, Post and Telecommunications 102, General Financial Services 65), and 3 advisers.

b This figure includes some advisers not strictly attached to a ministry but to other organisations, e.g. Tana River Development Authority. In such cases the expert has been imputed to the ministry appropriate to his work.

c This figure excludes personnel serving with research schemes, mostly in the field of agriculture and natural resources. There were 66 of these.

Technical assistance is a very important part of aid to Kenya, which gets some 45 per cent of aid disbursements in this form, and Britain is much the most important supplier. British technical assistance personnel can be classified in three groups. There are volunteers and experts, the latter being further divided into wholly- and partly-funded personnel. Volunteers are not part of the official aid programme, and we do not consider them further. The wholly-funded personnel are usually advisers to the Kenya government or a parastatal organisation whose salary is met entirely by

Britain. They work for a contract period and do not have established posts in the Kenyan administration. They are usually specialists with a particular, more or less technical, expertise rather than managers or administrators. The terms and conditions of their service are covered by the Special Commonwealth African Assistance Plan (SCAAP).[17] Partly-funded personnel are British nationals who hold established posts in the Kenyan administration. The Kenya government pays them a 'local' salary and the British government adds an inducement allowance or 'topping up' to UK levels. The terms and conditions of these personnel are covered by the Overseas Service Aid Scheme (OSAS) and the British Expatriates Supplementation Scheme (BESS). At independence, there were large numbers of British people working in the Kenyan administration. The OSAS scheme provided a device whereby they were induced to stay and others were recruited. It provided a means for HMG to support Kenya's general administration at a time when there would have been grave difficulties for the independent government in finding adequate executives and administrators to man the civil service. In the early independence years, therefore, most British technical assistance was OSAS and many of the people concerned were involved in the general running of government departments. BESS supports British nationals employed outside the central government in local authorities, universities and state corporations.

While OSAS people are still more numerous than other technical assistance, their numbers have declined more or less steadily. There were about 1,600 OSAS personnel in 1965 compared with about 1,000 now. The numbers doing general administrative work under the scheme have gone down much faster than OSAS numbers as a whole. One group, teachers, increased in absolute numbers for eight or nine years after independence, and has begun to fall only in recent years. There has been no clear trend in the numbers of expert advisers supplied under the SCAAP scheme, which was roughly the same in 1965 and 1973, although it had been much higher in between. Disbursements on British technical assistance are given in Table 8, and the numbers of British technical assistance personnel by Kenyan ministry in Table 9.

Britain still supplied over half of expatriate personnel in Kenya in 1973, but only two years before, the proportion was as high as 64 per cent. The cash value of Britain's technical assistance effort is, however, a lower proportion of the total as the areas in which British personnel work are rather atypical. There are more relatively low-paid teachers and fewer highly paid expert advisers.

The Commonwealth Development Corporation

The statistics in Table 6 include investments by the Commonwealth Development Corporation (CDC). Although this body has come under the authority of the Minister of Overseas Development since 1965 and it lends for projects in less developed countries at concessionary terms, its activities are regarded as separate from the aid programme proper. The CDC was established by Act of Parliament in 1948 as the Colonial Development Corporation to assist in the economic development of dependent territories and took its present name in 1963. It operates on commercial lines and has a statutory obligation to pay its way taking one year with another. CDC obtains money on loan, largely from the UK Exchequer from which it can obtain £205m. of a total statutory borrowing capacity of £225m. The Corporation may negotiate any interest rate but generally aims to lend at some two or three per cent above its Treasury borrowing rate. Most of its loans are currently made at interest rates of 8 to 10 per cent although for agricultural projects it can lend at 5 to 6 per cent. It can also take equity in projects.

The Corporation's investment in Kenya has been substantial. The book value of its outstanding investment there in 1973 exceeded £30m. At independence it was just under £10m. in current pounds. The lending of CDC is not subject to the Country Policy Paper[18] which guides the allocation of ODM funds, but like the official aid programme CDC has sought to concentrate funds in agriculture. At independence CDC was already involved in mining, electricity and water supply, housing, hotels and engineering. It held equity in hotels and manufacturing concerns; it owned the Kenya building societies and had made loans *inter alia* to the Kenya Power Company (£3.5m.), the Kenya Meat Commission (£250,000 with £135,000 outstanding) and Nairobi City Council for water works and housing schemes (£250,000). It was committed to providing finance, a manager and accountant-secretary for the Development Finance Company of Kenya.[19]

CDC was also involved at independence in the beginnings of its most successful venture in Kenya, the development of small-holder tea-growing which, from 1954, had been developed to 1,600 acres and one tea factory by the Kenya government on a proving basis, using funds derived from the British government grant towards the development of African agriculture. In 1960 CDC committed £900,000 to the Special Crops Development Authority, redesignated the Kenya Tea Development Authority (KTDA) in 1964, to develop small-holder tea-growing and lent some £480,000, two-thirds of the cost of six tea factories, to process the small holders' output. West Germany provided £212,000. A second KTDA scheme increased the number of factories to seventeen by the end of 1970 and a third brought total tea acreage planted to 64,500 acres by the end of 1972. By then CDC had committed some £1.35m. for field development and the IDA had committed £1.875m. Neither of these loans was fully drawn as crop yields and cesses exceeded estimates and KTDA costs were kept down. CDC had also contributed a substantial part of the finance for ten of the factories in operation, some £800,000. In 1973 the Corporation agreed support for three more factories and committed nearly £7m. for the Fourth Plan to expand acreage by a further 36,000 acres and for the construction of an additional twenty-two factories. The factories in operation are partnerships between CDC, the KTDA and commercial companies.[20] Under the Fourth Plan a factory management training and marketing department has been set up within KTDA which will design, arrange construction and undertake the duties of managing agents for future factories.

The success of the scheme in developmental terms lies in its involvement of large numbers of poor African small holders, over 90,000 of whom now supply tea to the factories that CDC has helped finance. Tea-growing brings them an income of perhaps £60 a year compared to about £5 a year that many earned previously. Prior to 1954 tea had been regarded exclusively as a plantation crop and the demonstration that high-quality leaf could be grown by small holders was very important. CDC claims that the scheme has become a model for the successful organisation of similar projects in other tea-growing countries. The operation is a valuable source of foreign exchange to Kenya as almost all KTDA output is exported. In 1973 it accounted for 18.1 per cent by value of Kenya's exports (up from 12.9 per cent in 1963). A social cost-benefit analysis of the Third Plan found that it had very high rates of return – over 38 per cent. The return to the small holders, counting their own and family labour as a cost and imputing a cost to the land, was rather less – 13 per cent; but their rate of return in cash terms was very high – over 40 per cent in some areas.[21]

CDC is now involved in the Mumias sugar factory which also received official British aid.[22] Other large schemes include the Bura Bura housing estate of some 5,000 houses in Nairobi. CDC has agreed to commit a £1.5m. revolving fund for construction and £3.5m. for mortgage loans to buyers, for a first phase of the project, and equivalent sums of £1.44m. and £1.75m. for a second phase. Part of the CDC interest in agriculture takes the form of investments worth a total of £200,000 in two estates producing largely horticultural crops for export, and owned by British and Kenyan business interests.

Older investments include £3.5m. lent in 1969 to the Tana River Development Authority for construction of the Kindaruma power station and a loan of £2.6m. to the East African Power and Lighting Company Limited for transmission lines.

Aid From Other Sources

This section gives brief descriptions of the activities of some of the important donors to Kenya shown in Table 3. A discussion of the policies behind these donors' programmes follows that on British aid policy in Chapter Four.

United States

Until quite recently the overwhelming bulk of US aid was either technical assistance or food aid. Between 1962 and 1972 the US Agency for International Development (AID) extended grants of $ 29.9m. to Kenya. These were almost all for technical assistance, although there were some small 'commodity' grants supporting the technical assistance and fully tied to US procurement. Aid was overwhelmingly in the field of agriculture, with a smaller number of advisers in education and vocational training. Only two capital loans were extended during this period: $ 2.2m. in 1964 to improve the Nairobi water supply and $ 3.5m. in 1970 for vehicles and construction equipment for the Kenya National Youth Service of the Ministry of Labour. Apart from AID's activities, $ 30.6m. was extended up to 1972 under 'Food for Peace' schemes, just over half of which was classed as emergency relief. The remainder was food loans repayable in US dollars. Volunteer assistance by the Peace Corps was recorded at $ 12.3m. for the period.

Since 1972 the US has become a more active donor. Technical assistance has continued at roughly the same levels with back-up in the form of vehicles and other equipment. Grants totalled $ 2.2m. in 1973. Teams of advisers are operating in the areas of livestock and range development, agricultural credit administration, rural development and family planning, among others. In 1973 the US also extended a programme loan of $ 10m. – 'to help fill Kenya's recently emerged resource gap and maintain development momentum'. The counterpart funds realised by domestic sales of imports financed by the loan are to be used for the Kenyan development budget. A further loan of $ 10m. was extended in 1974 for a livestock development programme. The money was to finance ranching development and *abattoir* and cold storage schemes as part (about one-fifth) of a larger livestock development programme to which the World Bank, UK and Canada, among other donors, were contributing.

West Germany

Since Kenya's independence West Germany has committed £23m. (DM 189.9m.) in capital aid to Kenya and succeeded in disbursing £9m. (DM 76.8m.) of it.[23] The largest single project, accounting for over 20 per cent of total commitments, was the Chemelil sugar factory which also received UK aid. Provision of tourist roads accounts for almost another fifth. Germany has concentrated more on industrial development than most other donors. About 13 per cent of its commitments have been to the Industrial and Commercial Development Corporation of Kenya to help finance industrial estates at Nairobi, Nakuru and Mombasa. In the agricultural field, nearly eight per cent of total capital aid commitments have been for a rice cultivation project and further sums have been committed for a pilot irrigation scheme and for a scheme to provide credit to small farmers. In earlier years, Germany provided money for the promotion of tea-growing. The most recent large commitment, nearly 10 per cent of the total, has been for water supply and sewerage to Nakuru, Kisumu and three other provincial towns.

All German capital aid is loan and the current terms are 30 years maturity with a 10-year grace period and 2 per cent interest. Technical assistance is grant. It has been worth £4.5m. (DM 36.2m.). It is quite widely spread across economic sectors, often associated with German capital projects. A higher proportion has gone into the agricultural sector than is the case with financial aid. The aid is not source-tied. However, many capital aid projects, especially in earlier years, were import-intensive and used goods which German industry was well able to supply. The Germans were also reluctant to finance local costs out of a desire to involve the Kenyans in all projects and 'make them feel responsible for them'. More recently a more liberal attitude to local costs has evolved.

Sweden

In the period 1964-72 the Swedes disbursed only £10.5m. in aid to Kenya but in 1973/74 and 1974/75 they committed sums of £5m. to projects. For the first ten years the sectoral breakdown of Swedish disbursement was: public administration and other services, 35.3 per cent, agriculture 25 per cent, education 18 per cent, water and power supply 10.7 per cent. The 1974 disbursement pattern was: agriculture 22 per cent, education 19 per cent, health, including family planning, 15 per cent, rural water 13 per cent, import financing 10 per cent. Most Swedish capital aid used to be loan, although on very soft terms with 25 or 50 years to maturity, ten-year grace period and either 0.75 per cent or 2 per cent interest charges. More is now grant; some three-quarters of current commitment is grant and the remainder is interest-free 40-year loan. The money is all untied in respect of procurement. Even technical assistance funds are untied in principle although Swedes do tend to be recruited.

Like the US and UK, Sweden made a balance of payments loan to the Kenyans in 1974 to counteract the deterioration in the world economic situation. This is supposed to be for imports for rural development, but the Swedes realise that that is semantics and free foreign exchange is just that.

Uniquely among donors to Kenya the Swedes disburse their aid in advance of expenditures by the Kenyans and merely require subsequent documentation to show how the money was spent.[24]

The World Bank Group

The World Bank group has long been one of the largest donors to Kenya. Between independence and 1975 it had committed $ 144.8m. in IBRD loans, $ 122.8m. in IDA credits and $ 25.9m. in IFC investments[25] for a grand total of $ 293.5m. The IBRD also lent a further $ 229.8m. to the East African Community. Much of this investment has been in large capital-intensive projects, and continues to be so although the Bank now lays emphasis on rural development in its policy pronouncements.[26]

An examination of the Bank's lending to Kenya since 1970 illustrates the difficulty of changing the pattern of loan disbursements away from infrastructure. Less than a fifth of commitments were to agriculture. In 1974, however, the influence of the new policy became clear with most of the money going to rural-based productive enterprises.

Table 10: World Bank commitments to Kenya 1970-74

			$m	
Loan	Year	IBRD	IDA	IFC
Education	1970		6.1	
Pulp and Paper Mills	1970			15.81
Nairobi Water Supply.	1970	8.3		
Highway Maintenance	1970		12.6	
Tana River Development Co. (power)	1971	23.0		
Highways	1972		22.0	
Tourism Promotion Services	1972			2.42
Nairobi Airport	1972	29.0		
Agricultural Credit – second loan	1972		6.0	
Roads	1973	29.0		
Industrial Development Bank	1973	5.0		
Kenya Hotel Properties Ltd. (Tourism)	1973			2.83
Pulp and Paper Mills	1974			1.77
Population Project	1974		12.0	
Tea development – third loan	1974	10.4		
Livestock development – second loan	1974		21.5	

The Costs of Aid

It is sometimes argued that much aid is swallowed up in a bureaucracy of its own creation. We consider here some of the costs of being an aid recipient. The focus is quite narrow and we are not, for the moment, concerned with any distortions in policy that aid may be responsible for, but purely with the direct costs of administering the receipt of aid and direct expenditures associated with technical assistance. We consider the latter first.

The receipt of technical assistance is associated with expenditures by the Kenya government, which often cites them in an attempt to get donors to foot more of the technical assistance bill. Some of these expenditures are real costs of technical assistance in the sense that if there were no technical assistance they would not be incurred. Other expenditures would be incurred to some extent if no technical assistance were received. They cannot really be viewed as costs attributable to technical assistance. Total counterpart expenditures, fresh costs or not, are considerable. By and large, all donors expect similar facilities for their personnel. Advisers get a house or housing allowance or pay no rent. The Kenya government meets internal travel and transport costs and provides office facilities. Advisers can import one car duty-free. For operational personnel the Kenya government pays a local salary which is liable to income tax. OSAS personnel receive part of their gratuity payments, pensions, or compensation from the Kenya government. Operational personnel from Denmark, Norway and UNDP are also paid gratuities.

A study in 1970[27] worked out that counterpart expenditures to Kenya were just under £4m. for a total technical assistance disbursement of £9.5m. Eighty per cent of this sum was on local salaries and housing. If anything, housing costs may have been understated because most expatriates stay in Nairobi where costs are higher than the national average. The 20 per cent of expenditures not salaries and housing, however, was overstated because costs were imputed to technical assistance not only for office space, secretarial support, and other back-up facilities but also for their share of the Kenya government's total social overhead expenditure, for example on public utilities. Both these sets of costs, however, were worked out by taking average spending per head for relevant groups in the country, whereas the marginal cost of the expatriates concerned in the case of most expenditures was almost certainly less than the average cost per head of the services. The receipt of one more expatriate does not require extra water supply for Nairobi, for example.

In 1970 the local expenditure on British advisers per head was roughly £2,380 and on OSAS people £2,790. If the Ministry of Education was excluded (mainly teachers), the latter figure rose to £3,740. How much of these expenditures can truly be called costs depends on what arrangements the Kenyan government would have made to fill posts if technical assistance had not been used. If local people would have been recruited, part of the housing expenditure on expatriates is a cost Some Kenyans might arrange their housing privately and in general they would house themselves at less luxurious levels than expatriates. Also in a poor country like Kenya there is a difficulty in raising tax revenue, so public money may be worth more than private.

The guesstimate for the pure administrative cost of receiving technical assistance, including preparing job specifications for donors and meeting and entertaining them, was about £10 a head, which seems on the low side. Most of that is presumably a genuine cost, although some job specification would have to be done in any event. At any rate such administrative costs were less than 0.5 per cent of counterpart expenditures.

If competent Kenyans are available for posts the Kenya government should not request technical assistance, so the alternative to it is generally doing without the services involved or recruiting abroad. In the latter case practically none of the counterpart expenditures are true costs of technical assistance. However there is some suggestion that sometimes Kenya government departments apply for technical assistance because they do not have adequate budgetary allocations to take on the staff they require even when people are locally available.[28] That would presumably apply mostly to jobs done by wholly-funded personnel because if a budgetary allocation is available for the local salary of an OSAS officer it should be available for a Kenyan, although it could apply to established posts if the salary required to recruit a competent Kenyan exceeded the going rate of pay. Surprisingly, in view of Kenya's school-leaver unemployment problem, we gathered that the Kenya government did indeed have difficulty in recruiting for many jobs at existing pay rates because of private sector competition. Technical assistance might be made more cost-effective in some cases by allowing Kenyans to compete for OSAS posts.

The true direct costs of technical assistance in 1970, therefore, were between nil and the cost of housing, administration, and gratuity payments (some £2m.), the precise sum depending on how many posts could have been filled adequately from local manpower.

The pecuniary costs to Kenya of administering aid are tiny in relation to the sums received. Total expenditure on the Capital Aid and Technical Assistance Division of the Ministry of Finance and Planning in the Kenyan fiscal year 1973/74 was £41,700 and the estimate for 1974/75 was £53,000.[29] These are not the only expenses as quite a lot of the time of senior personnel in the headquarters administration of the Ministry is taken up with aid matters. It is very difficult to evaluate the time of a Permanent Secretary in a country like Kenya where administrative skills are scarce; it would be preposterous to suppose that his salary really measured the opportunity cost of his services. Aid negotiations do take up an appreciable amount of the time of a Permanent Secretary (salary in 1975, £4,940) and two Deputy Permanent Secretaries (combined salaries £9,490). In addition about two-thirds of the headquarters administrative services division's travel and entertainment expenses are incurred in the course of aid dealings, i.e. about £6,700 in 1973/74 and an estimated £10,000 in 1974/75. Operational ministries, owing to the policy of the Ministry of Finance and Planning, are frequently involved with aid. The total cost of being in receipt of aid could well exceed £100,000[30] – the cost of a modest project. This is very low in comparison with the sums disbursed under aid.[31]

Notes

1. *Economic Survey 1974*, Table 10.5, p. 151.
2. J. R. Nellis, 'Expatriates in the Government of Kenya', *Journal of Commonwealth Political Studies*, Vol. XI, No. 3, November 1973, pp. 251-64.
3. See Chapter Four, pp. 89-90.
4. *Economic Survey 1966*, Table 8.11.
5. Underspending is considered further in Chapter Four, pp. 88-93.
6. These percentages were compiled by considering projects one by one and allocating them to a sector. They are necessarily somewhat arbitrary and approximate. An agricultural college, for example, could be classified either under agriculture or education (social services). We classified it under education but many similar border-line decisions are involved.
7. See below, pp. 63-5 and 99-100.
8. This is difficult to do for yearly British disbursements because different aid agreements with Kenya have resulted in loans on different terms (see Table 5), and disbursements have been delayed so that money might be extended on various terms in the same year. The terms of the current British loan agreement, 2 per cent interest, 25-year amortisation with an eight-year grace period, have a grant equivalent of over 80 per cent, if future charges are discounted at 10 per cent – the rate used by the Development Assistance Committee (DAC) of OECD. DAC records the grant equivalent of all bilateral aid to Kenya at 85.7 per cent in 1972 (*Development Co-operation 1974 Review*, Paris, 1974, p. 278). With inflation now above 20 per cent in Britain and likely to stay in double figures for some time, 10 per cent is a very modest discount rate. A more appropriate one would give a grant equivalent for current loans of over 90 per cent. Future British aid is to be entirely grant.
9. Aid flow deflator from Table 11, p. 209, Statistical Appendix of *Development Co-operation*, op. cit. Modified by dividing 1968 and subsequent values by 1.143 to remove effects of devaluation, and changing the base year to 1964.
10. See Table 5.
11. See *Proceedings of the UN Conference on Trade and Development*, Feb-Mar 1968, Second session, Vol. IV. Problems and Policies of Financing.
12. Bhagwati, in UNCTAD, op. cit., 'The Tying of Aid', para. 8, p. 46.
13. Quoted from Clive Gray, 'Tied versus local cost foreign aid', *East African Economic Review*, Vol. 3, No. 2, December 1971.
14. There are the same difficulties in calculating the extent of tying of any disbursement as in calculating its grant equivalent. As the amount of tying has varied between different agreements, it is hard to tell precisely how much tying is involved in any year's disbursement. Furthermore, the proportions tied are average figures. While, say, 50 per cent of a given loan must be spent in Britain, a single project financed by part of that loan can have less or more than 50 per cent import content.
15. The costs incurred by ODM in advertising for and interviewing personnel are counted as part of the aid programme, so there is no direct subsidy here.
16. The average proportion of Kenyan imports coming from Britain for the three years 1965-67 was 31.7; for the three years 1968-70 it was 30.6, which suggests a price elasticity of less than one, but clearly other factors were at work, and we cannot infer much from that.
17. See Chapter Four, p. 82.
18. See Chapter Four, p. 79.
19. Other subscribers were the Kenya government, the West German development agency, and the Dutch aid agency. There was some public subscription. CDC's 1973 commitment of £1,278,000 represents about a quarter of the DFC's

finance.

20. Brooke Bond Liebig Kenya Ltd., Eastern Produce Africa Ltd., James Finlay & Co. Ltd., George Williamson Kenya Ltd.
21. N. H. Stern, *An Appraisal of Tea Production on Smallholdings in Kenya*, OECD Development Centre, 1972.
22. See Chapter Five, Part Two.
23. The Sterling-Deutschemark exchange rate has been moving in favour of the latter for much of the period so Sterling equivalents are approximate.
24. See Chapter Four, p. 97.
25. IFC is the bank subsidiary that undertakes indirect (portfolio) investment.
26. See Chapter Four, p. 98.
27. Conducted by the Commonwealth Secretariat (unpublished).
28. That raises the question of what such people are doing if not employed by the government. The answer probably lies in the phenomenon of 'bumping'. Qualified people might be hired from the private sector, to leave jobs there to less qualified people (or possibly expatriates brought in by private firms – this cost eventually borne by shareholders). This sets up a chain reaction with people being upgraded, and at the lowest level some of the urban unemployed obtain unskilled work.
29. This and all other figures in this section are from the Government of Kenya *Estimates of Recurrent Expenditure 1974/75.*
30. Taking the view that the time of senior administrators is worth some multiple of their emoluments.
31. We shall argue (Chapter Six), however, that aid has had a deleterious effect on Kenyan administration, giving rise to heavy costs in a more general sense.

4 BRITISH AID POLICY AND ADMINISTRATION IN KENYA

British aid policy, towards Kenya as elsewhere, exhibits a dichotomy. Decisions about the allocation of aid between countries are strongly influenced by precedent and original allocations were usually subject to political and commercial considerations. These may also be important in determining some of the general features of the aid a country receives, how far, for example, aid is tied to specific projects and how far it is tied to procurement of British goods. When a sum has been agreed, however, if it is to be tied to projects, as it generally is, developmental issues become much more important in determining which projects receive assistance. That is noticeable in the case of Kenya. While commercial and political pressures are sometimes brought to bear on individual project selection they appear to have become less influential at this level over the past decade. British project selection in Kenya has become more oriented to development, as it is conceived within the Ministry for Overseas Development (ODM). The changes reflect the varying importance of different Ministries and Departments of State at the different stages of aid policy formation. The institutional arrangements within the UK government machine have changed since aid to Kenya began and with them has changed the importance of different strands in aid policy. An analysis of aid policy, therefore, must be partly historical.

The Early Years, 1963-69

No great decision was involved when the UK began to aid Kenya on the latter's independence in 1963. As a colony, Kenya had received funds from the British government. Grants in aid of both cash and technical assistance were annual features of the Kenya budget. Almost £5m.[1] was given in 1961/62, excluding payments for military forces – worth a further £1.9m. The Colonial Development and Welfare Act (CD&W) of 1945, and its precursor the Colonial Development Fund Act of 1929, provided the Colonial Office with funds to be spent on development programmes in the colonies, and Kenya received its share of these. In 1961/62 it received development grants and loans of £6.8m.

By 1963 the policy of continuing payments to independent Commonwealth countries was well established. At the Commonwealth Finance Ministers' Conference in Montreal in 1958 a policy statement expressed Britain's readiness to continue financial aid to poor independent Commonwealth countries. This policy had been applied in the cases of many countries reaching independence before Kenya, such as Ghana in 1957 and Nigeria in 1960. In the circumstances of the time, therefore, a decision not to aid Kenya would have been incomparably more significant than one to do so.

Britain did have, however, particular interests in Kenya which dictated some form of aid programme anyway and ensured that it would be larger than in other countries. The most obvious was the large number of white settlers of British stock who remained in the country. Many of them were well-connected and found champions on the benches of the Conservative Party in Parliament. The aid which received the greatest attention at the Lancaster House Conferences which preceded independence was that for the Land Transfer Programme (LTP).[2] The only other finance discussed at Lancaster House in any detail was assistance for the independent Kenya government in taking over the cost of military forces. Just over £1.1m. was loaned for that purpose. These two preoccupations show the nature of British concern with independent Kenya which was chiefly that law and order should be preserved and British property protected. Entrenched clauses were included in Kenya's independence constitution against expropriation without compensation.

It has been argued[3] that aid was one means of luring Kenya into a neo-colonial situation. On most definitions of 'neo-colonial' that probably credits the British with too much ambition. Their aims were of a limited nature. The Conservative government of the day would certainly have preferred a Kenya government made up of members of KADU – representing in the main the smaller Kenyan tribes with little tradition of involvement in the Mau Mau rebellion and believed to have a more amicable approach to the former colonists than African nationalists in the other party, KANU, which was dominated by the Kikuyu and Luo. Yet when elections in 1961 and 1963 made clear the strength of KANU support, HMG did not attempt to install its own client government. It realised the folly of establishing any government that would be overthrown when the British presence was withdrawn, and political engineering was restricted to trying to commit KANU to the LTP.[4]

HMG had no great confidence in the KANU leader, Jomo Kenyatta; many people seemed to believe the rhetoric of former Governor Patrick Renison that he was a leader to 'darkness and death', and foreign investment plummeted at the approach of independence.[5] Anarchy and ethnic strife rather than revolution was the fear. Kenya did not possess great strategic or political significance in Cold War terms. Despite anti-Mau Mau propaganda the British knew there was little evidence of Communist penetration, and although Oginga Odinga, the Luo leader and deputy leader of KANU, was thought to have Communist-bloc sympathies he was not taken seriously as a contender for national leadership. At that time there were British bases near both ends of the Suez Canal, at Aden and in Cyprus, and Kenya did not appear either a promising or a necessary place for a military base.[6]

It was hoped that the general friendliness of the new Kenyan government would be secured by military assistance (quite significant in a new state with fissiparous tendencies). In 1964, following an army mutiny, the assistance was extended to include arrangements to train Kenyan forces. The explosive issue of land was meanwhile anaesthetised by the LTP. Otherwise capital assistance was rather meagre. The independence settlement included a commitment of £34.2m. of aid. But £12m. was loan and grant for the Land Transfer Programme and almost all of it was the unissued balance of commitments made before independence; £4.3m. was the unissued balance of development grants and loans, again committed before independence; £13.6m. was a loan to enable the Kenya government to pay the pensions of British colonial civil servants and while it was right that the pensions should be paid, it was barely short of scandalous to class that as aid to independent Kenya; the civil servants were the responsibility of the British government and their pensions brought no benefits to Kenya. £1.25m. was a budgetary grant continuing colonial practice, but the last of its kind. Only £3m. was a new loan commitment of money for general development. More significant in the running of the new Kenyan state and in helping it to take the course it did was technical assistance. Expatriate advisers and civil servants who by their advice helped to delimit the range of policy options considered as real possibilities were probably more influential than promises of capital aid in shaping independent Kenya.[7] At the end of 1965 there were 1,716 publicly financed Britons in Kenya; 1,674 were under the OSAS, of whom nearly half were teachers. Technical assistance accounted for around 40 per cent of gross British aid.

The British continued to put small money on the Kenyan horse as it began to show signs of running strongly in the right direction – against the predictions of some political tipsters. The political conservatism of the Kenya government and its hostile attitude to nationalisation and free land distribution became apparent and the *Sessional Paper No. 10 of 1965* contained impeccably moderate social-democrat expressions of policy.[8] As business confidence revived, Kenya continued to provide a profitable base for foreign-owned enterprises. The excess of Sterling Area (largely UK) investment income over private long-term Sterling capital flows to Kenya in 1965 and 1966 was £4.2m. and £3.4m. respectively, and much of the 'inflow' was re-invested profits of Kenya-based firms anyway. These were tiny sums seen in the context of the British economy and certainly not sufficient to make any great neo-colonial conspiracy worth while. The general course of the Kenyan economy was, however, modestly favourable to British interests and it was therefore natural for HMG to continue supporting President Kenyatta's government. LTP remained a major portion of the aid committed in 1966/67 and general development aid did not increase in real terms. The Land Transfer Programme on the capital side and the OSAS scheme in the technical assistance field were the two chief pillars of British aid.

In 1963 British aid was under the control of the Foreign Office and the

Commonwealth and Colonial Office. There was a Department of Technical Co-operation in charge of technical assistance, jointly responsible to the two ministries. In 1964, the ODM was set up, headed by a Minister who for two years had Cabinet rank, and it took over responsibility for all aid. The effect of this for Kenya was not appreciable for some time. Britain entered a period of continual economic crisis, and the conflicting influences of more concern for development and reduced national circumstances were resolved by the British Treasury insisting that Kenya spend large proportions of British aid on British exports. Money for colonies under the old CD&W Act had not been tied to British goods and had been disbursed in advance against short-run projections of expenditure.[9] For independent countries, procurement-tying was introduced along with the principle of reimbursement of expenditures after they had been incurred.

Britain often complained in negotiations with the Kenyans during those years that the projects they proposed for assistance did not include enough imports and pressed them to find more import-intensive schemes. This pressure was rationalised by pointing to the British balance of payments difficulties and the fact that British aid to other countries (including the other countries in East Africa) was tied two-thirds to British goods, and an exception could not be made for Kenya without creating ill-will. The Kenyans replied with pleas that their development plans should not be distorted in an import-intensive direction, and by pointing out the favourable trade balance that Britain enjoyed with Kenya. They argued that although money for land adjudication and settlement in Kenya was necessarily local-cost, some 60 per cent of money for land purchase found its way back to the UK. The Kenya government could also argue with justification that the prevailing trade pattern meant that Britain's trade benefited substantially from any money lent to Kenya, whether it was tied or not. During the middle of the 1960s almost 40 per cent of Kenya's visible imports and an even higher proportion of her invisibles were from the UK. It has been estimated[10] that, on the assumptions that any foreign exchange received by Kenya would be spent quickly (with no leakages caused by excess domestic saving or budget surpluses leading to an accumulation of foreign reserves), and that average and marginal import patterns were similar, Britain could expect to receive back in payment for exports between 40 and 50 per cent of any foreign exchange accruing to Kenya, and that within three years.[11] Other aid donors knew the matrix of trading relationships was in Britain's favour, and Britain's insistence on tying her aid, according to the Kenyans, influenced unfavourably the policies of other donors. In fact with hindsight it is possible to see that aid-tying did not have some of the effects that the British hoped and that the Kenyans feared. The lack of competitiveness of British industry has ensured it a declining share of the Kenyan market over the past ten years despite aid-tying and other donors, notably the Swedes and West Germans, have unilaterally untied their aid at least formally.[12]

In other ways, British practice in the disbursement of the independence settlement grant and loan and the two subsequent loans was very helpful. The Kenyans published a Development Plan and Britain, having agreed in advance a total sum with the Kenyans to be spent over a number of years, lent money for expenditures consistent with the Development Plan. These were usually on equipment for quite small projects which were not scrutinised before aid was allotted in anything like the detail that has subsequently become the practice. There were a few large projects where consultants' reports were a necessary prerequisite for aid disbursement but in general the technique of aid-giving was very similar to the former practice with CD&W finance. The three aid tranches helped to finance 31, 17 and 56 projects respectively. The smallest disbursement was only £7,200 – equipment for Egerton agricultural college. The average disbursement size was only about £150,000. The Kenyans found the readiness of the British to provide finance for small unglamorous projects, to act in a sense as donor of last resort, a distinct advantage. It enabled them to spend money piecemeal that they might not otherwise have been able to spend, especially in view of the import requirements of British aid. Some of the projects were not conspicuously developmental. Police radio equipment, broadcasting equipment and prison staff housing were all aided. The former two, of course, had the advantage of a 100 per cent import content.

ODM, however, was anxious to move away from simply giving annual apportionments of aid for equipment for a large number of projects. It was keen to tie aid to specific projects that could be examined in detail by its own experts. This, it thought, would enable it to ensure a sound use of funds. A corollary was that HMG after 1966 began to press the Kenyans to put forward fewer and larger projects in order to ease the administrative burden implied by such an interventionist approach. There also seemed to be a feeling that aid spent on lots of small projects was being dissipated and if it were concentrated it would have more 'impact'. This policy was to lead to increasing underspending by Kenya which as a result had to identify large projects and prepare proposals including plans and evaluations to a level of detail it would not itself have bothered with, perhaps rightly in view of its shortage of skilled administrative personnel. The import requirement was more onerous when aid could not be spent in penny packets but more important were the administrative demands made by large projects. Towards the end of the period of the Number Three loan, 1966-70, and subsequently, the difficulties of finding large projects with a sizeable import content which yet met ODM's 'development' criteria became serious. And the difficulties of finding the administration and expertise to conduct adequate evaluations and make plans for a project submission were worse. This tendency in aid policy wiped out many gains in administrative capacity as Kenyans settled down in posts and acquired experience following the outflow of expatriates in 1963.[13]

Aid Administration Today

The Machinery

After 1969 the planning and administration of British aid to particular countries became more systematic with the introduction of the Country Policy Paper (CPP).[14] This was drafted mainly by economists attached to the relevant geographical department of ODM. It is an internal working document which describes the economy and policies of the country concerned and discusses the main constraints on development and other relevant factors in its relations with the UK. The CPP sets out the proposed amounts and forms of UK aid for the next five years – 'showing how this fits in with the recipient country's development priorities and the likely future aid programmes of other donors, taking into account any political and commercial considerations which are relevant.'[15] The CPP also indicates the main sectors of the economy towards which the aid should be directed and lays down relative priorities. It indicates, too, the proposed terms and conditions of the aid in relation to the recipient's debt servicing capacity and the practice of other donors. Between 1969 and 1972, in the case of Kenya, the draft CPP was sent to the High Commission in Nairobi (BHC) for comments, particularly on the political, commercial and investment aspects. The draft was (and is) then circulated to the Treasury, FCO, Departments of Trade and Industry and the Bank of England. Their representatives meet ODM as necessary to settle any differences of view which arise. The commercial departments and the Treasury are thus consulted at an early stage of the formation of aid policy to particular countries, and Kenya is no exception.

Such meetings result in the proposed aid programme to a particular country being fitted into the overall Aid Framework – the detailed breakdown of the UK's expected aid disbursements of all kinds for four years ahead, the years covered by HMG's Public Expenditure Review. The figures in the aid frame for a particular country showing planned disbursements for a number of years ahead will reflect expected spending of funds already committed in past agreements with the recipient country, and will also influence the extent of future commitments.

While policy towards a particular country is devised at ODM in consultation with other government departments, the British Mission in the country concerned has some responsibility for administering the aid programme. BHC Nairobi has two First Secretaries dealing with aid, and up to the end of 1974 one was in charge of technical assistance and one in charge of capital aid including both general development and LTP. There was then a reform which left one First Secretary in charge of aid with the other subordinate to him in charge of aid administration. A third First Secretary is now responsible for LTP, reporting directly to the Deputy High Commissioner. The two First Secretaries are directly responsible to the Economic and Commercial Counsellor who at present is also Deputy

High Commissioner. Project proposals for capital aid are made by the Kenyan government to the appropriate First Secretary in the High Commission. Up to 1972 the applications were then communicated, with the comments of BHC personnel, to ODM in London. Requests for over £400,000 have to go before the Projects Committee – an internal ODM body chaired by a Deputy Secretary. The Committee also considers smaller applications if they are not in line with policy expressed in CPP. Project submissions to the Committee are circulated to other government departments. It is, apparently, unusual for them to make strong representations at this stage as most of their leverage is exerted at the earlier stage of drafting the CPP.

After 1972 the situation was changed by the setting up of a Development Division for East Africa in Nairobi. This is an out-station of ODM and consists of a number of ODM experts in various fields who act as advisers to the High Commissions in their region. They are in a position to carry out on-the-spot appraisal of project proposals rather than these having to be sent to ODM in London, or an ODM team having to fly out to Nairobi. On the advice of the head of the Development Division, the High Commissioner was given delegated authority to commit sums of up to £250,000 to projects without reference to London as long as they are in accord with the policy outlines of the CPP. In 1975 this was increased to £400,000. The economists in the Development Division have also become responsible for preparing the first draft of annual revisions of CPP. The setting up of the Development Division has had a number of very beneficial effects on the Kenya aid programme. It enables projects of less than £400,000 to be authorised with much less delay and introduces more flexibility into the aid programme; it speeds up the whole business of project appraisal; and it greatly strengthens the hand of ODM if there are inter-ministry disputes about the desirability of certain projects. The FCO can no longer claim a monopoly of local up-to-date experience, so the political considerations weigh less heavily compared with the developmental.

Technical Assistance Administration

The policy towards technical assistance, as well as capital aid, is set out in the CPP, and the Development Division advises on it. The administration of technical assistance[16] is, however, rather different from that for capital aid. There are, in the first place, the two quite separate sets of arrangements for wholly- and partly-funded personnel. To obtain OSAS personnel each Kenyan ministry makes a 'bid' to the Kenyan Public Service Commission giving requirements for expatriate officers with projected localisation dates of posts. These are vetted and passed on directly to ODM in London. ODM used to be very permissive about meeting these Kenyan requests but it discovered that the rate of localisation of posts by Kenya was less than it expected. Consequently the OSAS commitment looked like running on, scarcely diminished, indefinitely. In 1970 an annual manpower review was instituted. The Kenya authorities are asked to forecast for three years ahead their needs for expatriates and to explain what they are doing about localisation of each post. This means there is scrutiny of requests both for new officers and the continuation of old ones. Every other year an ODM team from London has visited Kenya to assess the needs and requests. The latest review was the most thorough ever, involving considerable discussion with the Kenyans. After reviews, ODM sets a ceiling number of personnel for each ministry or organisation. These ceilings need not be lower than the Kenyan bids; that depends on ODM's view of requirements. However, ODM is trying to phase OSAS out over a longish period, perhaps ten years.[17] The aim is to eliminate lower-level posts first. Teachers, mainly in secondary schools, have been a considerable part of the OSAS complement and ODM has been bearing down on their numbers.[18] This is a source of continuing contention between the two governments as the Kenyans wish to retain as many teachers as possible owing to the rate of expansion of their secondary school system. This battle, like the ODM ceilings, is sometimes otiose as the planned numbers cannot be recruited anyway.

While the OSAS numbers have been falling, the HMG contribution has been rising. The British supplementation is intended to cover the difference between the Kenya government's local salary and what the equivalent post would pay in the UK, plus a local cost-of-living allowance, inducement to serve abroad, and an element in lieu of employers' pension contributions. This supplement is non-taxable and payable in the UK. ODM calculates that its share of the costs of an expatriate under OSAS is now 60-70 per cent. This means they are cheap labour to the Kenya government which, as noted in Chapter Three, might well have trouble filling some posts with Kenyans while paying a local salary perhaps 60 per cent below what the expatriate gets.

Up to now BHC and the Development Division have not been directly involved in administering OSAS, at least in theory. In fact, much time of BHC officers has been taken up with OSAS matters, acting as assessors and go-betweens and dealing with personal problems of OSAS people. Now local officers in BHC and the Development Division are to take over responsibility for the manpower planning reviews, and play a greater role in formulating ODM policy towards OSAS in Kenya. They may have some delegated decision-making power on individual applications beneath the set ceiling. Such developments would be entirely consistent with the drift of ODM policy towards decentralising decisions and, in our view, could speed up administration and perhaps improve decisions.

For advisory posts of limited duration, as opposed to an established post with executive duties, ODM supplies people under the Special Commonwealth African Assistance Plan (SCAAP), the details of which were renegotiated in 1974 – after seven years of discussion. Requests for this type of technical assistance are made by Kenyan operational ministries to a special division in the Ministry of Finance and Planning. If acceded to by the Ministry of Finance and Planning, they are sent to the appropriate First Secretary in BHC. ODM operates a yearly financial ceiling for SCAAP. The ceiling, like the CPP, is for internal guidance and is not communicated to the Kenyans. Two reasons are given for this secrecy. One, if the yearly ceiling were announced the Kenyans would invent requests to take up all the funds, resulting in a number of inferior projects, which it would be difficult to turn down; with the ceiling not announced, financial stringency can be used as an excuse for not supporting poor projects. Two, if good projects arise in the course of the year (as they sometimes do without warning) it is good to have money in reserve for them, and if countries are not told the full extent of their SCAAP provision, funds can be switched from one country to another. This adds flexibility and is supposed to reduce under-utilisation. We are completely out of sympathy with the first argument, if not the second. In the first place, if the Kenyans were really determined to take up all available funds they could simply invent applications anyway until they exhausted them, thus establishing the ceiling by trial and error. If a false ceiling is established because ODM uses it as an excuse to turn down some projects, that totally negates the second argument as far as it applies to Kenya. It is not very winning to plead financial stringency one month, then announce that it has magically disappeared the next because a better project has appeared. (Although this can happen owing to forecasting errors as well as duplicity.) In addition that sort of diplomacy appears to be quite self-defeating on two counts. Many of the reasons given for project-tying aid, both capital and technical assistance, are invalid.[19] One of the valid ones is that it enables the donor to demonstrate rational methods of project selection to the recipient in the hope that he will emulate them. That advantage is lost if the recipient dissembles the reasons for his preferences. Secondly, diplomacy of that sort makes for unpopularity rather than the reverse. It will become clear that we regard ODM as, developmentally, a much better donor than average in Kenya, yet it does not seem to be among the most popular donors with the Kenyans themselves. One reason is that they find the British unpredictable and do not understand why ODM rejects some projects and accepts others. They also suspect ODM of killing projects by prolonged delays while simulating interest, when a flat 'nothing doing' would be preferable. For all the harm that, in our opinion, more thrusting donors do, many Kenyans prefer to deal with the Americans, for example, who are blunt and straightforward in saying what they will not support and why. As the framework figures are guidelines, not commitments, it is not even clear that secrecy is necessary for flexibility between countries. Britain as the former colonial power is in a more difficult position diplomatically than other donors. Nevertheless a more open style of operation would pay dividends. There is some indication that it is happening with the establishment of the Development Division. For example, the yearly framework figures for disbursements of capital aid are also supposed to be secret but somehow the Kenyans seem to know what they are.[20] It is noteworthy that they seldom succeed in spending them all, although, of course, British appraisal of capital aid projects is usually more stringent than of applications for SCAAP personnel because of the different scale of sums involved.

Even though the administration of capital and technical aid is being integrated more, the funds for the two forms of aid are kept separate. The reason given for that has been that technical assistance funds are grant and capital funds are loan. This will not be so in future but in any case the inefficiency of this separation is manifest. Occasionally technical assistance funds have been spent up to the ceiling and a moratorium has had to be declared for the remainder of a financial year on this kind of aid. Meanwhile capital funds were underspent. It is an obvious reform to introduce some flexibility so funds can be transferred between the two heads. Better still would be to abolish the distinction, making particular aid agreements for a certain sum to be disbursed in any form agreed between donor and recipient. That would not obviate separate technical assistance agreements being made to establish terms for technical assistance which would apply when the recipient opted to take part of an agreed aid commitment in technical assistance form. Neither would it necessarily involve changes in the administration of British aid with separate sections looking after OSAS, SCAAP and capital aid. Co-ordination already exists, although it might have to be stepped up.

Despite these flaws the Kenyans have in general found British administration of SCAAP more to their liking than that for capital aid, because as long as requests for technical assistance are roughly in line with the CPP they are processed quickly. One British administrator explained that the general principle was that if the Kenyans asked for someone, they probably needed him, and it was unrealistic for ODM to argue about the merits of filling individual posts. As long as Kenya's allocation of technical assistance funds for any year was not on the point of exhaustion, therefore, there was a tendency to provide expatriates on request as long as they could be recruited. Extensive cost-benefit analysis is not worth while in view of the small sums involved compared with capital projects. Not only is project approval by the donor quicker, there is also a *pro forma* for the Kenyans to complete when applying for technical assistance, so they are told precisely what information is required and are used to making requests in a standard form. This does not apply in the case of capital aid.

Technical assistance administration has clearly shown the benefits of having a specialist aid agency. Some years ago, when there were nearly 2,000 British expatriates in Kenya, the programmes were administered by a single officer based in London with very junior people on the spot. Now there are more officials in London, more, and more senior, officers in BHC

Nairobi, and the Development Division all involved with technical assistance. The programmes are certainly not over-administered now. The additional manpower is necessary if ODM is to form policies about the economic sectors in which technical assistance is to be concentrated and to direct the programmes acccordingly.

It is sometimes argued that provision of technical assistance helps to mould recipient government policy in favour of the donor state. We discuss later the effects of various aid forms but here, in discussing British policy and administration, we can say that whatever the effect, there is no sign of such an intention on the part of ODM. There is almost no liaison at all between BHC and technical assistance personnel once they are in post. Many experts working in Kenya have been surprised at how unsupervised their work is. SCAAP personnel make an annual report on their assignment to the Kenya government and BHC. It is copied to ODM. In the case of OSAS officers the only report HMG receives of their assignment is the one they write themselves on completing it. This is on the grounds that it would be invidious for civil servants in post with one government to report to another. These reports are filed and add to the store of knowledge of experienced aid administrators, but there seems to be no procedure for collating and periodically considering them in order to inform future technical assistance policy. Even SCAAP personnel sometimes feel a sense of isolation as it is rare for their reports to lead to a request for a meeting with ODM for any re-assessment or rebriefing. A couple of SCAAP men confessed to being mildly shocked that British money was being spent on them without their feeling accountable to anyone.

The most important reason is that the two or three BHC officers dealing with technical assistance at present simply do not have the time to monitor the reports of several hundred British experts, far less the terminal reports of a thousand OSAS personnel. Despite the improvement in the running of technical assistance programmes they are certainly not over-administered – rather the reverse – and proper ex post appraisal would require more staff. Procedures for enforcing a higher general standard of technical assistance reporting, and for assimilating the information would be advantageous in improving technical assistance policy even if they attracted accusations of 'neo-colonialism'.

Policy Issues

Perhaps the first issue to be settled in determining aid policy towards any country is how much to give. The UK extends to Kenya slightly more aid per head than its average for Commonwealth Africa and three times the average for all Commonwealth countries. One reason is the importance of historical precedent. Reductions in aid, not agreed with the recipient, can be damaging to political relations, so other British ministries apart from ODM have been quite keen to see the volume of aid to

Kenya maintained at least in nominal terms. The FCO, for example, is aware of the problem of Kenyan Asians who are British citizens. The Kenya government is committed to Kenyanisation of the economy. So far it has reached an agreement with the UK for British Asians to leave Kenya and come to the UK in a gradual stream. Yet the possibility remains that Kenya, like Amin's Uganda, could simply expel all non-citizen Asians, leaving Britain with difficulties in absorbing the refugees without harming domestic race relations. This is a tacit bargaining counter for Kenya in relations between the two governments and provides the UK with an incentive to maintain friendly relations. Yet a number of facts up to 1972 persuaded some British aid administrators that on developmental grounds capital aid to Kenya could be allowed to fall in real terms. The considerations were the slow rate of disbursement, the absence of any very severe balance of payments difficulties, and the readiness of other donors to aid Kenya. Of course, in so far as this last factor indicated foreign penetration of a country and markets that had previously been a British preserve, it provided a reason for stepping up aid on commercial and political grounds.

In 1972 a World Bank analysis of the Kenyan economy concluded that while up to then Kenya's chief growth constraint had been administrative, from then on shortages of capital and foreign exchange would emerge. The economic analyses in ODM's CPPs are usually greatly influenced by IBRD findings, and these conclusions persuaded aid administrators that aid to Kenya should not be cut, quite apart from the Asian and commercial issues. Since then, the oil price rise has heavily accentuated the deterioration in Kenya's balance of payments, and Britain agreed to the programme grant of £2.5m. for essential imports.

Another issue is whether aid should be concentrated on particular economic sectors. It is now explicit British policy to concentrate more on aiding the rural areas. Other donors are following suit.[21] Most donor agencies, including ODM, have been persuaded by many of the arguments of the ILO report[22] and subsequent World Bank analyses pointing to the unequal mode of Kenya's economic growth. The concentration on the mass of rural poor is not simply because they are more numerous than the urban poor but also because relative improvements in urban conditions could cancel themselves by causing more poor people to migrate from country to town. Rural development is necessary to help both groups, therefore. Symptomatic of ODM's emphasis on rural development is the project to assist in the construction of rural access roads, both for their own sake, and as a pilot scheme for a larger World Bank and bilateral donor consortium project to build many such roads by labour-intensive methods. The pilot project cost £250,000 and was the first authorised by BHC Nairobi under the new delegated authority. The UK's ability to do this and get the project under way greatly impressed other donors who were unable to respond so quickly. On the other hand ODM will not now finance trunk roads between urban centres or heavy infrastructure primarily serving urban areas. In the rural areas the concentration is on agriculture or at least directly productive enterprises. ODM is less eager to assist with social services as the Kenya government is capable of providing these itself and is under some political pressure to do so. These preferences are far from being hard and fast, however.

The accent on rural development indicates the predominance of ODM's conception of development over other considerations in aid-giving. It means a departure from projects that diplomats and British businessmen can see from their Nairobi windows, and appears to go against Britain's immediate commercial interests, as the import content of rural development projects is often low. Insistence on the policy conflicts with short-term political interests, because rural projects are less visible, and despite the statements in Kenya's Development Plan about the priority of rural areas, the Kenyan government still frequently requests aid – but increasingly in vain – for urban-based projects such as airport improvements and trunk roads. Money has been requested for the Industrial Development Bank to invest in large industrial projects – some of them perfectly good and viable ones – but apart from CDC's seconding a management adviser and ODM putting IDB in touch with commercial credit sources, Britain has refused to aid this body. ODM officials have persuaded other departments in HMG to support the policy by arguing that it is in Britain's long-term interests. Whatever can be said for aiding projects which will give business to British exporters, or accommodating some shift in Kenya government policy, Britain's real interest, it is argued, is in helping to build a stable and prosperous Kenya.

While this view is uppermost it does not always get a free run with the money. It is not all that long since there were differences of view within the British administration. Certain projects which the Kenya government has wanted strongly have been backed within HMG because of the political returns from doing so but have conflicted with ODM ideas of development priorities. An example may have been a project costing £260,000 in 1971 to extend television to the Coast Province of Kenya. It was known to be greatly favoured by President Kenyatta, and support for the project might therefore have been helpful in maintaining good relations. Aid administrators might also be expected to favour it because of the very high import content. The required import content of an aid agreement loan is an average figure, so if some projects that are almost 100 per cent imports can be found it makes it possible to accept others with a high proportion of local costs, and this facilitates disbursement and removes some of the difficulties of administering the aid programme. This means of course that procurement-tying regulations (favoured by the British Treasury) can deform decisions and modify the commitment to development. The difficulty in the television case was apparently that a great deal of sophistry failed to convince some ODM advisers that the project had much to do with development, for it was accepted only after going before the Projects Committee. Ironically, it may be this or similar incidents which have led some diplomats to describe ODM's readiness to oppose its conception of development to that of the Kenya government as 'neo-colonial', although they admit the legitimacy of project selection in order to ensure 'value for money'.

Other donors as well as ODM are concerned that the mode of economic progress achieved in Kenya since independence is not viable in the long run, and a more egalitarian course should be pursued if political tensions within Kenya are not to grow. It may seem odd that donor agencies, including ODM, should take a longer view than the Kenyan government of what is in Kenya's interests. If there really is a threat of serious political instability, for example from the present economic and social policies, that would appear to concern the Kenya government before anyone else. However, perhaps the situation may be compared to that in Britain, where governments have been notoriously prone to inflate the economy at the approach of an election, irrespective of the long-run wisdom of doing so. In Kenya the need to maintain a short-run balance on the political scene may preclude taking a long-run view, at least without authoritarian measures to suppress interest groups that benefit from the *status quo*. And it is not clear which interest groups would provide the will for such measures and the means to carry them out.[23]

A question which immediately arises is, what is the point of having strong sectoral preferences and attempting to act on them, if they are not really shared by the recipient government? The Kenya government has declared itself for more poverty-oriented rural programmes. And there is no doubt the commitment is taken seriously by many Kenyan civil servants. It is fair to say, however, that there is some doubt among the donors how far the Kenya government as a whole does share such preferences, and how far it merely pays lip service to them. Many claim to observe a discrepancy between policy statements and the pattern of project applications they receive. To insist on one's own priorities in such a situation and to try to enforce them by project-tying aid may achieve little except to alienate the recipient. The usefulness of project-tying aid to secure a certain use of resources depends entirely on how fungible[24] the resources in question are. We analyse fungibility and discuss its application to Kenya later,[25] and here merely note ODM's attitude towards it.

The feeling in BHC and the Development Division is that one has to support good projects irrespective of political pressures or the possibility of fungibility, because doing so sets a good example to the recipient and persuades him to evaluate possibilities rationally, and ultimately it is necessary if the aid agency is to maintain morale and self-respect. The cynical would observe that this argument tends to vindicate the view that many arguments for project-tying are founded in the organisational interests of aid agencies. In the case of Kenya, however, ODM personnel believe that the recipient's scope for shunting funds around is limited.

At this point all we would say is that they appear to consider fungibility as largely a phenomenon concerning British and Kenyan funds. But where there are other donors British funds may be displacing other donors' aid. If the other donors then aid projects of which ODM disapproves, some (not necessarily all) of the point of project-tying is lost. There is a donor practice, shared by Britain, of insisting that Kenya puts some money into any project aided by the donor. This ties up much Kenyan money, reducing the scope for fungibility. UK administrators and those of other countries, however, insist that such is not the intention; they simply want to ensure a genuine Kenyan commitment to anything they undertake.

Underspending

Unquestionably, the British practice, shared by other donors, of tying aid both to projects and partially to procurement has reduced the rate of capital aid disbursement. This means that a lot of aid which Kenya is going to the trouble of negotiating for is not being received. British funds not spent in one year cannot be automatically carried over and added on to the framework figure for disbursements the following year. Money extended under an aid agreement that is not taken up during the period of the agreement is added on to the value of the new agreement. So in 1973, for example, Britain signed an agreement to extend to Kenya £17m. of 'new' money to be disbursed in the period 1973-77 plus £7m. to be carried over from earlier agreements (mainly the 1970 one) which had not been taken up. This division into 'old and new' money is, however, fairly clearly a matter of semantics; the amount of new commitment can vary depending on how much remains to be spent of a previous tranche. ODM officials insist that no crude 'netting' takes place, but they also admit that over the years Kenyan underspending has been a factor in determining the size of aid agreements. If underspending continues, as the aid programme is continuous, the money not being spent is pushed continually into the future and is lost in some real sense. Even if spent eventually, its real value is eroded by inflation.

There are two components of underspending. One is a slowness in the Kenya Treasury in making disbursements against commitments already made. The second is a slowness in committing to specific projects funds assigned to Kenya in an aid agreement. To eliminate the first problem the Development Division would be prepared to see Kenya's Ministry of Finance and Planning use 'overcommitment', that is, authorise more expenditure in any year on 'British' projects than Britain's framework figure for disbursements. Then natural slippage of projects behind schedule would mean that the available aid would get taken up, probably without much, if any, exceeding of the framework figure, rather than it being underspent as at present. The Ministry does occasionally commit in advance of an aid agreement but generally it displays a very conservative, bank-like attitude to finance. Indeed, one project supported by another donor was held up because the Kenya Treasury refused to authorise expenditure on certain items, although they were fully covered by promised aid. That was because the aid had not actually been received, and there was a general proscription on expenditure from Kenyan funds on the items in question as part of an economy measure.[26]

Much the more serious underspending problem, however, is the one of getting enough project applications to which to commit all the funds that have been agreed. This is emphatically not a problem peculiar to British aid. All donors share it. The most important constraints are the shortage of ideas for sizeable projects in some of Kenya's important operational ministries, and a lack of capacity to prepare project proposal and evaluation documentation to the level of detail required by many donors, including ODM. Hence the paradox, not unique to Kenya, that in a poor country lacking just about everything required to raise its people's material standard of living there appears to be a surfeit of capital aid.

The problem in Kenya will be intensified by the growing fashion among donors for favouring rural development. Productive investments in rural areas are harder to plan than simply putting up a factory or building a trunk road, and in truth when worth-while opportunities for development can be identified, they probably do not require very much money anyway, but rather improved administration and specialised skills and perhaps the release of some constraints imposed by adverse government policy, such as unfavourable agricultural pricing. Apart from these intrinsic difficulties is the fact that the Ministry of Agriculture is one part of the Kenyan administration that finds it hardest to plan projects, unlike, for example, the Ministry of Works.[27]

Donors' reactions to this situation take a number of forms. One is to diagnose the problem as a shortage of human capital and to attempt to inject technical assistance into the Kenya administration in a general way. A second is to take over some functions that strictly are those of the Kenya government; these include identification of projects and, usually in collaboration with a Kenyan operational ministry, preparing the project to implementation. This is done either by aid agency officials or by consultants or technical assistance teams specially engaged. A third is to relax requirements in some way, perhaps accepting vaguer or otherwise poorer project submissions, or easing the donor agencies' own rules, accepting higher local-cost elements in projects, or more recurrent expenditure, or perhaps abandoning sectoral preferences to some extent. The ultimate in this line is to abandon project-tying and give balance of payments support grants or loans. A fourth is to give up and reduce capital aid allocations.

Nearly all aid agencies in Kenya have done one or more of these at some time or other. ODM has shown some sympathy for giving general technical assistance. Despite its running down of OSAS it has, as noted, been permissive in its attitude towards SCAAP personnel. ODM has been shy in the past of the option of preparing projects itself, being much less interventionist in that sense than many other donors, although that policy is not changing. We suspect the option of lowering standards must have been taken from time to time although any moderating of ODM's own rules has been only marginal. The import requirement provisions are no less steep than they were, and the aversion to recurrent costs remains. In some cases, however, non-preferred projects have been undertaken to spend money. The recent programme grant may have been exceptional, rather than an extension of a tendency to compromise with principles, but future aid agreements between the two countries may include programme aid as part of the package. As for the option of reducing capital aid, we are confident that Kenyan requests for more aid would have been more successful if disbursement rates had been higher in the past.

We believe that an inability to spend capital aid is more likely to mean that technical assistance cannot be used properly either, than to mean it is bound to do good. Many donors have attempted to release the bottleneck in the Ministry of Agriculture by giving technical assistance. The UK, Canada and the World Bank have all done so at various times. The Ministry has a Project Planning Unit, which is largely staffed by expatriates, and it is beginning to jib at taking more. Some of the older advisers with a good knowledge of the country have done excellent work, but in general expatriates sitting in Nairobi, even if skilled in writing up project applications, are unlikely to get fertile ideas for projects or to be able to evaluate information they receive without the local knowledge and experience that many of them lack. The fate of the Unit provides an object lesson in the limitations of technical assistance when there is a weakness in the administration of a recipient country. The expatriates work and plan *in vacuo*, a tendency accentuated because there are clusters of them. The lack of political drive, which meant that indigenous Kenyan administrative resources and recurrent expenditure were not directed into agriculture, nullifies the efforts of expatriates even when those turn out to be more than jejune and inexperienced. They are reduced to justifying their position as fulfilling an educative function – demonstrating certain management and planning techniques – because they know that at present little is coming of their work. Even that benefit is reduced if a unit consists largely of expatriates, as then much of their educating is of each other.

ODM does not have such a penchant as some other donors for putting in teams of planners,[28] although it has more than one expatriate planner in Education and has provided a team for the Tana River Development Authority. Both of these ventures may well prove fruitful, but in general experience does not support the view that Kenya's absorptive capacity can be usefully improved by inserting cliques of expatriates. In this context two may be company but three is certainly a crowd.[29] There are perhaps two exceptions. One is in the field of research, which by its nature is an activity which can be more isolated from other government functions, and which often requires close co-operation of similarly oriented people. ODM has supported successful research teams in agriculture, especially in maize-breeding and agronomy. The second is the provision of short-term teams to tackle technical problems relating to the preparation of a single project. Consultancies may be the best means of doing this.

ODM appears to have a reputation for being more difficult than most other donors in the amount of information and documentation it requires before supporting any project. In ODM's view Kenyan operational ministries are supposed to evaluate capital projects on the lines of ODM's *Guide to Project Appraisal*[30] and to send applications to the Treasury to forward to appropriate donors. The ministries do not do that much, and when they do, Britain is not a favourite donor to approach first. A common informed view is that ODM asks for information that it is impossible to supply in advance of a project being implemented; the assessment of a construction project, for example, may call for building plans. ODM asks for such details simply in considering whether to support a project. However, the Kenyan government does not have the manpower resources to justify preparing a queue of thorough project applications. It is only worth working up a project to the implementation stage if the Kenyan government is sure it is going ahead. British practice, it is alleged, necessitates the Kenyans sinking precious administrative and planning resources and bearing the risk that the British will then turn the project down or insist on unacceptable modifications of the plans.

Other donors are thought to be easier to deal with in that they accept a project in principle and then, if they want further details and plans, offer a technical assistance team to work with the Kenyan ministry concerned in preparing these. While this view is very widely held, it does seem that the Kenyans misunderstand the procedures of some other donors. The Germans, for example, 'earmark' projects for support at the time of general aid negotiations. The Kenyans regard this as a commitment but in fact the Germans do not and could, in principle, refuse to support a project which emerged in a form they disapproved. In fact such a politically embarrassing situation has never arisen, evidence perhaps of the influence foreign experts can have over the form of any particular project.

The British approach, however, does have its positive side. ODM claims that its policy is to strengthen the Kenyan Treasury in its dealings with operational ministries. So ODM in principle expresses interest only in projects proposed by the Kenyans, either directly in negotiations, or more commonly by publication in Part Two of the Development Plan,[31] or in a Public Sector Projects List circulated to donors. Traditionally, expression of interest is made to the Kenya Treasury, usually to the External Aid Division which is asked to obtain an application from the appropriate ministry. Delays frequently ensue, punctuated by British appeals to the

External Aid Division and by Treasury appeals to the operational ministry for expedition. Applications are produced, and in the past they have been referred back by HMG or ODM as inadequate. Eventually an application is produced that is regarded as adequate. It is examined by the staff of the Development Division and, for sums over £400,000, sent to London with their recommendations. In the early months of the Development Division further delays occurred because ODM experts in London on the Economic Planning Staff queried facts and recommendations. Gradually the worst duplication of this kind is falling away as the Development Division becomes established. If the project is a large one, however, it has to wait for the next meeting of the Projects Committee. Even then it may conceivably be referred back. Eventually the project may go through but not always before mutual irritation has been engendered between British and Kenyans.

This contrasts markedly with the procedure of some donors, not, as Kenyan Treasury officials may be excused for believing, because their requirements for project write-ups are less onerous than those of ODM – we do not think they are much – but because their procedures are less formal. Other donors may see a project they fancy in the Kenyan literature or they may dream up their own. An approach is then made to contacts in the operational ministry concerned. Promises are made of money for the project and support is won. The donor may well practically write the application he wants to receive on behalf of the operational ministry and get the latter to send it to the Treasury with the information that the donor is prepared to finance the project. (No wonder the Treasury is not plagued by requests for more information.) The application is sent off to the donor country for approval. When the Kenya Treasury gets around to forwarding the application to the donor agency in Kenya, it is accepted and the project can be put in hand.

Clearly this procedure leads to more rapid project preparation and implementation than the British method, but equally clearly it has dangers of its own. It means that only a minimal attempt is made to devise the projects the Kenyans want, rather than those the donor wants to support. The Kenya Treasury finds itself receiving applications for projects that may or may not have the same names as those in the Development Plan, but if there is donor money behind them, it is hard to turn them down. The Planning Department in the Ministry of Finance and Planning has no opportunity to establish any kind of priority ordering of projects, and to direct donors' attentions to the top-ranking ones; it is reduced to saying yes or no to what donors propose. British administrators claim that some other donors have bitten off more than they care to chew by using this technique, and that some projects forced through the Kenyan machine have been flops on any criteria. Pressure can also increase friction and one administrator summed up: 'Aid must be partly about goodwill, so what is the point of a procedure that alienates the Kenyans straight away?'

Unfortunately, that argument does not accord with the views of Kenyan civil servants. Treasury men in particular are only too well aware of the limitations of some operational ministries. Being constantly chivvied by the British and having to chivvy other ministries in turn is not a comfortable position, and they would welcome the British doing some of their own pressing. Furthermore they are concerned with disbursement and they know that dealing directly with operational ministries speeds a donor's programme. They recognise the argument for not undermining Treasury control but, strangely, give it much less weight than BHC and ODM. In fact Treasury civil servants do not seem excessively concerned to establish priorities. As long as projects are in the Development Plan, they are content to handle them on a first-come, first-served basis. Evidence of this is a practice, enshrined in a number of intra-ministry circulars, that Treasury approval shall not be given for any project – even if in the Development Plan – unless some aid finance is assured. This amounts, in effect, to an admission that the Ministry of Finance and Planning is content to let donors do some pre-selecting for it. It would thus like to see the British take a more active role in aid-giving and make their own contacts with the operational ministries. There is evidence now that, since the setting-up of the Development Division, the British have realised this, and are doing so. The staff of the Development Division have discussed applications with an originating ministry before they were submitted, to ensure that the application arrived in a suitable form, and have actually helped in drafting applications.

What is comfortable for Treasury officials, of course, is not necessarily best for the country in the longer run. ODM is therefore in a considerable dilemma. The desire to disburse aid faster and to promote better projects has to be balanced against the further weakening of Treasury control and the implicit infringement of Kenya's sovereignty.[32] The trouble is that a self-denying ordinance by ODM does little good if other donors are piling in.

Donor co-operation

Projects in which a number of national donor agencies co-operate are still a tiny minority in Kenya. Multi-donor consortia, when they occur, are usually under the auspices of the World Bank. An example is a livestock promotion scheme where the UK is aiding the marketing component. The exception is the co-operation of Sweden, Denmark and Norway in 'Nordic' schemes. The UK is not antipathetic to co-operating with other donors and has done so occasionally for years, although it is fair to say that consortia are not its preferred mode of operation. ODM keeps in touch with the World Bank, and in one case turned down a project for a teacher training college after discovering an IBRD appraisal had gone against it. In general, however, the UK follows rather than initiates moves towards donor co-operation, leaving those to be started by the World

Bank and UNDP which organises a monthly get-together lunch for donor agencies in Nairobi. ODM's considered view is that a bilateral agency, especially that of the former colonial power, is ill-placed to set about engineering joint action by donors, especially as the Kenya government is thought to be suspicious of any signs that donors are 'ganging-up' on it.

There is a Consultative Group for East Africa which holds periodic meetings of donors, chaired by IBRD, in respect of individual recipient countries. It is attended by bureaucrats of British Under-Secretary level and below from donor agencies' headquarters. Some discreet carving up of donor areas of interest goes on but disputes as such are not resolved. The Kenyans who attend emphasise those aspects of their policy which please the donors, and diplomacy reigns supreme. The occasions appear to be of no practical importance in shaping anyone's policy, although they are said to improve the atmosphere in which donors operate. However, senior staff of the Kenyan Ministry of Finance and Planning are said to have devoted most of two months to preparing documentation for a Consultative Group Meeting in 1972.

The present state of donor co-operation appears to be an advance over the former situation. Some years ago the UK seemed excessively suspicious when the USA, for example, noticed that the Special Rural Development Projects[33] were likely to founder on the indifference of important ministries in Nairobi. UK representatives refused to take part in joint donor representations to the Ministry of Finance and Planning. The US had made its own mistakes in the field of rural development and these were notorious but it should have been clear they were irrelevant to the point at issue. Although the US was quite right in its forebodings, some UK administrators wanted to assure the Kenya government of their continued confidence. This may have been an instance of the pervasiveness of ODM and FCO 'diplomacy' as much as suspicion of other donors.

Other Donors' Policies

So far we have considered British aid policy, referring in passing to other donors. In Kenya there are many such, a fact that greatly affects British policy, and arguably should do so still more. The popularity of Kenya among other donors is probably best explained on organisational rather than political grounds.[34] The decision to 'have an aid programme', like the decision to operate a national airline, is taken in many countries as evidence that they have graduated to a higher stage of political and economic maturity. An early decision may be taken to spend some of the money in Africa. (Why not?) The country that gets the money will then have certain features. It will not have a desperately objectionable government to Western capitalist countries; it will not be too poor or small (it is impossible to spend much money in countries like Chad or Mauritania without practically taking them over; things are hard enough in Kenya), although publicity given to the plight of the 25 'least developed' countries, which are generally small, may change that slightly. Unless the prospective donor is France or Belgium it will prefer an Anglophone country as more of its technical personnel are likely to speak English; the scale of French aid, however, provides a more reasonable rationale for this tendency. It will be a useful bonus if the recipient provides an acceptable locality for European administrators and technical advisers in terms of climate and social life. It is evident that Kenya meets these requirements – perhaps best of all African countries. In addition, Kenyan politicians and civil servants have acquired considerable skill in dealing with donors. Their skill in this direction outstrips that of the rest of the government machine in finding productive uses for the aid on offer.

In this section we give brief descriptions of the policies of a few of the more important donors.

United States

The United States Agency for International Development (AID) is an agency of the State Department of the world's largest economic and military power, and as such is conscious that its actions have implications other than the purely humanitarian. AID personnel, however, insist, with plausibility, that military, political and commercial considerations are much less important in US aid to Kenya than they are elsewhere like Latin America, where US interests are more directly involved.[35] Although there is considerable US investment in Kenya it is small compared to that of the UK, and the area has no particular strategic significance. In Kenya humanitarian motives for aid are the ones stressed by AID personnel. In its emphasis on agriculture the US has anticipated the common fashion among other donors and more recently it has rationalised this emphasis and declared it as a policy for US aid in general of developing 'poverty focused aid'.[36] The AID mission in Kenya is currently planning and negotiating a sector loan of $ 10-15m. for agriculture.

If the US has been a leader among donors in terms of sectoral emphasis, however, its methods and procedures have been among the most backward. Each technical assistance project is the subject of separate agreement that has to be signed afresh each year. Capital loans are also subject to separate agreements that lay down strict guidelines for disbursement. Funds are withdrawn if an agreement is not signed within six months of funds being earmarkéd, if prior conditions are not met, or if a project is not completed in three years. The chief difficulty is that AID gets a country-by-country annual vote in Congress and does not know beforehand how much aid will be available for each country. Activity is assumed to go on at the previous year's level until the Bill is passed and new commitments can be made.[37] The need for each loan or grant to be negotiated independently meant in the past that the US was rarely approached for funds by the Kenyans, who preferred to submit projects to other donors.

In recent years the US has been getting around this by being the most initiatory of aid donors. Sometimes the AID Mission in Nairobi writes project submissions of behalf of Kenyan operational ministries and sends them almost simultaneously to the Kenya Treasury and AID in Washington. The US does not restrict itself to projects in the Kenya Development Plan. Project ideas 'consistent with Kenya and US policy' can emerge in informal dialogue and then they may be taken up by AID who put technical assistance in to assist with project preparation. For example, the US is 'concerned to help the Kenyans with their equity problem and help the marginal farmer'.[38] The Kenyans approached AID for a loan for small-farm credit, but the Americans did not consider credit to be the binding constraint on rural development. They got Kenyan approval for a technical assistance project to work up a general agricultural programme dealing with many factors including credit, and that is to be the basis of their sectoral loan. As an AID man put it: 'Once we decide to get involved, we push.'

West Germany

West Germany has as much difficulty in spending its aid as ODM. At the end of 1974 not a Mark had been spent on some projects agreed two and a half years earlier. This is partly owing to Kenyan administrative delays and partly because there is little local delegation by the Germans, so project applications have to go to Germany or teams from there have to visit Kenya for the assessment of projects. The Germans are now interested in switching more to programme or sectoral aid partly to help disbursement.

German aid is fixed in two-yearly negotiations with the Kenyans at which individual projects as well as the total sum to be given are discussed and funds are earmarked for projects up to the level of the total commitment. Agreements are made for the two-year period without even 'planning' figures being given for longer periods. One advantage of the German approach, however, is that the programming is done entirely in terms of commitment without stipulation as to rates of disbursement. The Germans have a very high tolerance of deviations in disbursements for any given year. They claim that experience is enough to guide them in estimating the rate at which commitments will be disbursed, and there is no need to be more rigid. The Kenyans do not have to worry about how much or how little they are spending in any year; they can just draw on a commitment until it is exhausted.

Capital aid and technical assistance are discussed at the same negotiations although there is a separate commitment framework for each. Unlike the British the Germans tell the Kenyans what the TA commitment is. They are clear-sighted about the division of aid into two exclusive funds. German officials admit it has no rationale and explain it as historical accident: capital aid was the responsibility of the Treasury while technical assistance came under the Ministry for Economic Co-operation. Vested interests are involved and it is not likely that the two frameworks will be amalgamated in the near future. At present capital aid is loan and technical assistance is grant.[39]

It has been suggested[40] that in the early years of the aid programme the Germans were intoxicated with the post-war success of their own market economy and anxious to proselytise others. There is little indication of it currently in Kenya, although West Germany is not among those donors that prefer aiding Tanzania to Kenya. The Germans disavow the approach of giving aid primarily to regimes with whose ideology the donor agrees – 'as long as the recipient government is a reasonable medium for assisting poor people it's all right'. A move to programme aid would, however, involve some political interventionism in the style of the IBRD. This is acknowledged within the German aid agency.

Sweden

In many ways the Swedish administration of aid is more liberal than that of any other donor. Like the UK the Swedes agree a block sum of aid for disbursement over a period (of three years in their case) before discussing particular projects. A firm figure is announced for disbursement in the imminent financial year with planning figures for the two following years. The Kenyans can apply for aid for projects at any time against the sums agreed. Unlike the UK Sweden has full carry-over of funds to following financial years if they are not disbursed on time. Uniquely among donors in Kenya the Swedes also disburse their aid in advance of expenditure by the Kenyans. Detailed estimates are requested for spending over the next six months, and disbursement is made against the estimate. At the end of six months the Swedes request reporting on the expenditure. They are primarily concerned that the balances they have advanced have been committed by the Kenyans and are not so concerned about whether the money has actually been paid out. Then they make further advances against spending estimates for the next six months. There is an eventual check on expenditure in the Kenya government's own audited reports. This is necessary to compute the following year's budgetary allocation.

The Swedes are not neurotic about financing recurrent expenditure. A number of their projects, an artificial insemination programme, a foot-and-mouth control programme, and the Kenya Science Teachers Training College, included provision for recurrent costs to be met, then to be gradually taken over by the Kenya government.

The combination of three-year aid agreements, carry-over of undisbursed funds, advance disbursement, no procurement-tying, recurrent cost financing and soft terms makes the Swedes popular donors but has not prevented underspending. Undisbursed aid balances have built up, and when advance disbursement began in 1973 the Kenyans were asking for the next tranche while being unable to show they had fully committed the previous one. However the system is said to be working more smoothly now.

The Swedes are explicit about their conception of development and their greater willingness to aid governments they believe to be pursuing it. The Swedish aid agency, SIDA, prepares an equivalent of the ODM Country Policy Paper stating a view of recipient government development policy, and it is shown to the recipient government. SIDA's policy is to promote economic equality and economic independence. In recent years in Kenya this has led SIDA to favour rural development projects. It has agreed to contribute to the Kenya government's Rural Development Fund.[41] However, many Kenyan civil servants believe Sweden favours Tanzania on ideological grounds, preferring that government's approach to economic development.

The World Bank

In his Nairobi speech in September 1973, Bank President Robert McNamara repeated the view that the tendency to concentrate resources on a 'modern sector' using capital-intensive technology had encouraged dual economies with few benefits percolating down to the rural poor.[42] A new strategy was required, spreading benefits among rural masses even at the expense of some economic growth as conventionally measured. The Bank has encountered problems in beginning to implement such a strategy in Kenya.[43] Many of its projects are still for heavy infrastructure, the reason being that the Bank has been doing what it can. Proposals for productive rural sector investment have not been forthcoming. The Bank regards its interest in livestock development in co-operation with other donors as typical of the way it wants to go and is taking a less accommodating view of requests to give large sums of money for trunk roads.

As an international agency the Bank is less inhibited than most bilateral agencies in making recommendations on general policy to the Kenya government. It has conducted a series of reviews of the Kenya economy complete with recommendations on the pattern of public sector investment and fiscal and other issues and incorporating IMF views on exchange rate policy. Its views are very similar to those outlined in Part One of the current Kenya Development Plan but they are not really reflected in the pattern of projects for which the Kenya government requests foreign assistance or the pattern of projected recurrent expenditure. In 1974 the Bank was negotiating to give a programme loan to Kenya, and a prelude to doing so was a close examination of Kenya's macro-economic policies.

As well as extending programme loans and intervening in economic policy, the Bank is among the most punctilious of donors when assessing single projects. There are seven different procedures for making loan disbursements, one of which has to be followed to the letter in any particular case. Disbursements are usually in respect of expenditures already incurred by the Kenyans, although sometimes the Bank can supply letters of credit direct to suppliers in other countries on provision of shipping documents. High standards of accountability are enforced for Bank projects, including three-monthly reports on their progress. Bank loans are, however, not procurement-tied to any particular country, although in the past they have been for 'offshore' expenses.

Despite this the Bank has been quite a popular donor with the Kenyans. There seem to be two reasons. Most important is the fact that it is prepared to advance larger sums for a single project than many bilateral donors and if necessary, in the case of very large projects, can organise consortia better than bilateral donors. Secondly, whatever the difficulties imposed by rigid administrative procedures, they do leave recipients knowing where they stand. The Bank is very straightforward and is always ready to put in consultants to help with difficulties in project preparation or implementation. IDA loans are also softer than those of many bilateral donors.

The Commonwealth Development Corporation

The rationale for having a body like CDC as well as an aid programme proper is not perhaps obvious at first sight. It appears to involve two administrations instead of one. And while the CDC uses what is in effect aid money, the requirement that it should pay its way[44] would appear to conflict, at least potentially, with the aim of development. For one thing it entails somewhat harder terms which have to be borne by the recipient. For another, given the price distortions in ldcs, projects which are socially beneficial in a macro-economic sense and those that make a profit are not necessarily the same thing. It might also appear strange, if the British government takes seriously the policy priorities devised in ODM, that these are not reflected by CDC. The Corporation does meet the Minister of Overseas Development and takes account of his views as to which countries are to be regarded as high priority for lending. It can go into new countries only with his approval. Yet on terms and project selection it goes its own way.

The arrangement does have advantages. The fact that it is not a government department gives CDC a number of important freedoms. It can insist upon preconditions before supporting a project, with a directness that government agencies do not find easy. Its requirement to pay its way gives it, in effect, a *locus standi* for being forthright with recipient governments. In this its demeanour, where necessary, can resemble that of the World Bank rather than that of a bilateral donor agency. This also applies to the nature of technical assistance supplied. As an investor, rather than simply an aid-giver, CDC monitors projects after they have been launched, as noted in the case of tea projects.[45] While perhaps irritating on occasion to the Kenyans, this after-care can be a valuable form of technical assistance. Technical assistance supplied by ODM to operate capital projects works for the Kenya government, and if its advice is ignored has little recourse but to write a gloomy report to ODM at the end of the year. The CDC technical assistance is often from people still working for that organisation and their recommendations, if ignored, can be taken up at a higher level. There is very little of this ex post evaluation and discipline in the case of projects financed by ODM.

CDC funds are not attended by all the rules that have circumscribed ODM. Money, for example, is not partly grant and partly loan, partly 'capital' aid and partly technical assistance. If CDC wishes to appoint consultants it can do so without concern as to which heading the expenditure should come under. In addition its funds are not source-tied. Commonly CDC will be financing a venture in conjunction with a sponsoring commercial company. That company will generally obtain supplies from the best source. CDC often tries via its Supply Department to find a competitive British supplier, but does not insist upon it. Most of the tea factory equipment in Kenya is British, but so are the commercial companies concerned. CDC is also involved in textiles in Kenya with 10 per cent of the equity (£44,000) and £80,000 in loans committed to Kisumu Cotton Mills Ltd. The Development Finance Co. of Kenya holds another £10,000 equity. Private interests in the company are Indian and most of the equipment is Indian, although there is also some Dutch and German machinery.

The Corporation's closer contacts with the private sector mean that there seem to be more project ideas at a concrete stage competing for its funds than is the case with ODM, which has to rely solely on the Kenya government bureaucracy. In 1974, for example, CDC was fully committed world-wide and was turning down projects in Kenya. The majority of approaches for funds come from the private sector but the trend, in Kenya at least, is increasingly for the government or para-statals to make the approach. CDC is aware that many areas of the economy are so sensitive that it is preferable for the government to be involved from the start. Anything involving land is an obvious example. State involvement also means that the government is less likely subsequently to introduce policies that are detrimental to the interests of CDC ventures or to argue about the interpretation of agreements made with such ventures. Any tension in government policies or objectives can perhaps be resolved at an early stage. CDC activities are thus being drawn more into the public sector.

On the other hand in 1971 the Conservative British government attempted to integrate official aid more closely with British private investment. In a White Paper[46] a number of measures were announced to encourage British private investment in ldcs. The most important were:

> Encouragement for joint ventures involving British private capital. This was to be done after a request from the ldc government. HMG could then supply aid funds, through it, to local investment banks

and development corporations for use in British joint ventures. ODM could also help British firms to make the necessary contacts.

Encouragement for British firms to investigate investment opportunities in ldcs. British aid funds were to be made available for part of the cost of pre-investment studies by private firms considering either a financial investment or participation in management of ldc enterprises.

Provision of government-to-government aid for infrastructure – road or rail communications, electricity, water, sewerage or drainage etc. – where facilities would otherwise be inadequate for a British private investment or joint venture.

These provisions are still in existence, but with the change of British government in 1974 little or no emphasis is given to them in Kenya or elsewhere. The one outstanding case of HMG providing aid funds for the Kenyans to invest in a joint venture with British private enterprise was the Mumias Sugar project and that pre-dated the provisions.[47]

Notes

1. The figure was somewhat higher than usual as some money was given for flood relief. *Kenya 1962*, London, HMSO, Ch. 3, p. 25.
2. See Chapter Five, Part One.
3. E.g., by Colin Leys in *Underdevelopment in Kenya: the Political Economy of Neo-Colonialism 1964-1971*, London, Heinemann, 1975.
4. See Chapter Five, pp. 106-7.
5. Private long-term capital movements: 1961, £2.2m.; 1962, –£0.2m.; 1963, –£9.4m.; 1964, –£15.0m.; 1965, –£1.5m. *Kenya Statistical Abstract 1967.*
6. Duncan Sandys made this clear in the House of Commons on 22 November 1963 (*Hansard*, Col. 1396).
7. However, an ODM official makes an interesting point: in the early years of independence there were as many advisers in Tanganyika but they did not constrain policy there. The influence of advisers is proportional to the congeniality of their advice. The greater complexity of the Kenyan economy and administration, however, may have made expatriates less dispensable.
8. See J. R. Nellis, 'Expatriates in the Government of Kenya' in *Journal of Commonwealth Political Studies*, Vol. XI, No. 3, November 1973, who records that this seminal expression of policy was framed by a foreign adviser.
9. However, some CD & W balances are still unspent, and ODM has stated that their use is 'limited to British goods unless strong reasons can be given for relaxation of this rule'.
10. Clive S. Gray, 'Impact of Foreign Aid for Local Costs on the Donor's International Receipts', *Eastern Africa Economic Review*, Vol. 3, No. 1, June 1971.
11. The Kenyans were not committing the Mercantilist fallacy in pointing this out. The British Treasury's insistence that aid should be at least partly tied was rational only if Sterling were overvalued. If it is so, however, exports are overpriced and it is good to promote them. Of course, the argument had more force when the Kenya shilling was fully convertible.

12. Their currencies, of course, were not overvalued.
13. The backlog in spending capital aid has always been a problem. In 1970 only two-thirds of the £18m. committed in 1966 had been spent and £0.5m. was still unallocated to any project. The trend in ODM policy precluded any improvement. See p. 88.
14. See R. B. M. King, 'The Planning of the British Aid Programme', *Journal of Administration Overseas*, January 1972.
15. King, op. cit.
16. Some confusion is possible because within ODM the term technical assistance is sometimes used to refer only to wholly-financed advisers as distinct from those partly-financed people in established posts with the Kenya government covered by OSAS. We use technical assistance in the 'outsider's' sense as a general term covering both groups.
17. The difficulty in doing it more quickly, even if desirable, is the scale of the programme. In 1974/75 OSAS expenditure in Kenya, including EAC, was £4m. SCAAP expenditure was £½m. and capital disbursements £3½m.
18. See Chapter Six, pp. 206-7.
19. See Chapter Six, pp. 184-9.
20. Other agencies, notably the Swedes, tell the Kenyans what their disbursement framework figures are for technical assistance and capital aid and indeed communicate the contents of their equivalent of the CPP. As one Swedish administrator said: 'If you are only going to give so much aid in a certain way because, for example, you dislike certain policies of a recipient government it seems only fair to tell it so and give it a right of reply.' The UK does not do so. This seems to be another example of the obsessive and malfunctional secrecy of British government departments.
21. See pp. 94-9. Rural development has always been a strand in HMG thinking since the Swynnerton report.
22. ILO, *Employment, Incomes and Equality: A Strategy for Increasing Productive Employment in Kenya*, Geneva, 1972.
23. See Chapter Six, pp. 217-22.
24. Fungible is defined in the *Hamlyn Encyclopedia World Dictionary* as: 'of such a nature that one instance or portion may be replaced by another in respect of function, office or use: usually confined to goods . . . as money or grain'. Hence, as one bit of money is as good as another, the effect of aid may be to displace domestic or other funds from a project to be used for another project altogether.
25. See Chapter Six.
26. Information from an official of the Ministry. The Swedes are the only donors who disburse aid in advance of expenditure by the Kenyans. One possible advantage of doing this is its psychologically liberating effect on the Kenya Treasury.
27. As one Treasury man ruefully put it: 'Works . . . you tell them how much money they've got and they'll tell you where the road stops'.
28. It did try to infiltrate the Ministry of Lands and Settlement which was spending much British money, but without success. See Chapter Five, pp. 119-20.
29. For further discussion see Chapter Six, pp. 209-14.
30. This proposes cost-benefit analysis on the general principles of I. M. D. Little and J. A. Mirrlees, *Manual of Industrial Project Analysis for Developing Countries*, Vol. II, *Social Cost-Benefit Analysis*, Paris, OECD Development Centre, 1968, but with many simplifications in procedures. Use of the guidelines is not obligatory for all sorts of projects.
31. Kenya's four-year development plans are in two parts. Part One gives general policies and overall expenditure projections of different ministries. Part Two

is a list of projects grouped by ministry which are supposed to make up the development expenditure.

32. See Chapter Six.
33. See Chapter Five, Part Three.
34. Another popular recipient is Tanzania, whose ideological attitude is rather different. Of course it could be that aid has a supporting role here, a subverting role there; it could be that such considerations are simply over-rated.
35. This is a source of relief to them; as one said, 'It's nice not to be the big kid on the block for a change'.
36. *AID Program Budget Submission Guidance to Missions FY 1976.*
37. See G. Cunningham, *The Management of Aid Agencies*, for a general account of US and other country aid procedures. London, Croom Helm, 1974.
38. As told to one of the authors in an interview with USAID personnel.
39. See Chapter Three, p. 67.
40. Paul Streeten, 'Aid to Africa', Geneva, UN Economic and Social Council, mimeo., 1970, p. 5, para. 10. The change in German aid policy has been credited to the period when the Social Democrat Dr Eppler was Minister of Economic Co-operation. See Cunningham, op. cit.
41. A form of programme assistance for decentralised rural development. See Chapter Five, p. 181.
42. For a summary and discussion of this speech which itself summarised earlier ones on similar lines, see A. Bottrall, 'The McNamara Strategy: Putting Precept into Practice', *ODI Review 1-1974*.
43. See Chapter Three, p. 68.
44. See Chapter Three, p. 64.
45. See Chapter Three, p. 65.
46. *British Private Investment in Developing Countries*, Cmnd 4656, April 1971.
47. 'Joint venture' may give a somewhat wrong impression as the British company involved, Booker McConnell Technical Services, has a management contract to run the project and only a very small equity stake of 5 per cent. See Chapter Five, Part Two.

5 AID IN ACTION

It is a familiar fact that the influence of aid on a country, even when it is completely project-tied, cannot be assessed by observing individual aided projects and cumulating their effects. That is because of the fungibility of resources. Aid, although it might be provided for specific uses, is an addition to total resources whose effect could be to free existing resources from the uses to which aid is then put. The freed resources are then available for other uses. If the aid had not been provided therefore, it is perfectly possible that the projects it ostensibly financed would have been undertaken anyway and it is other expenditures that would not have occurred.

Of course, development projects are not born fully formed. It may be that a project would have been carried out in some form, even without the aid that ostensibly financed it. Yet because this aid was offered, a donor may have come to exercise influence over the specification of the project. It is, therefore, possible to divide the effects of aid into two: the micro-level effects which consist of the donor's influence over the details of particular expenditures, whether these expenditures depend on him or not, and the macro-level effects which consist of the influence of his aid on the allocation of resources in a more general sense.

We postpone discussion of this distinction to Chapter Six and in this chapter we give a detailed account of three important British aid programmes or projects. In the case of two of the studies, the Mumias Sugar Project and the Kwale Special Rural Development Project, the focus is largely on micro-level effects. In the case of the first study, the Land Transfer Programme, the expenditures were on such a scale, the issue was so politically important, and the policy options so diverse, that decisions about the Programme more clearly had considerable macro-level implications.

Part One: The Land Transfer Programme

Almost 40 per cent of all Britain's aid commitments to Kenya since independence have been for the Land Transfer Programme, under which British farmers in the Kenya Highlands were bought out and the land was transferred to African ownership. The Programme was an example of a relatively large land reform, yet the finance for it, some £33m., represents perhaps the most controversial element of British aid. British diplomats and aid administrators commonly regard it as the most far-reaching aid Britain has given to Kenya, claiming that it 'saved political stability and democracy' and 'preserved law and order'. Yet many Kenyans dispute whether much of this money can be called aid at all. Parliamentary and press statements have referred to it simply as compensation for British farmers, and generous compensation at that. *Sessional Paper No. 10 of 1965, On African Socialism and its Application to Planning in Kenya*, hinted at a similar interpretation, and pointed out that as much of the money was loan, it was Kenya that was doing the compensating. Paragraph 103 stated:

> The settlement process was designed more to aid those Europeans who wanted to leave than the Africans who received the land. Our land problems should not be settled on terms decided in the United Kingdom . . . It is unlikely that Kenya, in accepting the debt burden, has obtained economic benefits of anywhere near the amount of debt incurred.

This section tests the latter assertion and considers what British policy interests were served by the Programme. An account of the Land Transfer Programme is followed by a suggested framework for evaluating it and some judgements. The account falls conveniently into two parts: 1960-65 and 1966-74.

1960-65

The Land Transfer Programme was instituted by the colonial administration.[1] In 1960 the State of Emergency which had existed for seven years was lifted, and at a constitutional conference at Lancaster House, London, in February of that year agreement was reached on a new constitution with common roll elections and progress to majority rule. Later in the year an Order in Council abolished the Scheduled Areas. These events stimulated considerable unease among European farmers who began to demand that the British government, which so recently had been encouraging them to settle, should guarantee their land rights under the African government which was now seen to be inevitable. While the British government had abandoned any notion of Kenya as a white man's country, it hoped to preserve a multiracial state where whites still had a large role to play in the spheres of politics and agriculture, among others. HMG therefore concurred with white liberals in the Kenya government in setting up the first Land Transfer Programme, the 'Yeoman and Peasant' scheme. The plan was to settle 6,000 African families on Peasant holdings designed to produce £100 a year net income above subsistence, and a further 1,800 families on Yeoman schemes designed to provide £250 a year net income above subsistence. This scheme, introduced in January 1961, was projected to cost £7.5m. Finance was to be provided by HMG, CDC and the World Bank. The Land Development and Settlement Board was set up to administer the scheme.

The intention was to ease tension over the land issue, and by taking over underutilised land on a willing buyer, willing seller basis to maintain or raise output.[2] There were, of course, settler communities in other British colonies, notably the Rhodesias, so HMG, with its eye on the wider colonial implications, wished to defuse the fears of whites while avoiding any suggestion that it was prepared to compensate settlers or guarantee their property. Compensation would establish an expensive precedent and might encourage expropriation by new governments. To this day British civil servants are at pains to stress that the Land Transfer Programme is not compensation. The forms of the transactions are designed to make that credible. Payments are made by HMG to the Kenya Treasury, after the purchase has been effected and the documentation complete. British farmers deal entirely with officers of the Kenya government in the Ministry of Lands and Settlement.

A general election in April 1961 led to the formation of a government dominated by the 'moderate' African party KADU, but including many white liberals. KADU made it a condition of taking office that it should receive more financial aid to appease African land hunger and so prevent the party being outflanked by more militant African nationalists in KANU.[3] To meet the requirements the 'New Scheme' was devised, doubling the acreage to be transferred with the intention of settling 12,000 families on higher density plots with net annual cash income targets of from £25 to £40. The programme was principally designed to meet the problems of unemployed Kikuyu families but it also showed the effects of pressure by European farmers. Allowance was made for one payment in cash to vendors, instead of a one-third cash payment and the balance in three equal interest-bearing instalments over five years, as planned for the original settlement scheme.[4] This scheme, too, proved inadequate. British farmers continued to write in to the government offering their farms for sale while African squatters were actually staking out areas to occupy on some European farms. By the time that the second Lancaster House Conference was held in February and March 1962, investment by Europeans and Asians had virtually stopped and it was feared that the economy . . . 'still greatly dependent on European farming, might collapse'.[5] The market in farm land had already done so.

As a result of the Conference, KANU members came into a coalition government with KADU, the *Majimbo* or regional constitution was promulgated, and the 'Million-Acre' scheme was born. This encompassed the 'New Scheme' and allowed for the purchase of 200,000 acres of land a year for five years at a cost of over £15m. The land, which included highly developed agricultural areas, was to be subdivided to provide net cash incomes in the range £25-£70 a year. Land was purchased in large blocks and settled according to tribal spheres of influence.[6] A few farms were also offered to 'freedom fighters' still in the forests to induce them to come out and accept the authority of the African government.[7]

KANU accepted the scheme, although there was some feeling in the party against it as appearing to accept the legitimacy of European land-holding. Some leaders believed the land should be acquired free after independence.[8] There was also uneasiness because the scheme was being implemented while KANU was not running the government. The party accepted the scheme on balance because its main ethnic support was receiving the bulk of the land, and because it did not wish to delay independence by disputes over the land issue.[9] While the settlement was regarded as imperfect it offered some resolution of the land problem which was explosive enough to threaten any government, even an independent African one. Another reason for acceptance which has transpired more recently is the conservatism of Kenyatta and other KANU leaders and their attachment to the notion of the sanctity of property, not to mention property itself.

A point at issue between KANU and KADU was the composition of the Central Land Board, set up to take charge of land purchase and conveyancing to new settlers. KADU and the European settlers, both fearing a Kikuyu-dominated government, wanted a board of regional representatives and representatives of the vendors, while KANU wanted a board under central government control. Initially, KADU had its way and Presidents of the Regional Assemblies set up under the *Majimbo* constitution were to nominate settlers. Settlement money became the responsibility of the Settlement Fund Trustees, a committee of the Ministers of Finance, Agriculture and Settlement. The Land Development and Settlement Board was wound up and its functions were taken over by the Department of Settlement in the Ministry of Lands and Settlement. However, the Republican constitution which became effective in 1964 abolished Regional Assemblies. The Minister of Lands and Settlement then had final authority in selecting candidates for all schemes. The Central Land Board was wound up in 1965, and its residual powers went to the Settlement Fund Trustees.

The pattern of land settlement was thus established for five years and policy did not change until after the reports of a British government mission to Kenya in 1965, led by Maxwell Stamp, which gave an account of the progress of settlement and made recommendations for future policy. The Schemes in existence up to that time were:

High Density Settlement: Planned to cover 987,000 acres, the settlers to be landless and unemployed, required to provide only £5 to £7 to include stamp duties, registration and conveyancing fees. Target incomes ranged between £25 and £70 a year.

Low Density Settlement: Planned to cover 180,000 acres of under-developed land of high potential. Settlers were required to have agricultural experience and a significant amount of their own capital. Target income was £100 a year. The earlier 'Yeoman' scheme with target income of £250 a year was absorbed into this programme. On both these schemes settlers were given Development Loans at 6½ per cent yearly interest for investment and as working capital. They were repayable over 10 years by 20 equal half-yearly instalments.

Large-scale Farming Units: Not all the land purchased within the Million-Acre programme was suitable for subdivision, being either too dry or having too poor soil. A small number of co-operative farms was set up in such areas, mainly to undertake ranching.

Assisted Owner Schemes: The Land Development and Settlement Board sold some farms to buyers with capital, intending to finance the scheme with IBRD and CDC money lent for the 'Yeoman' schemes. The lenders vetoed the scheme as not conforming to the loan agreements, but only after 125 settlers had been settled on 34,000 acres.

The Nandi Salient: The Central Land Board bought 17,008 acres for £179,563 and handed it back to the Nandi tribe as having been wrongly alienated.

Compassionate Farms: The Central Land Board began a programme of purchasing farms owned by aged and disabled people who because of their infirmity or location were thought to be in danger from squatters but who were unable to sell up and retire because there was no land market. The farms were either re-sold to Africans or included within settlement schemes.

The Ol Kalou Salient: Here the Kenyan government asked Britain to finance purchase of some farms that were being abandoned and were overrun by squatters. The request was agreed because both governments feared a precedent from squatters establishing themselves freely on alienated land, and the risk to law and order of a forcible eviction was considerable. The Department of Settlement has since carried out large-scale farming as the area has so far been considered unsuitable for small holdings.

Finance for the schemes was provided as follows:[10] The British government provided a grant for one-third of the value of land purchase and a loan for the remaining two-thirds repayable over 30 years at 6½ per cent interest. It also provided an administration grant and development loans for the settlers.

Table 11: HMG Finance for Million-Acre Scheme

		£'000	
	Loan	Grant	Total
High Density Scheme			
Land purchase	6507	3283	9789
Development loans	4101	–	4101
Other costs	–	4320	4320
			18210
Low Density Scheme			
Land Purchase	1263	632	1894
Other costs	–	1221	1221
			3115
Nandi Salient	–	195	195
Total HMG funds			21520

Of the total sum, slightly more than £10m. had been disbursed before independence. At independence and in 1965-66, a further £2m. was lent to the Kenya Land and Agriculture Bank to make commercial loans to Africans for purchase of European farms on the open market without subdivision. Another loan of £1,275,000 was made in August 1964 for land purchase by the Land Bank in the Ol Kalou salient. The Department spent some £490,000 in 1962/63 for Compassionate Farm purchases, also funded by HMG.[11]

IBRD and CDC committed £2,471,000 for development loans on the Low Density Schemes in the ratio one-third from CDC and two-thirds from IBRD. The organisations imposed stringent conditions on the supervision and administration of the schemes before extending the loans. IBRD was not interested in any plan that did not allow for a net cash income above subsistence of at least £100, so reinforcing the pressure for low density schemes with greater agricultural extension services. Participation from international organisations was said to be desired by the colonial and British governments for political reasons – the leverage they could exert on an independent Kenyan government.[12] The full IBRD and CDC commitment was never spent, and in 1972 the IBRD and CDC had disbursed K£1,080,000 and K£676,000 respectively. The West German government also committed development loans for the High Density Schemes amounting to £1,218,000.

The Settlement Schemes had a number of objectives which sometimes contradicted each other. The Van Arkadie Report, commissioned by the Kenya government, identified five policy objectives[13] which can be condensed into three: to redistribute income and wealth in favour of Africans, especially the destitute; to increase agricultural production by more intensive working of the land; to bring about a structural transformation of the economy.

The first objective was politically necessary, and was the dominant principle behind the High Density Schemes. British farmers were paid for the land at 1959 prices – the last year in which the land market was regarded as normal. Valuations were sympathetically carried out by expatriate personnel. Only 141 farms changed hands in 1959 and those transactions became the basis for hundreds of later purchases.[14] Part of the British finance was grant because it was realised that many of the permanent improvements and installations on the land, although affecting its valuation, would be of no use in the small-holder agriculture that was to succeed the British farmers. For the rest, the Kenya government had to repay the loans, and the new settlers were required to pay the Kenya government for their freehold, on the same terms as the British loans to Kenya. Instead of the African settlers receiving subsistence wages as labourers while the European farmer took the profits of the enterprise, the European farmer now took the profits in a capital sum, financed by HMG, which was then partly repaid via the government of Kenya from the profits of the new settlers working the same land. The Africans were theoretically to get subsistence still, plus a cash income of between £25 and £250 a year. It is not hard to see why the scheme commended itself to the British government: the European farmers could be kept reasonably happy, being paid for their land partly by the new settlers and partly by the British government. In the event it was the latter which did most of the paying because the implicit discount rate that capitalised the flow of future farm profits at the 1959 market price greatly exceeded the real interest rate on the British loan. The prices averaged roughly eight times annual profit, implying a discount rate of about 12½ per cent, while the loan was at 6½ per cent over 30 years and no allowance was made for inflation. Even without inflation the grant equivalent of the loan for land purchase was about one-third of the value of the land. Inflation changes that radically. If inflation of the money profits of the land averages 4-5 per cent a year over 30 years of the loan – which looks a very modest estimate at present – the grant equivalent of the loan equals almost two-thirds of the price of the land.

The second objective was the one that exercised the Kenya civil service most and made it favour low density settlement which was thought much the more likely to further development. The then Director of Settlement, in his Department's *Annual Report* of 1962/63, argued strongly that the optimum size of holding allowed for subsistence plus £100 a year, and nothing less, and the government should accept the selection of small holders and 'not draw from a cadre of landless and unemployed'.[15]

Criticism of the schemes came from what might conveniently, if loosely, be termed the left and right. From the left it was argued that settlement in the form it was taking was 'Rolls Royce in nature',[16] and free distribution to the landless should be made with smaller plots if necessary. This view was current in a section of KANU, and articulated increasingly in 1964 and 1965 by several politicians, notably B. Kaggia.[17] From the right, after making ritual obeisance to the political and social imperatives, it was argued that subdivision was already going too far and too fast, that land was Kenya's most precious asset, and systems of tenure should be such as to ensure its optimum economic use, within the political constraints.[18] This was the 'developmental' view current among civil servants and the IBRD. This view, of course, interpreted the third objective of structural change narrowly to mean Africanisation of much agriculture with smaller holdings and more labour-intensive methods, but basically producing much the same crops for the market. During the middle sixties, the 'right-wing' view prevailed and has since dominated policy. It received definitive expression in the Stamp Report, published in October 1965.[19]

The Report emphasised that the transfer of land did not lead, of itself, to increased output and indeed caused a foreign exchange drain as it was a condition of the programme that the farmers could take their payment in Sterling. Kenya's problems, including unemployment exacerbated by a population explosion, could only be solved by general economic expansion. It stated that great success in expanding output had been achieved where consolidation and registration of land-holdings had been effected and concluded that an expanded programme of land consolidation should be undertaken. The returns to investment were thought to be greater in areas already farmed by Africans than in Settlement areas. A programme of land purchase 'at a much reduced level' was recommended as there was 'an immediate need . . . for the maintenance of a market in land'. However, a pause in settlement was recommended:

> Although the settlement has done much to alleviate a difficult social problem of landlessness, the high density settlement schemes have not so far produced the levels of cash income for farmers which are necessary for the progress of the Kenyan economy. A pause in settlement for at least two years should be made to enable past results to be analysed and present and future practice to be improved.[20]

1966-74

The Stamp Mission report was one of the bases for negotiations between British and Kenyan Ministers in London in November 1965. The Kenyan background to these talks was one of increasing political dissension in KANU between the 'radicals' led by Oginga Odinga and Kaggia and the 'conservatives' led by Tom Mboya and, as it later turned out, enjoying the support of Kenyatta. Only four months later Odinga was to leave KANU and form a new party – the Kenya People's Union (KPU) – one of whose platforms was the need for free land distribution.[21] It would be surprising therefore if the Kenya government did not argue strongly the political necessity of continued land settlement, and claim that Stamp had underestimated the political factor, although the view that land consolidation and registration had a lower cost-benefit ratio in purely economic terms was accepted and expressed in *Sessional Paper No. 10*. Political unrest was also a factor in making European farmers eager to leave at an undiminished rate. Kenya government estimates were that in the event of a collapse in the land market some 100,000 acres a year would be abandoned, although this was probably a 'negotiating' estimate rather than a serious projection. In the event a compromise was reached. An interest-free loan of £6.3m. was agreed for Land Transfer, including £0.55m. for further settlement schemes. Stamp had recommended further land transfer at a maximum of 85,000 acres a year, but a rather higher rate of 100,000 acres a year was agreed.

In April 1965, the Agricultural Development Corporation (ADC) was set up to undertake agricultural operations in the national interest on the direction of the Ministry of Agriculture. An ODM Mission went to Kenya as a result of Stamp's conclusion that a review and subsequent strengthening of the Kenyan administration of land transfer was required. The Mission recommended that the ADC should be the vehicle for further land transfer. The ADC acquired farms and leased the majority to appropriate tenants (often farms were leased back to the European farmer from whom they had been bought) or farmed them itself until they could be sold to African private buyers. Some farms were retained and operated as National Farms where a specialised activity was involved such as maintaining a pedigree herd or cultivating improved seed varieties. The money which HMG lent to the Kenya government interest-free was lent on to ADC at 5 per cent. ADC tenants in turn paid rent of 6½ per cent of the farm's valuation and 7½ per cent interest on ADC farm improvement loans.

Kenyan demands for some sort of subdivisional settlement scheme were met by the *Harambee* programme of low density settlement to be carried out at the rate of 20,000 acres a year for four years, a tenth of the rate projected for the Million-Acre schemes. The British were content that this should continue under the administration of the Department of Settlement only because the ADC was judged not ready to take it on.[22] Officers in the Ministry of Lands and Settlement regarded the ADC as the brainchild of the Minister of Agriculture, B. R. McKenzie, and his attempt to get in on the settlement business as he was becoming resentful of the growing power of the Ministry of Lands and Settlement. British support for the ADC signified a loss of confidence in the latter ministry and in settlement schemes as such. The Africanisation of the Department of Settlement did seem to coincide with a decline in administrative efficiency. While the Million-Acre programme was carried through quite successfully, the much smaller *Harambee* programme lagged from the first, and by the time it was overtaken by a policy change, little of it had been completed. To that extent, Stamp's belief that the Kenyan settlement administration was at full stretch was vindicated.

Some of Stamp's other conclusions, however, were subsequently falsified by events. An ODM team evaluating the *Harambee* settlements proposals in 1968 observed that there was little evidence to justify the widespread belief in the success of low density and in the failure of high density schemes in agricultural terms. Confirmation that in certain respects high density settlement had in fact turned out the more successful came in 1971 with the publication of the Ministry of Finance's Farm Economic Survey.[23] The Survey had sampled both types of farm on settlement schemes from 1964 to 1968. While the level of output per acre was higher on low density farms than on high density for three years out of four, the rate of growth of output per acre was much higher on the high density schemes. Net farm profits per acre were higher on the low density schemes for the first two years but were higher on high density schemes for the following two years. High density also showed a greater return on capital invested. And while most of the settlement farms failed to reach their target incomes, the shortfall was greater on the low density farm with targets of £100 and £250, than on the high density with targets of £25 and £40. The intermediate income group with a target of £70 a year did worst on this reckoning. Ironically, the *Harambee* schemes fell into this latter range. Later work attempting a cost-benefit analysis of the two forms of subdivisional settlement has tended to support the conclusion that the high density schemes have often given a higher economic return to investment than the low density schemes.[24]

The conventional wisdom came full circle in 1972 when the ILO report on Kenya quoted this survey and urged the further subdivision of settlement holdings, particularly on low density schemes, to increase labour absorption and the intensity of land use and thus raise output per acre.[25]

There were further changes in settlement policy in 1970. After McKenzie's retirement the ADC was phased out of settlement by the Kenya government and restricted to managing existing state farms. The practice of leasing farms back to their former owners was stopped, and all settlement and land to be settled became the responsibility of the Settlement Fund Trustees. The *Harambee* scheme was stopped and only 431 families were settled on about 16,000 acres. A survival of the Stamp period, however, is the definition of a mixed farm, an enterprise involving mixed arable and livestock production as opposed to either a ranch or plantation. Britain, for the earlier schemes, agreed to finance the purchase of mixed farms as these are suitable for subdivision. Ranches are in general too dry to provide a livelihood for small holders, and estate plantations growing permanent crops such as tea and coffee are usually on such fertile soil as to make their purchase prohibitively expensive. The Million-Acre Scheme was carried out on an *ad hoc* basis without 'mixed farm' being defined. A definition was laid down in 1967 that is still used.

Table 12: Britain's commitments to land transfer since 1970

	£m.	
	Grant	Loan
1970		
Land purchase for settlement:	2.5	–
ADC and Agricultural Finance Corporation		1.0[a]
Special Scheme	0.25	
Total	3.75	
1973		
Land purchase for settlement	6.0	
Agricultural Finance Corporation		1.0[a]
Total	7.0	

a 2 per cent interest.

The loans to AFC are for on-lending to private buyers making free-market purchases of European-owned farms. The Special Scheme was for the purchase of farms which were becoming dilapidated or over-run by squatters, to prevent the need for the Kenya government to impose a management order.[26]

The land bought with these later British funds has been settled differently from the earlier schemes – on the *Shirika* or co-operative principle. Landless and unemployed people are settled on large farms along with the original farm employees. Each family is allocated a plot of about 2.5 acres while the rest of the farm continues to operate on a large-farm basis with a manager supplied by the Settlement Fund Trustees.[27] Theoretically the responsibility for management is transferred progressively to the co-operative society of all the settlers. Originally they were supposed to be buying the land with a purchase loan but the policy may be adapted so that they hold the land on a lease, paying an annual rent of 5 per cent of the land value. The advantages of this form of settlement are continuity, the realisation of economies of scale, including the maintenance of large livestock herds and the fact that capital equipment on the farm, useless in the event of subdivision, can continue to be used and maintained. The co-operatives get development loans for the purchase of the farm's loose assets and for other investment. Each settler is required to be resident on the scheme, and the annual target income for each family is K£60 plus subsistence, the money coming partly from part-time employment on the large farm and the remainder and subsistence requirements coming from the small holdings.

While the scheme seems reasonable in principle, in many cases it appears not to be working as intended. One effect of providing the additional land for the subsistence plots is that the area of the original farm is reduced by perhaps a quarter. Labour requirements, far from being such as to provide work for the increased numbers of people on the farm, are therefore reduced. The majority of people who get jobs are those with specialised skills, like tractor drivers or mechanics, so the available work cannot be shared. The settlers are thus left on plots smaller than any on high density schemes and without the concentrated agricultural extension services available on the older conventional schemes. The farm manager has no time or inclination to concern himself with small-holder cultivation, being a paid official with no incentive to do so. When the development loan is paid off, the settlers should theoretically be in a position to ask the Settlement Fund Trustees to withdraw their manager so that they can run the farm themselves and take decisions about what proportion of the farm's net profits should be re-invested and what proportion they will take in the form of dividends. This is not a situation that has yet arisen, however, and it is one that is regarded with considerable trepidation by many settlement officers.

On some farms the lack of competence of the manager will maintain the farm in debt. One more able *Shirika* manager said that he just would not tell the settlers what the loan repayment position was until he thought they were 'ready'. Yet the settlers took no part in the running of the farm at all. As the land area had been reduced, the manager was laying workers off, not using more. Almost all the men on the settlement left to find work in a nearby town where they earned wages that made it uneconomic to employ them on the farm. In fact the manager insisted that mechanisation would remain more economic and efficient on a farm of that size (some 4,000 acres net of the settlement) specialising in dairy production, even if wage rates were much lower. In the circumstances there seemed no reason why the settlers should ever be 'ready'.

In practice, therefore, the *Shirika* farms are run much like ADC state farms with bits carved off to provide small holders with the barest subsistence. At present the system works reasonably smoothly because the new settlers, being previously landless, are grateful enough for the small plots. There is a fear, however, in the Department of Settlement that they may in a few years' time demand either a share of profits of the farm or an active share in its running, to both of which they are entitled, although both may be inimical to the farm's profitability as a large unit. We received conflicting impressions of what would happen then. Some civil servants seem committed to *Shirika* as a way of preventing much of Kenya's mixed farming land going to subsistence agriculture. Others maintain that the Department has an open mind and should *Shirika* prove unsuccessful, the farms will be subdivided. It is the IBRD view that subdivision should occur if *Shirika* encounters major problems, and it is our view that the schemes might very well do so, especially where they operate in areas where the most economic crop is not labour-intensive. The implications of *Shirika* do not appear to have been thought through to the point of reconciling the desire to maintain large-scale farming with the claims of the landless who have been given, so far notional, rights on these farms.

The other important form of government-organised settlement did not use British funds. In fact it led to conflict with the British which, the Kenyans allege, caused a delay in the negotiation of general development aid in 1970. The *Haraka* settlement schemes (formerly called Squatter Settlements) were carried out on farms from which the European owners had been excluded by a management order under the Agriculture Act.[28] This Act gives the Minister of Agriculture power to take over inadequately managed or supervised land. It obliges him to run the farm and pay compensation to the owner or sell it and give the owner the proceeds minus a deduction for the costs of sale, but neither was done in fact. Instead, in 1965, a Commissioner of Squatters was appointed to settle the land so taken over. People who could prove they were landless registered with the Commissioner who could provide land for them. About 45,000 people registered. Settlement began on the farms taken over, and it was done for the most part rapidly and cheaply with settler families getting small plots of about ten acres. In July 1971 the Department of Settlement took over the schemes from the Commissioner.

The government's action drew protests from HMG and eventually was contested in the courts where it was ruled that acquisition had taken place and the Kenya Land Acquisition Act of 1968 applied.[29] The Kenya government was required to pay the market value of the test-case farm plus a 15 per cent surcharge. Following negotiations it seems likely that the British government will allow the use of land transfer funds to pay for these farms, but not the extra 15 per cent above market price or interest payments owing because of the delay in compensation.

Originally, it was planned to settle some 45,000 families on *Haraka* schemes, but later this target was reduced and the programme was ended after 14,635 families had been settled on 35 schemes totalling nearly 140,000 acres. One reason was agricultural fastidiousness; the schemes were unplanned and looked scruffy. More important, the political situation cooled down with the successful suppression of the KPU (whose genesis had almost coincided with that of the Commissioner for Squatters). HMG, which held up subsequent aid negotiations to discuss compensation for the land-owners concerned, did not help and the transfer of the schemes to the Department of Settlement, where they were not popular, doomed them. Nevertheless, *Haraka* was a cheap form of settlement as no farm planning was done before settlement took place; the settlers got no development loans and little in the way of extension services. Marketing co-operatives, fostered from the start on Million-Acre settlement schemes, are only now being started on *Haraka* schemes.

The Director of Settlement commented in 1972, 'these schemes continue to be a problem to my department.'[30] Yet *Haraka* is not without its proponents. J. D. MacArthur, formerly of the Ministry of Agriculture, in an evaluation of settlement schemes,[31] states that in view of their cheapness they may well have a higher benefit-cost ratio than other schemes. In effect the administration and other inputs lavished on other settlement schemes have not had very high returns, so *Haraka* shows up well.

As the *Haraka* type of settlement might represent what the Kenya government would have done on a larger scale if British funds for land transfer had not been available, that is expropriate the land against some promise of future payment and settle it rapidly by subdivision into small plots with little planning, it is tempting to regard *Haraka* as a yardstick, an indication of what might have been on a larger scale. However it would not be appropriate to take yield estimates or estimated patterns of production on *Haraka* settlement and compare them with the results on other sorts of settlement scheme, because in general the land taken over for *Haraka* settlement was not mixed farming land. Many of the 50 or so farms taken over were formerly ranches or sisal estates. *Haraka* land is usually extremely marginal for small-holder arable cultivation, and as no development money has been available, the settlers have not been able to buy livestock. *Haraka* schemes in general seem to be less well developed than high density schemes of the same vintage but that is attributable less to lower initial expenditure and planning than to a harsher environment. On one scheme at Munyu, near Thika, Central Province, the rains had failed for four years out of five and the settlers had had to leave to get work to live. Not surprisingly most of the ground in the plots was uncultivated. It was the opinion of a good many settlement and agricultural officers interviewed, however, that when conditions were favourable, *Haraka* settlers achieved just as high returns per acre as conventional high density settlers, even with no high-grade cattle as supplied elsewhere, less extension advice, no special development finance, and inferior roads and other infrastructure. However a high proportion of output was consumed on the holding and less was sold for cash. These impressions do have implications for an assessment of the effect of British funds on post-settlement farming.

There are no reliable output figures from settlement schemes later than those given in the 1964-68 Farm Survey, although there are figures showing sales through settlers' co-operatives.[32] These are an imperfect guide to output as they obviously exclude subsistence output and private sales, which are important for many products. With these reservations, they appear to reveal increasing output which exceeds pre-settlement levels in many areas. This is partly due to technical advances, notably improved seed strains for maize, in particular. It is quite possible that output per acre would have increased even faster had there been no transfer and settlement.

The Effects of British Aid on Land Settlement

The Land Transfer Programme to many people simply means the Million-Acre Scheme. Yet over 40 per cent of British money for LTP and nearly 60 per cent of money for land purchase has gone on subsequent programmes, many of which involve little or no subdivision of landholdings. Quite a lot of the money therefore has financed not a land reform whereby the system of land tenure was changed, but a simple transfer of ownership. Large-scale farming has not been a great success in Kenya.[33] The transfer of large farms is also open to more serious corruption than the allocation of small holdings.

In retrospect it is probable that British policy took a wrong turning with the Stamp Report. There is clearly a role for a large-farm sector but given the shortage of experienced entrepreneurial farmers and the abundance of peasants, the balance between subdivision and ADC farms was too much in favour of the latter after 1966. While the Million-Acre Scheme was not a perfect land reform it was more thorough-going and probably more successful, socially and economically, than those aided programmes that have followed. It cannot be concluded however that HMG is entirely to blame for the systems of tenure that have evolved in the former Scheduled Areas. British aid has had a declining effect on the form of settlement that has taken place on transferred lands since independence. The Million-Acre Scheme was devised and largely executed by Europeans in the Kenyan administration in close consultation with the British government. The form of settlement in the Stamp period was partly determined by the unwillingness at that time of the British government to make more funds available for subdivisional settlement out of a belief, still regarded as justified in some circles, that settlement had gone too fast and strained the planning, administrative, and extension services available, and another belief, much more controversial, that high density cultivation was not a success, especially in the sense of not providing a basis for loan repayments.

The Kenya government itself, however, was ready enough to curtail *Haraka* and *Harambee* schemes once the political goad of the KPU had been removed, and *Shirika* is its own conception. Many influential Kenyans prefer large-scale farming because of its appearance of modernity, the supposed greater contribution to marketed output, and perhaps because of its consistency with an elitist political and economic philosophy. ODM has in any case increasingly opted out of intervening in land settlement as such. Since 1970, funds have been entirely for land transfer and no money has been available for settlement.

One reason given is that this is consistent with the general policy of insisting that recipient governments have a financial stake in any project undertaken using British aid funds, as a guarantee of continued interest in the project. It has been argued that transfer and settlement are a single project, and Kenyan finance for settlement is an appropriate division of financial responsibility. This argument appears to be a rationalisation. HMG decided that it was impolitic to interfere in the form and institutions of land settlement because of the high political sensitivity of land. LTP was regarded as different from other aid and ODM handed it over and asked no questions. Having relinquished influence over settlement, however, ODM did not trust the Kenyan institutions to administer development finance, so did not provide any. There was a feeling that the Department of Settlement had become a self-perpetuating body which continued to grow while its proper functions diminished. In fact that was partly a consequence of the way finance was provided for the Million-Acre Scheme, as we argue below. ODM eliminated the grant for administration because, as subdivisional settlement came to an end, it was thought that the administrative expenses should also fall. The progressively softer terms of British aid for LTP – interest-free loan in 1966 and grants after 1970 – were also seen as making a contribution to Kenya's administrative costs. It is true too that HMG did not have the capacity to monitor at all closely the progress of settlement schemes. British aid is administered in Kenya by relatively few people and there used to be fewer. The First Secretary at the High Commission responsible for administering the Land Transfer funds also had, for years, to administer the general development funds. Much of his time was spent acting in a consular capacity to British farmers who came in to Nairobi to offer their farms for sale, or to complain about pressure being put on them to sell, or the prices they were being offered. It was administratively impossible for him to check up on the fate of farms after settlement, and all monitoring of settlement was done by a single Agricultural Attaché, who also had other things to do.

HMG's desire to distance itself from the operations of the Department of Settlement is understandable. British recommendations that the Department should employ more economic expertise, and offers of technical assistance, were coolly received; no technical assistance was used by the Department from the time that its established posts were Africanised and it still employs no economist. However, it was the British government's insistence on financing land transfer for the Million-Acre Scheme largely by loan, and the financial structure devised by the colonial administration, consisting largely of British citizens, that was partly to blame for some of the subsequent problems. While the non-provision of funds for settlement, as opposed to purchase, can be justified, it does give renewed credibility to the claim that Britain's interest in land transfer is purely a concern for the welfare of European farmers – for all British money is now going to them. The cost of subsequent settlement is borne by the Kenyans alone. On most schemes land purchase accounts for nearly half of all expenditure; development loans and administrative expenses account for a quarter each.

The principal problem with the Million-Acre Scheme was that, although mainly inexperienced farmers, the new Kenyan settlers were required to pay for the land. Development loans were therefore considered essential if enough cash surplus was to be generated to make that possible. The development loans were made in kind, not cash, but they too had to be protected, hence for fiscal reasons the scale of extension services in the settlement area greatly exceeded that for Kenya as a whole. That remains true up to this day. The last count of officers in the Department of Land and Settlement in 1971/2 revealed there were some 560 agricultural extension officers of the rank of Assistant Agricultural Officer and above (including equivalent livestock and animal health officers) serving 35,560 settlers in ten Settlement areas, a ratio of just under 1:64. This did not include Settlement Officers proper or co-operative officers, also on the strength of the department. The establishment has not changed since. For the rest of the country the ratio of Assistant Agricultural Officers to farmers was 1:700-1,000. There were in addition some 5,000 Junior Agricultural Assistants in the field, many of them untrained. As they were serving some 1.2m. small farmers, that still meant a ratio of 1:240.[34]

Originally the Department of Settlement was supposed to administer the Settlement Schemes for two and a half years. It became clear that a longer period of intense supervision would be required to supervise the loans. It was believed that as the Department had extended the loans it had to retain control of supervision and agricultural extension on the schemes, and if the Ministry of Agriculture took over, sufficient priority for the schemes could not be ensured. The period of the Department's administration was thus progressively extended to five then seven years. It now seems to be accepted that the Department's suzerainty over the Settlement areas is indefinite. While the Van Arkadie report accepted the need for continued supervision, it recognised that the nature of the administration of the Settlement Schemes would change and agricultural extension would become more important than settlement *per se*. Consequently it recommended transferring the Department from the Ministry of Lands to the Ministry of Agriculture.[35] This never happened, probably because the Minister of Lands and Settlement, Mr. Jackson Angaine, was too well-established politically. It became increasingly necessary for the Department to obtain technical staff on secondment from the Ministry of Agriculture and other ministries. This was unpopular with the staff themselves, however, as they considered that they were being overlooked for promotion in their parent ministry while on secondment. The inevitable upshot was that they were established in the Ministry of Lands and Settlement to provide them with a career structure and promotion prospects in that ministry. The result is that rural administration and agricultural support in Kenya is sharply divided between Settlement areas and the rest of the country, with parallel pyramidical structures for the different areas. The Ministry of Lands and Settlement has become a quasi state-within-a-state, duplicating the functions carried out by a range of ministries elsewhere. HMG rightly noted and deplored this tendency but failed to realise, at any rate early enough, that the financial structure of support for the Million-Acre Scheme was partly to blame.

Of course, it was only partly to blame. The provision of loan rather than grant finance posed a fiscal problem for the Kenya government but it was not bound to attempt to solve it in the way that it did, although in doing so it was continuing on a course set before independence. Strictly speaking, the problem of where and how to apply agricultural extension services to achieve the greatest gains in output is a separate problem from how to tax output so as to repay an external national debt. It is highly unlikely that such an uneven provision of extension services as Kenya has is economically optimal, and if it is, that is no more than a lucky accident, for the allocation was not made on the grounds of economic rationality. Furthermore it seems unreasonable to attempt to fund the whole British debt by what amounts to a tax on the output of the new settlers. Although they obtained the land at subsidised rates they were far from being the only beneficiaries of LTP, as we shall argue in greater detail below. Charging the settlers much less, allocating rural services and credit on agricultural economic criteria, and using the administrative resources saved by winding up the Department of Settlement when its work was done, to expand the activities of the Department of Inland Revenue and later the Exchange Control division of the Central Bank, to reduce tax evasion of various kinds, would have been a better strategy economically and fiscally.[36]

That things were not done in a more sensible way must be explained on political grounds. The new Kenya government was just as anxious as the colonial administration to bring home to the Kenya masses that there would be no free land after independence. There was in any case considerable competition to get on to Settlement Schemes and had the cost to the settler been lower no doubt that would have intensified. By charging the settlers the government reduced the grievance of those not allocated plots and emphasised that land was not a birthright but an economic asset to be paid for. This also fulfilled the ideological function of suggesting that when it was paid for it was legitimately occupied by the payer, a matter of some importance to leading politicians, many of whom became large land-owners. Even after British funds became interest-free loans in 1966, subsequent land purchase and development loans to settlers carried interest at the old rate (e.g. on the *Harambee* scheme). And loans to *Shirika* farms have also carried interest although British finance has been on a grant basis since 1970. A possible justification is the need to relieve the fiscal burden caused by defaulting on the earlier loans. The Kenya government's insistence on the sanctity of private property and the need for land to be bought, however, was a plank in its campaign against the KPU in 1965, and it may well be that this was the more important consideration. Nevertheless, perhaps these political and ideological objectives could still have been achieved with lower charges on settlers.

The weaknesses of the strategy adopted are demonstrated by the poor repayment record of the settlers. Land and development loans to the value of about £16.7m. had been issued in 1972 (the latest available figures from the *Annual Report* of the Department of Settlement). From the first, the rate of repayment on bills due has been low. In 1964/65 it was 47 per cent. The Department, however, charges interest at the 6½ per cent rate on the arrears, hence increasing the indebtedness of the settlers. The total amount which had been billed to settlers at the end of 1971 was about K£10.4m., i.e. over 60 per cent of the full value of loans, although about 60 per cent of the loans were repayable over 30 years and the rest over 10 years. The settlers are still paying bills at the rate of around 50 per cent. In 1973 they were some K£5.3m. in arrears.[37] The Van Arkadie report[38] estimated that if settlers could make annual loan repayments of only K£800,000, by 1989 the interest owing on arrears would exceed their repayments and the scheme would be financially unviable – the settlers' debts would be increasing. Although the report regarded this as the outcome of pessimistic assumptions, reality has been even worse. Total repayments in 1971 were K£642,000 and in 1972 K£683,000. President Kenyatta's two-year moratorium on loans for new settlers, announced in 1967, has complicated the calculation but some observers, including a World Bank team, believe the scheme is already financially unviable. As a result, the 1974-78 Development Plan said the government was considering not charging interest on arrears, an overdue reform urged by the Van Arkadie Commission in 1966.[39] It is also proposed to offer settlers in arrears the option of converting their holding to leasehold, but that would probably be extremely unpopular.

The Commission also urged a tougher line on defaulters, with increased evictions. Despite the political difficulties involved, a number of evictions subsequently took place. The Department's *Annual Report* in 1966/67 recorded 76, compared with two up to the time of the Van Arkadie report. This policy was based on the premise that when all allowance had been made for the difficulty of settlers in meeting their loan repayments there was an element of refusal to pay based either on the belief that the land should be free or on a shrewd calculation that the government would be politically unable to evict. There were however quite sufficient grounds for predicting widespread payments arrears even if all the settlers had been anxious to repay. Billing was six-monthly, with the first bill arriving six months after the settler moved on to his plot. Few had by then generated enough cash income to be able to pay, so they started off in arrears. Even more important was the low level of production. This was owing partly to the inexperience of settlers and also to shortages in the early years of certain inputs and assets. Farm budgets were based on planned stocking rates, but in the early years of settlement there were fewer grade cattle available than the farm plans called for.[40] Not all the farmers therefore had the cattle they needed to generate the target income. When the target cash income above loan repayment and subsistence is only £25 to £40 a year with high levels of husbandry required, it is clear that a shortfall in production, which is likely to occur, will immediately jeopardise the loan repayment capability of the farmer. Certain household expenditures such as minimal food, clothing and, in Kenya, school fees, are likely to be given precedence over loan repayment in any case, so in the circumstances it is surprising that loan repayment was as high as it was on high density schemes in the early years, especially as in the case of loan repayment, defaults by below-average farmers are not offset by extra payment by the above-average. On the other hand it is perhaps surprising that repayment rates have not risen more since.

There have been other distortions. One of the channels for loan repayment was through a levy on earnings from sales through the settlers' marketing co-operatives. While this was administratively convenient, it probably had the undesirable effect of retarding the growth of the co-operatives by encouraging settlers to sell their produce privately. Some extension officers believe that this effect is smaller now that settlers are used to the idea of co-operatives and appreciate their benefits. As a few farmers approach the point where they receive their freehold, this is expected to provide an incentive to the others, and once the inevitability of repaying the loans is accepted, the farmers find the co-operatives a convenient P.A.Y.E. way of doing it.

The Evaluation of Aid for Land Transfer

Most of the British money has been given purely for land purchase and it is those funds we consider first here. Money for the administration of settlement or to finance development loans is considered further later. We consider the costs and benefits of the British finance for land transfer under two heads: the value and cost to Kenya; the value and cost to Britain.

The Value and Cost to Kenya

The net value to Kenya is the sum of the net extra benefits accruing to Kenya citizens as a result of the provision for land transfer of the finance, compared to the situation where it was not forthcoming. In order to assess these benefits, it is necessary to guess how the problem of foreign farmers would have been dealt with by the Kenya government in the absence of British finance.

One thing the independent government could have done in theory is nothing. This appears to be the assumption of those on the British side who argue that LTP 'saved law and order'. It would seem to be so that had the government stood by inactive, illegal squatting involving violence would have occurred on a large scale and, had the government attempted to resist it while offering no *quid pro quo*, the government might well have collapsed. For that very reason it seems completely at odds with the realities to assume the Kenya government would have done nothing, and the possibility can be dismissed. Assuming therefore that the Kenya government realised that it faced an absolute necessity to replace European farmers with Africans, there was more than one course open to it:

(i) It could have undertaken to buy farms from their owners at what they considered a fair price based on historical market values. This appears as a simple transfer payment, but the real cost to the economy is likely to have been high. Many of the farmers would have left the country (as they did) and taken the money, leading to a foreign exchange drain. Without labouring the point further, therefore, we can say that if this were the policy adopted, British funds were worth their full grant equivalent – the full value of the finance minus the present value of interest and loan repayments. It might be objected that the Kenya government could have imposed exchange control or otherwise restricted the ways in which the purchase money could be spent. The market price of the farm was, however, determined under the colonial system where there was no exchange control between Kenya and the UK from where most of the farmers came. Imposition of exchange control or any other restriction on their use of the proceeds of sale amounts simply to paying less than the old market price and is *ex hypothesi* excluded from case (i).

(ii) The Kenya government could have expropriated. Expropriation is here defined as the compulsory acquisition of assets at less than their historical market price (i.e. that before the process began). The expropriation of the farms would have reduced the costs to Kenya under (i) but would have given rise to other costs. Without proving the statement we can plausibly assume that these other costs would vary directly, but probably not proportionately, with the degree of expropriation – which becomes 100 per cent when the government kicks all the farmers off and gives them no compensation.[41] The costs of expropriation would take the form of certain flows of production forgone over time which can be reduced to a single figure by discounting at an appropriate interest rate, In practice the government will not be indifferent to the interpersonal distribution of those flows. For example, the consumption of European farmers can be subtracted from the flow of production forgone as the Kenyan government can be assumed not to value it.

There are a number of expropriation costs one can posit, but there may also be some benefits. The costs of expropriation are the net present value at the time of expropriation of the following effects:

(a) A loss of production owing to the possible accelerated departure of expert farmers at a rate exceeding that at which they can be replaced, whatever the organisation of land tenure, i.e. a managerial input is being lost.

(b) A loss of production owing to the running down and perhaps the deliberate destruction by farmers of productive assets during the time that they as a group are being removed.

(c) A more indirect cost, the acquisition by the Kenya government of a reputation for arbitrary action inimical to business confidence and foreign investment.

(d) A saving of administrative resources: if nothing had been paid for the land the government might have adopted a different pattern of settlement, e.g. it might not have attempted to retrieve the money from new settlers and so saved administrative resources spent on debt accounting and collection.

(e) An effect on the political popularity and hence authority of the government: the morale of Kenyans might have been improved by the spectacle of their government taking a firm line, but against this is the vestigial capacity of the white settlers to make political trouble. In fact a UDI by white settlers on the Rhodesian pattern is sometimes said by British civil servants to have been averted by LTP. The need for metropolitan troops to combat Mau Mau surely demonstrates that a UDI was not possible. A Kenya government would have had to disguise intentions to expropriate, however, if independence were not to be delayed.

Clearly if the Kenya government had done the best it could in the absence of foreign finance, it would have taken over the farms with just that degree of expropriation that balanced the marginal values of costs under headings (i) and (ii), i.e. when the loss in the present value of production owing to a bit more expropriation equalled the cash value of that bit of expropriation. The situation with which we might compare British-financed purchase at market prices, therefore, is the acquisition of the farms using the optimal degree of expropriation. The value of the aid for land purchase then is the difference between what transfer would have cost the government of Kenya expropriating optimally, and what the existing arrangements have cost.[42] Unfortunately, we do not know what this optimal degree would have been, and it is fair to doubt whether the Kenya government would have known it either.

At this range it is impossible to say what sort of deal a Kenya government acting in the majority interest would have offered the settlers. One Kenya civil servant insists that the full market price would have been paid in line with the constitution and the government's own ideology. That is perhaps the most diplomatic thing to say when one is relieved of having to make the choice. His superior guessed some fraction of the 1959 market value might have been offered – perhaps a half, with payment by a medium or long-term bond. Prices of the farms that did change hands on the free market in 1960-61 were at half the 1958 prices anyway. The provisions of the Agriculture Act might have been liberally applied to farms which it was possible to claim were underutilised or mismanaged, perhaps with an amendment to make subsequent settlement legally possible.

What would have been the expropriation costs of such an arrangement? If farms were simply taken over on being abandoned, while some payment were made on compulsory acquisition, it makes sense for all the owners to stay as long as possible in order to minimise their losses. In practice that does not appear to be the way people always behave. In Kenya in the early 1960s, there were some desertions anyway – for example, from many of the farms on which management orders were placed. If a farm is not making much money or requires new capital investment, the owners may not be prepared to make the necessary outlays in order to recoup what the government has promised, because their confidence has been shaken sufficiently to doubt the reliability of any deal proposed. Settlement Officers, usually white, ran the farms taken over for the Million-Acre Scheme before the land was settled. Such an arrangement on a larger scale could have stretched managerial resources. The competence and even honesty of the early Settlement Officers was very varied anyway.

Another source of loss is likely to have been the running down of the farm – not replacing capital equipment, allowing permanent improvements to deteriorate, and not using fertiliser, so reducing soil fertility. Some Kenyans have argued that the effect of expropriation on running down would not have been great because European farmers did it anyway. Every district settlement or agricultural officer has some story of a departing farmer who deceived valuers about the age of cattle or replaced his best stock with inferior animals after the valuers had called, and there are also stories of malicious damage by farmers. Apparently some allegations of malicious damage, especially in the Machakos area, have their origin in the floods of 1961 which naturally destroyed many groundworks like dams. In fact of all the cases of alleged stripping after the visit of the valuer, only two were established.[43] Usually the allegations related to farm houses rather than the farms themselves. This is not surprising as there was a ceiling price on farm houses that was below the market rate.

The Settlement Officer taking over any farm had the right and duty to query anything on the ground which differed from the valuers' report of which he had a copy. Nevertheless, it can be inferred that some cheating occurred from the fact that for transfer schemes after 1966 valuation procedures were tightened up. Veterinary inspection of herds was introduced along with a second inspection by the valuer who now returned to the farm with Settlement Officers on the day of the handover. Whatever the scale of cheating, most of it occurred in the early years of settlement.

A more important reason why the costs of running down could probably have been small in settlement areas is that much of the capital of farms was in any case useless for the kind of farming that followed: fencing and piping were usually in the wrong place for small holdings and could not be moved. Machinery was inappropriate and needed too much maintenance. A graphic example of this is provided by the experience of a farmers' co-operative at Endarasha in the Kieni West Division of Nyeri District, Central Province. The European farm which was taken over had an irrigation system depending on a motorised pump operating from a river dam. No one on the settlement scheme could maintain the pump, which fell into disuse. For ten years many of the small holders have walked several miles for their water. Now the co-operative is attempting to save Ksh3m. by a levy on its members to install a reticulated irrigation system depending on a hilltop reservoir and gravity feed.[44] The uselessness of much on-farm capital for settlement purposes was indeed the reason why Britain gave one-third of the Million-Acre land purchase money in the form of a grant.

The point that emerges is that the loss of production owing to expropriation would have been small or negligible after settlement. The effect would have been felt in the large-farm sector – in those areas not settled at all or in areas settled later, before they were settled. Without the land purchase money there would have been no recovery in land prices and no investment in the large-farm sector. In any event it took until about 1967 for money prices to reach the 1957 level again. The ways the Kenya government could have countered such an agricultural depression would have been to raise food prices considerably – with political dangers – or to increase the rate of settlement – *Haraka* style. More rapid subdivision might have involved breaking up breeding herds and could have led to other longer-run dangers such as increased soil erosion, owing to more intensive cultivation and less supervision of output. More rapid take-over of large farms by Africans could also have led to declining yields – as it did even at the rate experienced. Faster take-over might well have resulted in an output performance even worse than that of discouraged white farmers running their holdings down.

We cannot proceed rigorously and quantify the direct costs of expropriation,[45] but we can estimate the order of the value of production that would have been endangered by expropriation – the output of white farms for, say, seven years after independence – and compare it with the market price of the farms purchased. The first difficulty is knowing where to draw the line. The main effect of expropriation would have been on those mixed farms not bought up. Would it also have depressed output in the rest of the large-scale agricultural sector and on plantations and ranches not immediately threatened, and even expatriate business generally? It is highly probable, but we shall ignore it for the moment by assuming the government could have made clear its expropriations were confined to a 'special case' sector. This clearly imparts a considerably conservative bias to our evaluation.

The Van Arkadie report estimated the value of output from the mixed farming sector at £15m. in 1961.[46] We have used a similar method to estimate the value of output from the large mixed farm sector for the years 1963-71. (See Table 13.) Only a part of this came from European-owned farms, and it is necessary to estimate that proportion. The *1968 Economic Survey* and the 1970-74 *Development Plan*[47] give two estimates of the proportion of the mixed farming area still in white hands, and using these as benchmarks we have assumed that, of the remaining large farm areas after deductions for settlement, 7 per cent a year was taken into African ownership up to 1967 and 5 per cent a year thereafter. It would not be reasonable, however, to take these estimates of the proportion of the mixed farm acreage in white hands in each year as estimates of the proportion of output coming from white-owned farms, as the latter were undoubtedly more efficient than their African-owned counterparts during this period.[48] In the first place, it tended to be the more efficient white farmers who held on while the less efficient were content to be bought out and as surveys showed, African farmers who took over large farms often ran into difficulties.

On the basis of farm surveys we have assumed that the value of output per acre was 50 per cent higher on white farms than black. This assumption, combined with the acreage estimate, gives estimates of the proportion of total mixed-farm output coming from white farms.[49]

This output, however, does not represent the social value of continued production; a number of adjustments have to be made. The price of agricultural commodities does not always represent their true social opportunity cost. Many agricultural products are marketed in Kenya by Marketing Boards to which the large farmers often have privileged access. The prices charged to consumers often included a subsidy element to the producer to the extent that overproduction resulted and was often exported at a lower price than domestic output. Certain important commodities have been revalued at social accounting prices based on the import or export prices of traded goods in an attempt to get nearer to the true social value of output.[50]

Table 13: Estimated value of production by large mixed farms in Kenya, 1963-71

	(current prices)								
	£m. *1963-1967*					K£m.[e] *1968-1971*			
	1963[a]	*1964*[a]	*1965*[a]	*1966*[b]	*1967*[b]	*1968*[c]	*1969*[c]	*1970*[c]	*1971*[c]
Wheat	2.95	3.50	4.16	3.17	4.08	6.50	6.50	4.90	5.10
Maize	2.05	0.98	1.03	1.24	2.87	2.92	2.00	1.50	2.00
Other cereals	0.51	0.47	0.49	0.32	0.30	0.30	0.30	0.30	0.30
Total cereals	5.51	4.94	5.68	4.73	7.25	9.72	8.80	6.80	7.30
Cattle and calves[d]	0.61	0.56	0.53	0.55	0.54	0.60	0.60	0.60	0.60
Sheep	0.22	0.19	0.17	0.19	0.22	0.20	0.20	0.20	0.20
Pigs	0.50	0.48	0.47	0.54	0.44	0.40	0.35	0.30	0.25
Poultry, eggs	0.27	0.25	0.22	0.20	0.20	0.20	0.20	0.60	0.60
Pyrethrum	0.77	0.49	0.71	0.74	0.42		Immaterial		
Other temperate crops[f]	0.44	0.37	0.38	0.33	0.31	0.30	Immaterial		
Milk	1.86	1.78	1.92	2.70	2.88		Immaterial		
Butterfat	1.41	1.16	1.10	1.01	2.03		Immaterial		
Butter, etc.	0.01	0.01	0.01	0.01	0.01		Immaterial		
Total dairy	3.38	3.07	3.15	3.83	5.13	5.00	4.00	5.00	6.50
Total	12.08	10.69	11.64	11.53	14.97	16.57	14.40	13.65	15.60

Sources:

a *1967 Abstract of Statistics*, Table 74, p. 77.
b *Economic Survey 1968*, Table 4.7, p. 58.
c Estimated from total agricultural output figures, various *Economic Surveys*; large farm proportion in total taken as average of 1963-67 proportions for wheat, other cereals and livestock except for cattle; a slight decline in the large farm share of maize, cattle and dairy products was allowed for by rounding down.
d Van Arkadie's method (op. cit., Chapter 2, para. 113) was followed by assuming one-quarter of cattle sales came from mixed farms — the remainder from ranches.
e Average exchange rate: £1 = K£0.85.
f Pulses, potatoes, fruit, vegetables and flowers, plus oilseeds.

A deduction has to be made for the cost of inputs. The input-output table for Kenya for 1967 was used. Value added was taken as 0.82 per cent of the value of marketed output.[51]

Much of the value added, however, accrued to the European farmer in the form of profits. Input-output data show that in the agricultural sector some 60 per cent of value added is profits. This figure was assumed to rule for the European mixed-farm sector. About 13 per cent of these profits were taken by the government in direct taxation and are therefore of full value as a social benefit.[52] The rest of value added consists largely of wage payments and these, too, were valued at their full amount. Net profits were treated differently. In the first place the consumption of European farmers could be regarded as valueless from a Kenyan point of view. Their savings, however, especially after exchange control was introduced in 1967, probably financed some investment of use to the country. No data exist on the savings propensity of European farmers as a group. As self-employed businessmen they might be expected to save quite a lot in the ordinary course of events, but it is doubtful whether they were doing so in the early 1960s and if they were, they were probably remitting their savings abroad. In the end we assumed one-quarter of net profits went into investment useful for Kenya, so post-tax profits were valued at a quarter of their sum at accounting prices. This is clearly a rather arbitrary procedure but has to do in the absence of fuller information.

This adjustment completed the derivation of what might be called the 'social surpluses' realised in each year. These were deflated to 1963 prices using the middle-income consumer price index,[53] then discounted to a present value, as of 1963, using an accounting rate of interest of 10 per cent. Land purchase expenditure for 1963-73 was similarly deflated and discounted (see Table 14).

The calculations indicate that the present value of land purchase money expended was some £13m. in 1963. The 1963 present value to the country of European farm production during the forthcoming nine years was about £27m. Obviously both these figures are subject to wide margins of error. They indicate that the output safeguarded was worth about twice the cost of doing so, hence the saving from a 10 per cent degree of expropriation would have been wiped out by a fall in the 1963 present value of output of slightly less than 5 per cent. Of course, this says nothing about how farmers would have reacted to any degree of expropriation; we have no means of estimating any behavioural equation of that kind. This merely shows roughly what sort of response would have been necessary to wipe out the gain from any expropriation.

It seems that paying the market price or something like it might well have been good tactics for the Kenyans, even in the absence of British finance. There are many plausible scenarios. If, for example, the output of the white farms had fallen to half its actual figure for eight years after independence (owing either to the lack of interest of the whites or the inexperience of those succeeding them), the gain from a complete expropriation would have been wiped out even if output thereafter rose to the level it has actually reached. The optimal degree of expropriation, therefore, might well have been small.[54]

Some of the assumptions made in reaching the estimate can be varied to test sensitivity. If productivity on white farms had been merely average for the large-farm sector, for example, 1963 present social value of

Table 14: Costs and potential benefits of land transfer

A Social surplus from white mixed farms, 1963 prices

1963	*1964*	*1965*	*1966*	*1967*	*1968*	*1969*	*1970*	*1971*
5.47	4.42	4.36	3.58	3.91	5.02	4.05	3.27	2.96

Present value in 1962 of these flows with a discount rate of 10 per cent: £27.03m.

Source: Output as in Table 13: (i) each line multiplied by accounting ratios (see note 50, p. 143); (ii) yearly totals multiplied by a factor (as in note 49, p. 143), to obtain share of white farms; (iii) multiplied by 0.82 (proportion of value added in output) to give value added at accounting price; (iv) multiplied by 0.59 to derive social surpluses at accounting prices derived as follows:

$$\text{Social surplus} = \underset{\substack{\text{non-profit}\\ \text{component}\\ \text{of value added}}}{0.39(VA)} + \underset{\substack{\text{tax on}\\ \text{profits}}}{0.13(0.61)(VA)} + \underset{\substack{\text{25 per cent}\\ \text{of net profits}}}{0.25(1-0.13)(0.61)(VA)} = 0.59(VA)$$

(v) deflated by consumer price index (as in note 53, p. 144) to obtain social surplus.

B Land purchase expenditure, at 1963 prices

1963	*1964*	*1965*	*1966*	*1967*	*1968*	*1969*	*1970*	*1971*	*1972*	*1973*
3.1	3.91	2.788	0.897	0.884	0.925	0.914	0.893	0.840	1.008	1.653

Present value in 1963 of these flows with a 10 per cent discount rate: £13.24m.

Source: Basic statistics from Department of Settlement *Annual Report*; deflator price index: as above.

European farm production would fall to about £23m. If European farmers' savings, as well as their consumption, are valued at zero, the 1963 present value of production falls to £21m. If both of these new assumptions are made together, a figure of £18m. is obtained.

All of this merely considers possible production losses, but what about the effect on foreign and other investment? On independence foreign investment fell away but then recovered (see Table 15).

Table 15: Private capital flows in the independence period

	K£m.								
	1961	*1962*	*1963*	*1964*	*1965*	*1966*	*1967*	*1968*	*1969*
Net									
Long-term private capital movements	2.2	−0.2	−9.4	−15.0	1.5	1.0	8.0	9.1	16.0
International investment income	−6.1	−7.0	−9.2	− 9.0	−9.0	−12.5	−14.0	−14.1	−16.2

Source: Government of Kenya *Statistical Abstract*, 1967 and 1973.

The so-called 'direct effect' on the balance of payments of foreign enterprise is usually negative in Kenya because profit repatriation (international investment income in the national accounts) usually exceeds the capital inflow. However, to look at this net figure is to make the same error as in the netting of aid flows.[55] There is nothing more 'direct' about these effects of foreign investment, that show up as monetary flows in the balance of payments, than about those that are implicit in the trade figures. Foreign-owned enterprises are producing output that is either exported or would have to be imported or done without. While it is true that if the government acts competently in the national interest, it can usually prevent harmful foreign investment, in practice some sub-optimal and perhaps harmful foreign investment has probably occurred in Kenya – that in enterprises which are heavily protected and have a negative value added at world prices so that their influence on the trade figures is also negative. But it is not just that sort of investment that would have been discouraged by a reputation for expropriation. More than capital, Kenya lacks managerial and entrepreneurial expertise which is supplied jointly with capital by foreign investors. It is an open question whether Kenya has obtained these inputs as cheaply as it might have done in view of the adverse financial flows and the transfer pricing associated with foreign investment. It is also an open question whether the management obtained was employed in the best activities from a social point of view. Much management was, however, obtained and Kenya could have dispensed with foreign investment only with a totally different kind of economy.

Now we consider finance for the administration of settlement and for development loans. These cannot really be divorced from the land purchase money because they would certainly not have been forthcoming if Kenya had taken over the mixed farms with more than a small degree of expropriation. The development loans and administrative grant could quite simply be valued at their grant equivalent. However, that would probably be incorrect. The sums cannot be evaluated separately from Land Transfer money, for all the money helped to induce the Kenya government to a misallocation of resources, as we have argued. If it had not been forthcoming, and a more rational system of rural administration and agricultural extension had been adopted in the country, there would almost certainly have been considerable net savings to the Kenyan exchequer and possibly gains in agricultural output. These ought to be subtracted from the grant element of all the funds for the LTP in assessing their value to Kenya. While that is easy to state in principle, it is impossible to do in practice.

Nevertheless the implication of considering all likely costs and benefits is that Kenya would probably have been well advised to pay close to the market price for farms taken over and British aid for land purchase was actually worth something near to the grant equivalent of the sums advanced. To this must be added the grant equivalent of the development and administration funds, minus something for a misallocation of resources. Even if we make the strong assumption that these cancel out and the development and administrative funds were worthless, we are left with a substantial sum. Over £12m. of the £20m. for land purchase has been grant anyway, and inflation has greatly reduced the real interest and repayment burden of British loans. Even assuming average inflation of only 4-5 per cent a year for the period of the loans, the £20m. of British funds were worth £18-19m. as aid to Kenya. The contention of *Sessional Paper No. 10* is false. The benefits of these funds to Kenya greatly outweighed the debt burden.

There is an objection to the foregoing analysis which takes as its starting point the fact that the rate at which settlement could proceed safely was itself a decreasing function of the money paid to the European farmers. The more compensation they received and repatriated, the more the Kenya government had to tax future output in order to pay the compensation. Had the European farmers received nothing at all, the land could have been parcelled out free to new settlers with a minimum of planning. Then, it is argued, the whole of the mixed-farming area could have been settled very rapidly. Marketed output would have fallen, and Kenyan agriculture would have moved largely to a subsistence basis, but the majority of the population would not necessarily have been worse off.

There is, of course, nothing inherently illogical about this. In 1961 Kenya had a typically colonial economy and in many ways the structure of the economy has hardly changed. Expropriation of all land and its free distribution would have destroyed this economy and led to the atrophying of many industries that existed in Kenya. Such a policy was not even considered by the colonial civil servants who framed the LTP. More recently much thought has been expended on how the existing economy might be made to serve the interests of the majority better, perhaps in the teeth of the interest groups spawned and maintained by it.[56] Of course an agriculture given over to peasant subsistence, while it might have supported the population as a whole at better nutritional levels than the export enclave agriculture has done, equally well might not. It would have been less diverse than the current economy and perhaps less resilient in the face of natural disasters like drought. It would have posed grave developmental problems of its own. Notably, it would have been difficult to tax such production or realise the savings necessary for productive investment or industrialisation. The effect on the price of foodstuffs to the small but politically vital urban population would also have been critical. But perhaps it is not necessary to speculate here whether it would have been better from the majority viewpoint to thus 'go back and start again' rather than attempt to develop along the existing lines, because this was not really a live political issue in Kenya at the time of independence. What we are prepared to say is that once the line of existing development was chosen, the optimal economic policy in the early years of independence, if not later, was to pay expatriate farmers something close to a market price for their holdings.

If, as we suspect, Kenya would have developed on similar lines even without the money provided for land purchase, then it is not necessary to judge how far British interests were in conflict with those of the Kenyan masses (i.e. to evaluate the suitability of a capitalist form of development for Kenya) in order to conclude that LTP funds were a useful form of aid.

The Value and Cost to Britain

Much of the money that Britain forwarded for land purchase was of course repatriated. The Exchange Control Office of the Central Bank of Kenya has a record of remittances of proceeds of sale of farms bought with British aid funds. In the period January 1967 to August 1974, K£5.15m. was remitted, of payments by Settlement and Trustees, ADC and AFC. British disbursements in the period 1967/68 and 1973/74 (British financial years) on the Land Transfer Programme were £7.83m. (ODM figures). At an average exchange rate of £1 = K£0.85, this gives a repatriation rate of 77.4 per cent. However, this figure assumes disbursements from Britain are in respect of purchases during roughly the same period, whereas there is usually a lag between the British national taking his proceeds in Sterling and repatriating them and the Kenya government requesting reimbursement from HMG, so some of the repatriations have been covered by subsequent disbursements. A more accurate figure is probably obtained, therefore, by omitting remittances made in 1974 as those were almost certainly in respect of disbursements not registered in the statistics. That reduces total remittances to K£3.93m. and the repatriation rate to the region of 60 per cent. It would not be accurate to say that the money repatriated was not a net cost to Britain, especially if the Kenyan government would have bought the farms anyway. In any case some has been subsequently re-exported to Australia, South Africa and other places.

If the costs of the programme have been modest, the advantages to Britain are largely political and psychological. A Conservative government was relieved of an embarrassing situation involving land-owners who had strong connections with its own supporters, and some of whom could justifiably claim to have been misled by the British government.

It could also be argued that by making the money available, Britain influenced the political and economic direction that an independent Kenya would take. It was certainly in British manufacturing, ranching and plantation interests that the Kenya economy should continue on its predetermined path, but it is impossible to know what the importance was of these funds in themselves. Aid is only one of a complex of relations between developed and emergent states and is usually given too much importance by commentators. As the ILO report says, '. . . Kenyan attitudes and aspirations had perhaps been moulded more than was realised by the style and ethos of the divided economy, by the colonial experience of having had to accommodate oneself and to work within the existing structure of the economy rather than to change it. Thus, when national independence was achieved, the political aim of taking over the economy became merged almost imperceptibly with the individual aspirations to take over the jobs, positions and life-styles which the economy made possible.'[57]

That acculturisation of the Kenyan elite had already occurred. At the time of independence, was there a politically significant group aware of the implications of a radical land policy and prepared to accept them? There was certainly a populist group in favour of free land distribution, but there was not much debate on the issue before independence and it was not until 1965 that the populists left KANU to form the KPU. This may have been a result of the LTP, of course. Even then, however, the KPU policy had not been thought through to the extent of accepting the revolutionary social and political changes it entailed. Consequently it was easily stigmatised as irresponsible.[58] While it is clear therefore that the provision of LTP finance on concessional terms was absolutely consistent with a policy of protecting British interests in general, it is not really clear that the provision was critically necessary for the protection of those interests. We cannot know that the degree of expropriation would have been high in the absence of aid, or if it were, that this would have permanently undermined British capitalism in Kenya.

Appendix: A Model of Expropriation

In this appendix we justify, rather more formally, the assertion that the optimal degree of expropriation was probably low in Kenya's mixed-farm sector in view of the output at stake. What follows may have application to other land reforms or expropriations.

Information in markets is never perfect so the notion of a market price is usually vague. It seems plausible to assume, therefore, that farmers' reactions in terms of reducing investment, running down their holdings or even leaving, would be moderate in response to a small degree of expropriation. As the degree of expropriation increased, the reactions would intensify as more farmers reacted to the low prices being paid and as the reactions of individual farmers became more violent. At a certain degree of expropriation almost all the farmers would be running their holdings in an extractive manner if they had not left altogether, so further increases in the degree of expropriation could give rise to only a small further reaction. We define e, the degree of expropriation, as (M − P)/M, where M is the market price and P is the price actually paid for farms, and we define r, the reaction, as measured by the loss of farm output compared with normal running. Given the pattern of response hypothesised, plotting e against r diagrammatically would give a rising curve with a point of inflexion.

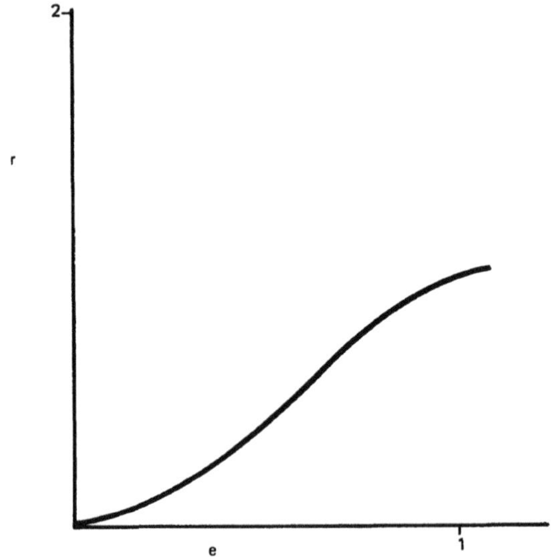

Figure 1

So far we have said nothing about time. The curve could be drawn in Figure 1 on the assumption that the government took over farms at a constant rate of acres per year. That would not be very intelligent, however, because the optimal speed of expropriation from the government's point of view almost certainly varies with the degree of expropriation. It is well known, for example, that if a complete expropriation is planned ($e = 1$) it is better to do it very quickly. If the government varies the speed of taking over land so that the speed of expropriation is always best, given the degree of expropriation, then the curve in Figure 1 will be rather flatter. Then the reaction curve would indicate the loss of output owing both to the discouragement of the farmers being expropriated and the inexperience of those succeeding them. In what follows we consider only the degree of expropriation and assume the government expropriates at the speed appropriate to the degree. Our reaction curve therefore charts the smallest possible output losses for any degree of expropriation. Having introduced time, we have to work in present value terms; savings on purchase owing to expropriation and losses owing to reduced farm output are considered as the present value of these cash flows at the start of the expropriation.

In the context of land transfer in Kenya the maximum value of e (= 1) is worth the 1963 present value of the Land Purchase funds, some £13m. (as the take-over was in fact at market prices). The maximum value of r is where all output from farms to be expropriated is lost and we have calculated that as having a 1963 present value of about £27m. Normalising the axes of Figure 1, therefore, with $e = 1 = £13m.$, the maximum value of $r = 2$ approximately.

The simplest form of reaction function having a shape as we have drawn is a cubic form. To identify it further we can specify the following boundary conditions consistent with our behavioural assumptions:

(a) $$r = ae^3 + be^2 + ce$$

i.e. there is no intercept term – the reaction begins with the expropriation.

(b) $$\frac{dr}{de} = 0, \quad \text{for } e = 0 \text{ and } e = 1$$

(c) $$\frac{d^2r}{de^2} > 0 \text{ for } e = 0; \quad < 0 \text{ for } e = 1$$

i.e. $e = 0$ and 1 are minimum and maximum points respectively of the function.

This defines a set of cubic functions of the form:

$$r = -\frac{2}{3}xe^3 + xe^2 \qquad (1)$$

where x is an unknown parameter. It is constrained to give a value of r between 0 and 2, as e ranges between 0 and 1, so it must lie between 0 and 6. As noted, in effect it is a function of the speed of expropriation, but we assume that that is chosen to minimise x. The task of the Kenya government in the absence of LTP would have been to minimise E, the cost of taking over the farms, where:

$$E = (1 - e) + r \tag{2}$$

To find the minimum value of E, set the first derivative of E with respect to e = 0 (the usual first order condition for identifying an extremum). This gives:

$$e^* = \frac{1}{2} \pm \frac{(4x^2 - 8x)^{1/2}}{4x} \tag{3}$$

where e^* is the value of e that satisfies the necessary condition for a minimum.

The second order condition for a minimum is: $d^2E/de^2 > 0$, from which we derive that:

$$e^* < \frac{1}{2} .$$

These results are, however, inadequate to determine the best policy which may be a corner solution, not shown up by calculus. In Figure 2 we plot reaction functions (1) with their associated expenditure functions (2) for three values of x. Note E = r when e = 1, so the curves meet at that point.

For values of $x = x_2$ and x_3 the minimum points on the expenditure function are at a_2 and a_3, equivalent to low rates of expropriation (e^*_2 and e^*_3). For the lower value of $x = x_1$, however, the point a_1, although a local minimum, has a higher value of E than when e = 1. For values of $x < 2$, (3) has no real solution – the expenditure curve falls monotonically in the relevant range and complete expropriation is optimal. Higher values of x still give a corner solution although real solutions to (3) exist. To determine the critical value of x below which a corner solution is optimal, reflect at e = 1:

$$E = r = -\frac{2}{3}xe^3 + xe^2 = \frac{x}{3} .$$

This must equal the value for E when $e = e^*$.
Hence substituting e^* for e, and (1) into (2):

$$\frac{x}{3} = 1 - e^* - \frac{2}{3}xe^{*3} + xe^{*2} .$$

$(e^* - 1)$ is a factor of this cubic equation which can be written:

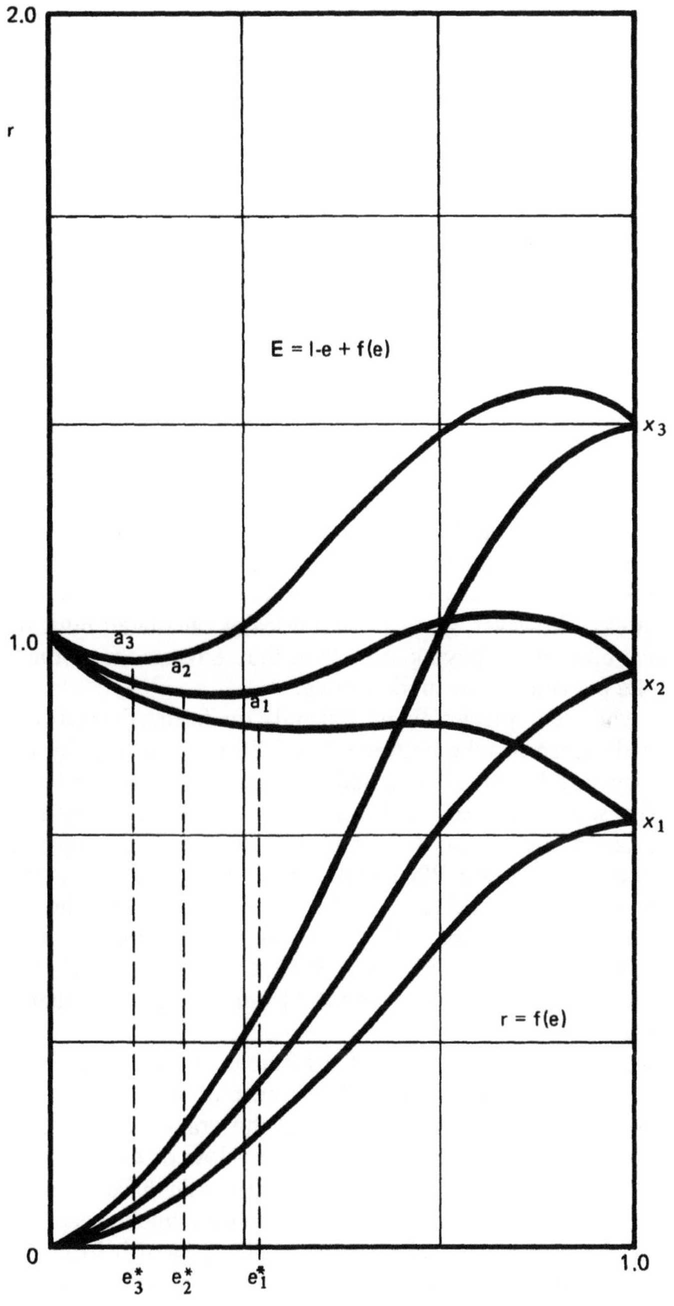

Figure 2

$$(e^* - 1)(2xe^{*2}/3 - xe^*/3 + [1 - x/3]) = 0.$$

Ignoring the solution $e^* = 1$, we can treat the quadratic expression in e^* as $= 0$. The solutions to the quadratic equation are an expression in x which must, however, equal the expression in x in (3). Equating the two expressions and solving for x gives the result that $x = 2.6\dot{6}$. That is therefore the critical value for x, below which complete expropriation becomes optimal.

Conclusion

If x in the farmers' reaction function is below $2.6\dot{6}$, it pays to expropriate them completely, making no payment. If x lies in the possible range 2.67–6.0 the optimal degree of expropriation is low. Where $x = 2.67$, for example, the value for e^*, the optimal degree of expropriation, is 0.25, i.e. the price paid to farmers should be 25 per cent below the market price. The savings entailed by such a course of action on paying the full price is, of course, the money saved by not paying the full price minus the value of lost output, or $e - r$. Where e is 0.25, $r = 0.139$, or almost 14 per cent of the market price and hence the saving is 11 per cent of the market price. As x increases, optimal expropriation falls until at $x = 6$, $e^* = 0.09$. That is, it is best to pay 91 per cent of the market price. In the Kenyan case, however, given the empirically calculated limit on r it could not have been worth paying more than that. Savings then would have been about 4½ per cent of the market price.

So, while the precise figure depends on farmers' reactions, it would have made sense to take between 9 and 25 per cent off the market price or to pay nothing at all. It could not have been optimal to do anything else. The savings on paying the market price achieved by any degree of expropriation are always less than the degree of expropriation by the amount of the reaction. When expropriation is total, the reaction becomes the whole cost of taking over the farms. Even then the savings over paying the market price will not be very great unless x is quite a lot below 2.67; when it is 2.66, and $r = 0.89$, for example, total expropriation, while the best course, is only about 11 per cent cheaper than paying the full price.

Now, British aid was worth the difference between the cost to Kenya of an optimal expropriation and the cost of the existing arrangements (viz. the market price of farms minus the grant equivalent of the aid). The value of the aid could have been very low or even negative if x was low or even $= 0$ (i.e. if an expropriation would have been costless). To assert that total expropriation would have been much cheaper than paying the market price, so the aid was damaging or worth little at best, is to assert in effect that x was very low. There seems to be no empirical warrant for this assertion. That is especially true when we consider that reactions to this expropriation might have extended outside the mixed-farm sector (which removes the limit on r). It may well be, then, that the best Kenya could have done without aid would have been to save some small percentage of the market value of the farms. British aid was then worth its grant equivalent – some 90 per cent of nominal value – minus this small percentage of land purchase costs. If the Kenya government had got its policy wrong and tried paying, say, half the market price, the operation might have ended up costing more than paying the full market price (a situation that arises when the expenditure functions in Figure 2 have points above $r = 1$, and the e chosen results in one of these points being reached), so British aid also prevented the possibility of expensive mistakes.

This model of expropriation is deficient in at least two ways. We have not treated the problem of the speed of take-over at all thoroughly. And we have assumed in effect that the Kenya government had to select e at the start of the programme and maintain it throughout the programme. In fact the best strategy may be to change e over time, paying different percentages of the market price in different years. Specifically, as fewer expatriate farmers remain to cause trouble and as more Kenyans acquire experience, the optimal degree of expropriation may rise. However, two considerations limit the importance of this. One is that if e is changing, what will determine reactions is not the present value of e set in any year, but farmers' expectations about its future course. The farmers would have spotted any tendency for e to rise and perhaps extrapolated on that trend in forming their expectations. Raising e steadily only works if the farmers are very stupid. Secondly, if the expropriation affects confidence outside the mixed-farm sector and expatriates remain important in other sectors, raising e over time may lead to greater losses elsewhere in the economy than it saves on the farms.

Notes

1. See Chapter One, p. 15.
2. C. P. R. Nottidge and J. R. Goldsack, *The Million-Acre Settlement Scheme 1962-1966*, Nairobi, Department of Settlement, 1966, p. 1.
3. G. Wasserman, 'The Independence Bargain: Kenya Europeans and the Land Issue 1960-1962', *Journal of Commonwealth Political Studies*, Vol. XI, No. 2, July 1973. The party initials stand for the Kenya African Democratic Union and the Kenya African National Union.
4. Nottidge and Goldsack, loc. cit.
5. Ibid.
6. Report of the Mission on Land Settlement in Kenya (Van Arkadie Report), Nairobi, December 1966, mimeo, Chapter 2, para. 32.
7. Warhuiu Itote, *Mau Mau General*, Nairobi, 1967, pp. 257-60. Also Van Arkadie, op. cit., Chapter 13, para. 543. *Kenya 1962* (HMSO), p. 130, relates: 'Kikuyu subversive activity came to the fore with the discovery of the activities of the Kenya Land Freedom Army.'

8. J. W. Harbeson, 'Land Resettlement and the Politics of Rural Development', Institute for Development Studies, Nairobi, IDS Discussion Paper No. 28.
9. Wasserman, op. cit., pp. 104, 105 and 116.
10. Nottidge and Goldsack, op. cit., p. 9.
11. Department of Settlement, *Annual Report 1962/63*, p. 7.
12. Wasserman, op. cit., pp. 106 and 111.
13. Van Arkadie, op. cit., Chapter 3, paras. 91-109.
14. Ibid., Chapter 6, para. 182.
15. Department of Settlement, op. cit.
16. Ibid., p. 2.
17. C. Gertzel, *The Politics of Independent Kenya*, London, Heinemann, 1970, p. 45.
18. Department of Settlement, op. cit., p. 3.
19. See ODA, *Aid Policy in One Country: Britain's Aid to Kenya 1964-68*, 1970.
20. Ibid., pp. 4-5.
21. Gertzel, op. cit., pp. 73, 84-85.
22. The source of this and other information in this section is interviews with British and Kenyan civil servants.
23. Statistics Division, Kenya Ministry of Finance and Economic Planning, *An Economic Appraisal of the Settlement Schemes, 1964/65-1967/68*. Farm Economic Survey Report No. 27, Nairobi, 1971.
24. M. F. Scott, J. D. MacArthur and D. M. G. Newbery, *Project Appraisal in Practice: The Little/Mirrlees Method Applied in Kenya*. Forthcoming.
25. International Labour Office, *Employment, Incomes and Equality: A Strategy for Increasing Productive Employment in Kenya*, Geneva, 1972, Chapter 10, pp. 165-72. These suggestions of the report were not well received by some agriculturalists who thought they underemphasised that land is not homogeneous and that many less fertile holdings would be non-viable if subdivided.
26. See p. 116.
27. *Development Plan 1974-1978*, Nairobi, Government Printer, p. 229.
28. Agriculture Act, No. 8, 1955, section 187.
29. New Mery Sisal Estates v. Attorney General, 1972.
30. Department of Settlement, *Annual Report 1972.*
31. Scott, MacArthur and Newbery, op. cit.
32. Department of Settlement, *Annual Report.*
33. See Chapter Two, which refers to the need for a rehabilitation programme financed by the World Bank.
34. Figures supplied by the Departments concerned.
35. Van Arkadie, op. cit., Chapter 16, para. 663.
36. Over half the employees in Kenya potentially liable were not assessed for income tax and nearly half the liability to graduated personal tax up to 1971 was evaded. The situation is worse in respect of the self-employed. ILO, op cit., Chapter 16, p. 272.
37. Figures taken or calculated from *Annual Report of the Department of Settlement*, various issues, 1962-72.
38. Van Arkadie, op. cit., Appendix G, Table V.
39. *Development Plan 1974-78*, Chapter 10, para. 116, p. 228.
40. Van Arkadie, op. cit., Chapter 9, para. 313.
41. The degree of expropriation expressed as a percentage is defined as: $(M - P)100/M$. Where M = market price and P = price actually paid. Note that the market price has no 'economic' significance; it is simply the price that the farmers' experience makes them consider 'just' and at which they will maintain their farms.
42. The latter sum presents no difficulties, being the sum paid out for the land minus the grant element of British finance.

43. Information supplied by the Department of Lands.
44. *The Nation*, 18 September 1974, and as told to one of the authors on a visit.
45. But see the Appendix to this section, pp. 137-4.
46. Van Arkadie, op. cit., Chapter 2, para. 113.
47. In 1961 all mixed farms were in European ownership. *Economic Survey 1968* (data relate to 1967), p. 55: Africans own 59 per cent of the mixed-farm areas in the ratio 14:12 large farms to settlement plots. Whites therefore still owned 41 per cent of the mixed-farm sector, and 56 per cent of the existing large mixed farms in 1967. *Development Plan 1970-74*, p. 200. Two-thirds of the mixed-farm sector had been transferred, half-and-half large farm and settlement, in mid-1968.
48. Yields per acre for white-owned farms in Trans Nzoia in 1959/60 were similar for maize to yields on African farms in the same area ten years later, despite the introduction of higher yielding varieties. Profits of white farms in the earlier year which were in the size range 800-999 acres (the average size of farm in the sample of African farms ten years later) were about 42sh an acre, double the figure for African farms ten years later, at current prices. Output per acre was similar, but white costs per acre were only 2/3 of those on the later African farms. See *Economic Survey of African-owned Large Farms in Trans Nzoia 1967/68-1970/71, Farm Economic Survey Report No. 28*, November 1972, Table 3.15. *A Report on an Economic Survey of Farming in the Trans Nzoia Area 1959/60; Farm Economic Survey Report No. 5*, April 1961, Table IV.
49. White farms were assumed to produce 50 per cent more output per acre than black farms. Proportion of output from white farms was: $O_e/O_t = 1/(1 + 2l_a/3l_e)$ where O_e = output of European mixed farms, O_t = total large mixed-farm output, l_a = percentage of mixed-farm acreage under African control and l_e = percentage of mixed-farm acreage under European control.
50. Accounting ratios were supplied by M. F. Scott, who calculated them for Scott, MacArthur and Newbery, op. cit., as:

	All years	1963	1964	1965	1966	1967	Succeeding years
Wheat	0.84						
Maize		1.23	1.69	1.33	0.84	0.58	0.87
Dairy cattle	1.30						
Milk and butter-fat	0.84						
All others	1.00						
Pyrethrum		1.41	1.32	1.15	1.07	1.08	0.00

We assumed the accounting ratio for pyrethrum to be zero after 1968 on the grounds that the Pyrethrum Board allocates quotas and after that date all quotas allocated to large farms could have been filled by small holders. The share of large farms in pyrethrum production was down to some 30 per cent by 1966 compared with two-thirds in 1963.
51. Central Bureau of Statistics: *Input-Output Table for Kenya 1967*, Nairobi, 1972, Table 1, column 3; value added is 0.80 of gross output. The ratio of output of mixed farms at accounting prices, to that at market prices, is 0.9. Using a standard conversion factor of 0.80 for the accounting price of farm inputs, and assuming that the mixed farm sector is typical of the agricultural sector as a whole, gives a ratio of value added to gross output, both at accounting prices, of 0.82.
52. M. J. Westlake, 'Tax Evasion, Tax Incidence and the Distribution of Income in Kenya', IDS, Nairobi, 1971, mimeo.

53. Price Index:

1963	1964	1965	1966	1967	1968	1969	1970	1971	1972	1973
100	101.0	102.2	105.9	107.4	108.1	109.3	111.9	119.0	123.9	136.0

Source: Abstract of Statistics 1967, Table 179, p. 157; *Abstract of Statistics 1973*, Table 247, p. 258.

54. On plausible assumptions about the pattern of farmers' reactions it is possible to draw firmly such a conclusion about the optimal expropriation policy. See Appendix to this section.
55. See Chapter Three, p. 55.
56. This we take to be one of the themes of the ILO report, op. cit.
57. ILO, op. cit., Chapter 6, pp. 87-8.
58. Leys, op. cit., p. 225. While Leys regards the Land Transfer Programme as an important instrument in smoothing the transition of the colonial economy to a nominally independent one favourable to British capitalist interests, he also brings out the political weakness of the 'radicals' in Kenya, before and after independence.

Part Two: The Mumias Sugar Company

The setting up of the Mumias Sugar Company (MSC) is the biggest ODM-aided project Kenya has undertaken since independence, excluding the Land Transfer Programme. The British aid contribution was a soft loan of £2.9m. in 1971 towards a total investment of some £7.5m. The Kenya government is now considering further cane-growing and processing developments in Western Kenya so the lessons of the project have an immediate as well as a general importance. We give a summary of the main features of the project and an account of its institution, followed by a description and evaluation of the outgrowers scheme, whereby much of the cane processed in the Mumias factory is produced on small-holder plots. There is a discussion of the lessons of the project for the question of appropriate technology, cost-benefit evaluation techniques, and the practice of aiding commercial ventures.

The Mumias sugar scheme consists of a factory processing cane, a nucleus estate of some 8,000 acres where roughly half of the factory's cane requirements are grown and the outgrowers scheme. The factory and nucleus estate employ directly over 2,500 workers. Operations began in July 1973 and in 1974 55,000 tonnes of mill white sugar were produced. Production is planned to increase to 75,000 tonnes over the next two years. The outgrowers scheme is scheduled to grow and provide all the additional cane required. There are currently some 3,500 outgrowers with about 14,000 acres under cane, in an area within an eight-mile radius of the factory. Eventually there will be 5,000 outgrowers with 20,000 acres under cane over a wider area. There are also about 1,000 people on a cane-cutters register, of whom about 600 are employed cutting outgrowers' cane at any time. Many of these workers are, however, outgrowers or their dependants doing extra work for cash wages.

Of the project's total capital cost of £7.5m., the factory itself cost £4.5m. The British government's loan extended at 2 per cent interest included £2.5m. 'for the factory' which was supplied by a British firm, Fletcher and Stewart, a Booker McConnell subsidiary. The money was used by the Kenya government to acquire equity in the Mumias Sugar Company, which was set up to own the scheme. The Kenya government holds 69 per cent of the equity. Other equity holders are: Commonwealth Development Corporation 12 per cent, Kenya Commercial Bank 9 per cent, East African Development Bank 5 per cent and Booker McConnell Ltd. 5 per cent. Bookers Agricultural and Technical Services have a management contract to operate the scheme.

Sugar in the Kenya economy

The scheme has importance for the Kenyan economy as a whole. Kenya's total production of sugar in 1973, when Mumias produced only some 20,000 tonnes, was 133,000 tonnes, or just over half of consumption requirements. Kenya has long been an importer of sugar. The setting up of two new sugar factories in Nyanza in 1967 was followed by a once-and-for-all drop in the volume of imports. However those factories have experienced teething troubles and the demand for sugar has increased more strongly than expected with rising national income. Table 16 shows how imports have risen after a fall.

Table 16: Imports of sugar

1968	*1969*	*1970*	*1971*	*1972*
		tonnes		
24147	8540	21223	71747	103816
		K£'000		
624	324	935	3768	7053

Source: Kenya Government, *Statistical Abstract 1973.*

The rising price of sugar on world markets in recent years has meant that imports have become an increasing foreign exchange burden. In 1972 sugar imports were over half by value of all food imports (K£12,836) and almost 4 per cent of total imports.

Consumption is expected to reach 285,000 tonnes by 1978 and with Mumias and the older factories at full stretch that would cut the import requirement to some 50,000 tonnes.[1] Thereafter rising demand would again increase imports, hence the plans for further sugar development.

This demand is partly the result of the Kenya government's own policy. It fixes the price which it pays to producers for sugar and adds an excise duty and a margin to allow for distribution costs via the Kenya National Trading Company. The price of sugar in Kenya has been considerably below the world market price during the upheavals on the world market over the past couple of years; it was briefly only a tenth of the world price. The difference between the import price and the consumer price is met from a sugar price stabilisation fund. Sugar is a very important consumer good in Kenya. Variations in its price, colour and texture arouse strong feelings among the Kenyan public. Because of this the government has maintained a price that does not always reflect the cost of the commodity to the economy, and is planning to meet a domestic demand predicated on that price. Sugar makes little direct contribution to the diet although it is argued that it makes more nutritious foods palatable and increases their consumption. Subsidisation is based, however, on its political importance rather than its dietary attributes.

History of the Project

The original idea for a sugar industry in Western Kenya came from the Swynnerton Plan in 1954. The modern Mumias development was the brainchild of the then Minister of Agriculture, B. R. McKenzie in 1965. The area north of Lake Victoria in the Western Province of Kenya was selected because it seemed climatically reasonable and although quite densely populated, with 222 people per square mile, it was very underdeveloped. The Abaluhya population depended on subsistence farming, and a number of state initiatives to introduce cash crops, including coffee and sisal, had all failed for a variety of reasons. Some cane was, however, being grown in the area for jaggery production.

After a preliminary study Bookers Agricultural and Technical Services was approached.[2] It declined to begin operations immediately but insisted on a pilot scheme to test the viability of commercial sugar production in the area. Eventually it was agreed to have a feasibility study run concurrently with a preliminary stage of the main project so that if the pilot project were successful there could be a rapid transition to commercial production. This pilot project was largely financed by the Kenya government with £450,000, and Bookers put up £50,000 to be repaid on presentation of the feasibility reports. The pilot project began in 1967 and a final feasibility report and social cost-benefit analysis appeared in 1970. They concluded that the project was a good one and the Kenya Cabinet gave the go-ahead at the end of that year.

There was some dispute over the financing of the project. The Kenya government wanted Bookers to put up a substantial equity stake while the company wanted simply a contract to supply the factory via their subsidiary Fletcher and Stewart and a management contract for their Technical Services Division to run it. HMG was keen to provide aid for the project which was an attractive one from the donor viewpoint; it was large and highly visible, the commercial involvement meant it was likely to be well run; and as it included a factory it had a high import content. Far from the Kenyans going cap in hand to HMG, therefore, they could afford to haggle. An attempt was made to obtain British funds for Mumias outside the agreed aid framework figure.

Some reservations were felt about Mumias within ODM because of its effect on East African economic co-operation. At that time Kenya imported its sugar requirements from Uganda, which had some advantages as a sugar-producer. At the price paid for Uganda sugar, the Mumias project did not have a very high projected rate of return (see below), and there seemed to be a case for leaving sugar production with the sister-state in the East African Community. This view did not prevail because it was clear that Kenya intended to go ahead with sugar production in any case. An attempt at leverage would have failed and would furthermore have been fiercely resented by the Kenyans. Finally there was the consideration that if Britain did not support the project some other donor would, and perhaps German management and equipment would be used. HMG succeeded in lending money to Kenya for the project within the aid framework, and the Mumias Sugar Company was formed in 1971. Bookers obtained the management contract but was obliged to take a small equity stake – about half what the Kenyans had pressed on them.

The British position in these negotiations was strengthened because the Kenyan government had been impressed with Bookers' handling of the pilot scheme. And the Chemelil factory which had been supplied from West Germany and supported by German as well as British aid funds had run into technical difficulties. As a *quid pro quo* which Bookers had to pay for the management contract at Mumias, it took over the management of Chemelil, which had been operating at a loss and running at well below capacity.

Equity in the Mumias company amounted to £3.5m. and loans of another £5.2m. were arranged, although only £3.8m. of loan finance was eventually used, as contingency funds built into the estimates were not in fact required.[3] The Kenya government had intended to on-lend the 2 per cent British aid loan to the Mumias Sugar Company at 3 per cent and put in about £1¼m. in equity. On ODM advice, however, it put in more equity – some £2.5m. This reduced the Kenya government's subsidisation of the project in the long run, as 3 per cent was much below the commercial lending rate, and it reduced the gearing and hence cash flow problems of the project in the early years. The Chemelil sugar factory, financed by German aid loans in Deutschmarks, had had a gearing ratio of 3:1, and this was one of the factors which caused it to show a loss in operation.

The Project in Prospect and Practice

Sugar production in Kenya had not been a success when Bookers began its pilot scheme at Mumias and the company approached the project with considerable care and circumspection. This, by general agreement, has resulted in a sugar complex that operates efficiently and outperforms all others in Kenya. The experience of Bookers in cane production elsewhere in the world was important. The Chemelil sugar factory, supplied from Germany, was based on designs that were insufficiently flexible for local conditions, and the factory suffered repeated breakdowns. The techniques and equipment at Mumias, drawing on experience in other tropical areas, were better adapted to its situation. The Wanga area of Western Province where the factory is situated is also technically better for sugar production than Nyanza. The rainfall is higher and more regular and the soil is more suitable, being more porous and draining more easily than the black cotton soils of Chemelil. These characteristics obviated the need for either irrigation or much drainage and reduced considerably capital costs of the nucleus as well as making for success with outgrowers.

While Western Province is in general densely populated, the Wanga area is much less so than surrounding districts. The land on which the factory and nucleus estate stand is rented by the Mumias Sugar Company from the government which had to acquire it from its owners, the area having been previously adjudicated and registered to private ownership. Much of the area for the nucleus estate was taken from lower-lying land in the Nzoia valley which requires extensive drainage and was in consequence little-used. The price which the government had to pay for the land, and the social cost of putting it under sugar, were lower than they would have been elsewhere in Western Province. There was however some difficulty when the land was being bought. The local MP urged small holders to hold out for a higher price, and the personal intervention of President Kenyatta was required at one stage to keep the project on schedule.

In carrying out their commercial feasibility study, Bookers worked with 1970 prices including a controlled sugar price of K£45.25 a tonne and controlled cane price to outgrowers of K£2.34 a tonne less transport and other charges.[4] They computed that the expected rate of return over 25 years would be 12 per cent. This incorporated conservative estimates of technical coefficients such as yields of cane per acre and tons of sugar to tons of cane. If a 5 per cent increase in production was assumed, it gave a rate of return of 13.1 per cent. The project was expected to be in deficit from 1970/71 to 1973, with a cumulative deficit of K£5.53m. Allowing for contingencies, therefore, over K£6m. was thought to be required to finance it.

These estimates were amended in various ways in calculation of the social costs and benefits. There were additional necessary costs incurred not by Mumias Sugar Company but by the government, of K£1.45m. for land acquisition, road construction, and township housing and finance of outgrowers. Bookers followed a policy of adjusting market prices as little as possible. This was reasonable as shortage of reliable data reduced adjustments to guesses anyway. Yet some prices were so clearly out of line with true social costs that some adjustments were required.

Sugar was valued at its c.i.f. import price, not the domestic consumer price. At that time Kenya imported sugar from Uganda at a price of K£40.4 a tonne. This was taken as the value of output. Since it was K£5 a tonne less than the Kenya price the benefits of the project had to be written down by some K£250,000 in an average year.

On the other hand the cost of untrained labour was marked down. The Kenya Union of Sugar Workers applied a minimum wage of 3.85s[5] a day although casual agricultural labourers in the district worked for between 1.50s and 2.00s a day. Bookers claimed that 'some research' suggested the opportunity cost of an unskilled man-year of employment was between 400s and 450s, less than a third of the wage it was paying, some 1,600s a man-year. To be on the safe side it fixed the shadow wage at 40 per cent of the market rate – some 1.70s a day or 640s a man-year. This adjustment reduced costs by K£96,000 in an average year. No adjustment was made to the wages of skilled workers which were also counted gross of income tax.

Some government-incurred costs were included, but road and housing construction were shadow-priced at 90 per cent of market cost to allow for the unskilled labour component and indirect taxes and duties. Compensation for standing crops and houses was included but not the cost of land for the nucleus estate. Nor was rent imputed for outgrowers' land being put under cane. This was on the grounds that there was no land shortage in the district, over half being uncultivated. Part of the nucleus estate area, being swampy, was particularly little-used, and the assumption was made that the purchase receipts would be used to buy unutilised land elsewhere in the area.

Finally the cash surpluses of outgrowers were included among the social benefits of the scheme. These added an annual amount, rising to K£452,000 in 1981, to the scheme's benefits.

Other benefits arising from road construction were not included, and costs and benefits were discounted over 25 years, making the conservative assumption that the project would have no terminal value after 25 years. The internal rate of return was found to be 12.6 per cent. A 5 per cent fluctuation in output gave internal rates of return of 11.2 per cent and 13.3 per cent for declines and increases respectively.

Obviously many of the estimates used in this cost-benefit analysis could be varied. As noted, a lot of carefully conservative estimates were made – of technical coefficients, of the reduction appropriate for the shadow wage rate; the extraneous benefits of road and housing construction were not counted. There is, however, one outstanding instance of an omission in the other direction. This occurred in the treatment of the outgrowers' surpluses. The social benefit was taken to be the outgrowers' cash surplus, making no allowance for the cost of their labour or that of their families. It may be that working on sugar, especially after initial planting and weeding have been carried out and the cane is big enough to look after itself, does not conflict much with growing other crops. Yet people's time usually has some value to them, and hard work has some disutility. The fact that small-holder land is so little utilised, which was used to justify its negligible shadow price, must suggest that labour might well be a scarce factor of production. If so, the labour of the small holder and his family cannot be ignored. Adequate input-output data are lacking to assess this cost rigorously. However, Bookers calculated that the return small holders could expect was between 152s and 136s an acre for a five-year cycle, taking no account of the farmer's labour. It added that a farmer making 152s an acre for a five-year cycle, if he used hired labour, would realise some 28s an acre less, i.e. the cost of hired labour would reduce his surplus by about a fifth.[6]

There seems no reason why the farmer's own labour should be less valuable than that of a casual labourer he hires. So we adjusted Bookers' own calculation by deflating outgrowers' surpluses by a fifth to allow for the value of outgrowers' labour. This significantly reduces the rate of return which could have been expected from Mumias – it then becomes some 8.5 per cent.

As a development project, as opposed to a commercial venture, therefore, Mumias *ex ante* did not appear outstanding.[7] Given Bookers' generally conservative treatment of costs and benefits, it was still adequate for the Kenya government, which, after all, hoped to get British loans at 2 per cent interest. Indeed as the carrying out of the project led to Britain extending soft loans to Kenya that might otherwise have remained undisbursed for years, given the current aid-spending problems, the grant equivalent of the British loan should be counted as a benefit of the Mumias project from the Kenya government point of view. From the British point of view, however, it might seem less clear why ODM was so keen. In fact given the conservative assumptions made, the rate of return is up to the average standard for aid projects. The point is that where there is a shortage of projects, donors spend money on what they can. And if the project includes a large factory dominating the landscape and entirely imported from the donor country, so much the better.

Whether the project was backed for sound reasons, however, now appears a somewhat cold speculation for in fact subsequent events have vindicated it absolutely. The project turned out to be profitable even before the rise in world sugar prices. Then came the collapse of Uganda as a sugar exporter after the political upheavals in that country, followed by the boom in the world sugar price already noted. Under bilateral deals sugar was imported into Kenya at about K£140 a tonne and the world free-market price soared to K£600 a tonne before subsiding to its level at the time of writing of some K£135 (£165). The Mumias project was very well run and technically its performance exceeded projections. Production in 1973 and 1974 was 163 per cent and 145 per cent respectively of the expected figure. And in 1975 it is expected to be 121 per cent of the original projection. This is owing both to better yields of cane per acre by both nucleus estate and outgrowers than expected and to the greater efficiency of the factory. The ratio of tons cane to tons sugar, for example, is commonly about 10 in a modern sugar factory, but at Mumias in 1973 it was 9.3 and in 1974 8.79. For 1975 it is now expected to be 9.2. Costs have also been lower than expected. For example, the actual cost of harvesting and transporting cane in 1973 and 1974 were 74 per cent and 96 per cent respectively of the projected figures, despite inflation and the greater output. The factory has also been economical in its use of fuel, running for most of the time on combustion of bagasse (the waste vegetable matter from the cane) and using no oil at all.

The rise in the c.i.f. import price of sugar has boosted the internal rate of return (IRR) of Mumias considerably. If output is valued at the year's average world market price in New York, deflated to 1970 prices,[8] it has been: 1973 K£1.17m.; 1974 K£11.57m., 1975 K£4.30m.[9] The project had paid for itself, therefore, at the end of 1974. However low the sugar price falls in future, the project will have been justified even if it has to be closed down. It is possible, if doubtful, that Kenya could have continued to import sugar more cheaply under trading agreements than the price being charged in the residual free market. Against that, however, is the fact that Kenya since the oil price increase has run into a severe balance of payments problem. The official exchange rate does not reflect the true scarcity value of foreign exchange. Computing a shadow foreign exchange price goes outside the scope of this study, but if, for example, it were 1.2 of the current par value, a perfectly possible situation, then the value of Mumias output to Kenya in 1974 could have been as high as K£14m. at 1970 prices.

Clearly the rate of return on the Mumias project depends on a number of factors that are wide open to different assumptions – what would sugar have cost Kenya over the past three years, what will happen to the world market price over the next 25 years, what is the true or shadow exchange rate? On any reasonable mix of assumptions, however, the Mumias IRR will be very high. For example, suppose that Kenya could have obtained sugar during 1974 and 1975 at the price ruling in June 1975 – some K£135 – and this price is on average maintained during the life of the project; Kenya remains short of foreign exchange for ten years with a ratio of shadow to actual foreign exchange price of 1.2. These assumptions would give Mumias an internal rate of return of over 75 per cent. Viewed technically and from the point of view of the Kenya balance of payments, therefore, Mumias has been an unqualified success. It has not, however, been immune from criticisms. These have concerned its impact on the development of the Wanga area, and whether the technology in use is appropriate to Western Kenya.

The local developmental effects of Mumias will largely come from the outgrowers scheme which involves twice as many heads of households as are employed in the factory or on the nucleus estate, so as a prelude to consideration of Mumias as a development project and the criticisms made of it, we give an account of the outgrowers scheme.

The Outgrowers

The 14,000 acres or so now under outgrowers' cane is made up of individual sugar holdings with an average size of 3.9 acres. This average hides some variation. Some farmers have as little as one acre and one is known to have 58 acres, despite a company policy to try to restrict the size of individual holdings. The average small-holding size in Wanga is some 10 acres, but it is considered socially undesirable for a farmer to have more than half his land under cane. The intention is to leave farmers with enough land to continue to grow their subsistence requirements. The individual holdings are grouped into blocks of at least 15 acres so that cultivation and transport can be viable. This means that a man cannot easily become a registered outgrower unless his neighbours wish to be so too, as contiguous plots have to be pooled to form a block.

The company surveys each potential farmer's plot to determine its suitability and the farmer is charged with clearing an agreed area. It is ploughed, harrowed and furrowed mechanically by the company cultivation unit. The company then provides appropriate disease-free seed cane and fertiliser, and the farmer himself is responsible for his own planting, fertilising and weeding. The company does, however, employ casual labourers and if a farmer cannot cope with his own weeding a gang can be sent along. Only about 10 per cent of outgrower weeding is handled in this way; most farmers make their own arrangements. Harvesting is undertaken by the company. The 1,000 people on the cane-cutter register work around the outgrowing areas. Cutting and stacking is done by hand and the cutters are paid by the task – some 5s a tonne in 1974. The idea is that people should turn up from the area where cutting is taking place, with outgrowers taking precedence, and about 600 cutters will be working at any time. There is considerable turnover of workers and no excess supply, so that someone could get work every day if he turned up. Once stacked the cane is loaded and transported mechanically. All the outgrowers' operations are checked by the company. There are three superintendents and a fourth responsible purely for harvesting. These posts have been Africanised. Under the superintendents there are 17 supervisors who have certificates in agriculture, and below them some 48 headmen who have basic literacy and have been given on-the-job training. So the company operates a lively extension service with regular inspection of outgrowers' plots providing advice and guidance.

All these goods and services are provided on credit to the farmer and the cost of plot development, planting material, fertiliser, weeding if necessary, harvesting, transport and maintenance of access roads is eventually docked from the money he gets for his cane. The company, at the Kenya government's request, charges the farmers interest of 8 per cent per crop for these services. At present each farmer has a contract with the company which specifies the conditions on which he becomes an outgrower and the costs of services. The contract obliges the Mumias Sugar Company to buy all the cane grown according to contract and to provide the specified services. The farmer is obliged to follow approved cultivation practices, to plant at the time specified by the company, to grow approved varieties of cane, to maintain standards of husbandry, and to sell his cane to the company.

At the end of 1974 the price of cane was 62s a tonne, transport and harvesting costs were 22s a ton. After other costs had been deducted the net payment was in the range of 15s to 22s a tonne. A yield of 55 tonnes per acre, which was average for the plant crop,[10] would give an income of over 950s an acre for the 22 months of the crop. The yield achieved varied from 28 to 90 tonnes an acre and the income varied accordingly – a few outgrowers were receiving over 2,000s net an acre a crop.

Both MSC and the Kenya government are anxious to regularise the outgrowers' position and provide a corporate body that could negotiate terms with the company and deal with it on behalf of the farmers. The outgrowers themselves were hostile to a co-operative and the intention has been for a long time to form an outgrowers' company, which would take over *inter alia* the financing of services for outgrowers from the Mumias Sugar Company. At the time of writing, however, the problems of setting up this organisation had not been solved, although CDC had agreed to provide finance.

Mumias and Rural Development

The picture that emerges from the above account is of a group of small holders whose activities are very closely regulated. In effect they rent a bit of their land and some of their labour time to the company for an assured payment. As a company employee put it: 'They have an assured market, no risk and no decisions to take. We take all the decisions.' Most of the farmers in Wanga regard this as an enviable position to be in, and the competition to be outgrowers is strong. In the eight-mile radius from the factory, only one small holder in five is an outgrower and most of the others would like to be. In one area the company was proposing to plough about 150 acres of land for sugar. So many farmers had come into the field office offering plots averaging four of five acres, however, that there were over 400 acres on offer and registered as available. Some farmers clear their land in advance of agreement, hoping to induce the company to plough.

It is too early yet to assess the developmental impact on the neighbourhood because production only started in 1973, and no farmer has yet received payment for more than one crop. In principle the scheme should boost agricultural output in the area generally. Financial constraints are being removed; after 22 months farmers are receiving lump sum payments, often of more money than they have seen in their lives. The agricultural extension service provided by Bookers for cane has also influenced agricultural techniques generally. In particular, farmers are aware now of the gains from planting in rows and using fertiliser. In fact the sugar company finds that some small holders have been embezzling fertiliser issues – half-dosing the cane and putting the rest on their maize crop. A black market in fertiliser has appeared following its rise in price, with people coming from other neighbourhoods to try to buy the small holders' fertiliser issues. The wage employment in the area should also provide something of a local market for food crops.

There are a few signs, however, that development might not proceed so smoothly. Most of the first cash from sugar was certainly not invested in agricultural inputs. Tony Barclay, an American sociologist resident in the area, has found that, on a sample of farms he studied, off-farm investment was preferred.[11] Sugar revenues were spent on children's education or acquiring a small shop as well as on durable consumption goods like wives[12] and tin roofs. There seem to be two reasons, one general to the Wanga district and one that may be peculiar to the sub-district he studied. The general reason is a local labour shortage in small-scale farming. The Abaluhya social structure is not conducive to certain kinds of co-operative effort. People regard it as demeaning to work for an outgrower if he is doing well financially but does not enjoy a higher traditional status than his fellows. People would rather work for the company, and if they are employed on a neighbour's plot are not above a little sabotage, for example putting dirt over weeds instead of uprooting them. Faced with a labour constraint therefore, farmers concentrate their labour (or that of their wives) on sugar and perhaps spend less time on the subsistence crops they previously grew. The less general reason is that the quality of soil is very low in that part of Wanga where Barclay was resident. Careful husbandry yields only 10 bags an acre of maize, and 2 bags an acre is not uncommon. Farmers do not regard it as a worthwhile investment to plough their earnings back into such soil. This observation is confirmed by Mumias Sugar Company employees. They notice that the farmers work much harder at their husbandry where the prospects of high yields are better.

Apart from the issue of whether the benefits from sugar will help to generate much local development (and we repeat that judgement is premature), there is the vexed question of the distribution of the benefits. After disastrous experiences with government-sponsored cash crops like sisal (the market collapsed), cotton (the area was too wet and pests proliferated), and coffee,[13] farmers were sceptical about sugar. The first to become outgrowers were therefore those who agreed to try it, either the most enterprising or the møst desperate. Now things have changed; everyone wants to be an outgrower and the company can afford to pick and choose, usually on the basis of soil suitability and ease of access. Farmers whose plots happen to enjoy these advantages can become outgrowers and receive a relatively large cash income without the exercise of any enterprise at all.

This has led to enormous pressures on the employees of MSC, especially the African staff. Kinship ties are called on, bribes are offered. Relatively well-to-do people from other areas, sometimes civil servants, attempt to acquire land in the district and then put pressure on to get the land ploughed. Even though MSC employees act with considerable probity it is difficult to get this widely believed in the district.[14] Refusal to plough someone's ground because, for example, it is too stony, is usually rationalised by the disappointed farmer as owing to nepotism, tribalism and bribery. Furthermore a process of cumulative causation may be under way. When outgrowers receive their money, although they have not used it much on their own plots so far, one of the assets they try to acquire is more land. This is because of the emotional significance of land but also because they hope to get the new plot ploughed too. The company has no hard-and-fast upper limit although it is not supposed to take more land off a single person than he can cultivate adequately. But of course it is very difficult to establish when it is dealing with a front man, either for an absentee owner or for someone who is already an outgrower (or in extreme cases both). Some indication of these trends is given by the rising price of land in the Wanga area. Variations in land prices are considerable, but broadly an acre of land changed hands in 1969 for 400-500s. In 1973 it cost 600-700s. Now over 1000s an acre is not unusual.

It is possible for people in Britain to be over-sensitive about inequality in a poor country. Almpst by definition, development entails making someone better off than he was before and therefore better off than some other people still in the boat he was in. You have to start somewhere. However, there are obvious disadvantages to the situation in Mumias just outlined. People may be getting better off not because of any quality that means they are more likely to make productive use of their opportunity than their neighbours, but because of the accident that their plot has convenient characteristics for the Mumias Sugar Company. Or worse, because they can wield some other sort of influence. There is little recourse for the enterprising man without these advantages, although a rising demand for food crops owing to higher cash incomes should help him somewhat. Because the Mumias factory turned out to have more capacity than expected some non-contract cane has been bought from freelance growers. About 13,000 tons has been bought in this way – about 4 per cent of the factory's requirements. However, this is being phased out. From this year on, the company has said it will buy no more cane from non-contract farmers, because planning of outgrowers' output now takes the factory capacity fully into account.

We are not idolators of the market mechanism who believe that it is bound to allocate resources to best advantage. In this situation, however, residual market purchases of cane would have one obvious advantage. They would give everyone some sort of chance to make a living from sugar even if non-contract growers were at a disadvantage. From that point of view the ending of non-contract cane purchases is a pity.

It is clear that no blame at all attaches to Bookers for these difficulties. Having sugar produced by outgrowers was itself a considerable experiment.

If the factory was not to suffer cane shortages leading to the kind of low capacity working that has blighted other plants in Kenya, it made perfect sense from a management point of view to take what steps were necessary to see the cane supply was smooth and ample. Indeed that was the first priority. However, we believe that the patterns coming to light should be taken into account in future sugar developments. A higher priority should be given at an earlier stage to setting up an outgrowers' organisation. This could perhaps make supporting services available more widely if less intensively than at present, leaving something to farmers' initiative. To compensate perhaps for the greater uncertainty about production a measure of overplanting could be encouraged. This might entail some subsidisation or at least easy financing for the outgrowers' company, especially in the early years. This would be an appropriate place for government support, perhaps with foreign aid. The organisational difficulties are formidable. Any arrangements must include provision for control of cane varieties and disease prevention. And it would be wrong to penalise farmers by refusing to buy their output in the event of overproduction. Perhaps the cane price should be set in advance each season on the basis of experience of supply response. This would require relaxation by the Kenya government of its strict price control of cane.

At any rate the present arrangements could prevent sugar boosting development as much as it might by concentrating land and money in the hands of a proportion of the local population who are not particularly deserving, and also in the hands of absentee landholders. It has led, and will lead, to an exacerbation of social pressures and enmities in an area already noted for its somewhat fractious politics and it places a heavy burden on company employees in charge of outgrowing who have to tread through this political minefield. However, any expansion of MSC should to some extent automatically mitigate these difficulties by increasing the proportion of local farmers who can participate in sugar production. And by increasing the amount of land under cane in the area it should raise food prices to the advantage of those still growing food crops.

The Mumias Sugar Company and Bookers are of course aware that their operations are likely to have profound effects on the district and they have offered between them to pay three-quarters of the cost of a sociological study of the area but at the time of writing finance for the remainder had not been forthcoming. That is unfortunate. Such a study would be an appropriate use of aid funds. A study of the situation in the neighbourhood before the effects of Mumias really appear is particularly urgent as it will provide the base line for later assessment of those effects. The developments in the Mumias area will have implications much beyond the case of sugar. Many of the supposed obstacles to rural development – shortages of liquidity for investment, of knowledge of correct agricultural techniques, of access roads, and of a market for cash crops – are all being removed for many farmers. The money and the roads and the knowledge, although arising from sugar, are there to be applied for other crops. What happens in the next few years must be instructive about rural development, probably more so than developments in the Special Rural Development Areas which have attracted the attention of aid donors in Kenya. It is important therefore that events in the Mumias area should be monitored.

Mumias and 'Appropriate Technology'

The traditional alternatives to sugar in Kenya were honey and jaggery, a dark substance which is basically sugar-cane juice, partially dehydrated. There are many small jaggery factories in Kenya but they are not encouraged by the government because jaggery is frequently used in making *changa'a*, an illegal spirit. As a simple sweetener jaggery is not popular, and a small survey has shown it is used for this purpose by only 2 per cent of Kenyans, while 98 per cent use sugar.[15] Although it contains trace elements removed from refined sugar, jaggery is said to have strong laxative properties so it does not today constitute much of an alternative to sugar.

It has been argued, however,[16] that palatable sugar can be produced in small factories on the scale of existing jaggery factories and with only limited refinements to jaggery techniques. The sugar, which is off-white in colour and more or less crystalline, is produced by open-pan sulphitation techniques and requires additional power and settling tanks to a jaggery mill. It is widely used in India where nearly 1,000 small plants have been set up in recent years. The Kenya government has asked IBRD to review the sugar industry in Kenya, and part of this review – an assessment of the feasibility of cottage sugar plants making *khandsari*[17] sugar – has been hived off UNIDO and FAO who are investigating the possibility of a trial conversion of a jaggery factory.

The advantages claimed for cottage sugar plants are that they are more labour-intensive and require less capital per unit of output, and are hence more suitable for a poor country like Kenya, abundant in underemployed labour; that they are small-scale so that, as well as wages accounting for a higher proportion of costs, profits will be less concentrated and more equal income distribution will result; that by scattering sugar production instead of concentrating it in one area they will even up development in rural areas and reduce cane and sugar transportation and distribution costs. We are not competent to assess fully all these claims, but the evidence suggests there is a *prima facie* case.

Using figures supplied by a Ghanaian consultancy firm proposing the installation of cottage sugar plants in that country,[18] it appears that a *khandsari* sugar plant in Kenya would cost about K£90,000 to set up with a cane-crushing capacity of 60 tonnes a day (Mumias crushes some 2,000 tonnes daily). The output of the factory in a ten-month season, working two shifts (16 hours) a day, would be just under 1,500 tonnes of sugar (Mumias: 50,000 tonnes from three shifts). The factory would employ about 143 people (of whom 23 would be supervisory), skilled or semi-skilled. The figures are based on Indian experience. Taking the cost of the Mumias factory complex proper as K£5m., it appears that the capital investment required for a tonne of output per year there is K£100 and for the *khandsari* plant K£60. These figures assume depreciation is the same on both plants. Taking the employment in the Mumias factory complex at 2,500 (an overestimate as some of these people are employed on the nucleus estate), the capital required per job created is: Mumias K£2,000; *khandsari* plant K£630. In other words for the capital investment represented by Mumias it seems you could have more than 50 *khandsari* factories which between them would produce over half as much sugar again as Mumias and employ nearly three times as many people. This capital-saving excludes the saving to the Kenya government of not providing housing for large clusters of workers.

In addition, the *khandsari* plants are not more prodigal in their use of skilled workers, shortage of whom is in fact a much greater constraint on output in Kenya than capital. The same output as Mumias (requiring say 33 *khandsari* plants) would require 759 skilled or semi-skilled workers. Mumias employs 175 management personnel, 275 skilled and 450 semi-skilled people – 900 altogether.

In some other ways the *khandsari* plants would be less efficient. The number of tonnes of cane used to tonnes of sugar produced would be in the region 13-14, compared with Mumias' 8-9. For the same output of sugar, therefore, assuming similar cane-yields per acre (and these are likely to fall without the close supervision arranged at Mumias), Kenya would need to put some 50 per cent more land under cane – perhaps an additional 10,000 acres, for the production of another Mumias. This is a considerable drawback in parts of Western Kenya where population densities are high on good arable land and population growth is rapid, so that land for food production could become scarce in the near future. The *khandsari* plants would also be less economical in their use of fuel than Mumias, as they would not operate 24 hours a day and would use fuel to restart production even if running afterwards on combustion of bagasse.

There are other considerations: it would be more costly to collect and levy an excise duty on the produce of a large number of smaller factories compared to doing it with a handful of large ones. The taxing difficulty, plus the fact that Mumias is largely government-owned, might take some of the substance out of the distributional argument for small-scale factories, though clearly not all. The present technology does have favourable implications for public finance, as well as unfavourable ones for concentration of economic power.

In addition the types of skills required in the two sorts of factory are not entirely similar. Some of the workers in a *khandsari* sugar plant, in particular sugar boilers, would require 'craft' skills requiring 'touch' and not easily systemised. These skills are less generally usable than those of the mechanic and accountant, and in fact are specific to sugar production, while many of those acquired at Mumias are common to much modern industry. Whereas training at both sorts of factory should yield some external benefits to the economy as a whole by adding to 'human capital' these would be less therefore in the case of *khandsari* plants.[19]

The sugar produced by *khandsari* plants would be less white than that from a larger factory and while marginally more nutritious would probably meet with consumer resistance. To maintain consumer welfare it would have to retail at a lower price. In India the market price has been 10-25 per cent below white milled sugar.

However, by introducing more flexibility into production, as running at below full capacity would be less expensive in the case of the less capital-intensive techniques, *khandsari* plants would obviate the need for such close regulation of outgrowers, and could be supplied perhaps by local farmers individually or in co-operatives. So there may be a case for establishing a number of cottage sugar plants near large-scale factories to cope with variations in cane supply that might result from a desirable reduction in the control of outgrowers' activities.

In conclusion, there are clearly a large number of factors affecting the relative social profitability of large-scale and *khandsari*-type sugar production and they do not by any means all point in the same direction. The greatest question mark over *khandsari*-type production is simply that if it is so simple and profitable, why has it not been widely undertaken or indeed undertaken at all by private enterprise? As we have seen, existing large-scale sugar plants do not supply all of domestic demand.[20] There should have been room for small-scale enterprise, especially given the presence in earlier years of so many Asian entrepreneurs themselves coming from a *khandsari* area. The Kenya government and aid donors should, however, be aware that much more large-scale sugar development is likely to pre-empt the market and close the gate to what might be a profitable avenue of development, given recent advances in small-scale techniques. Now that the sugar price is lower, therefore, it is important that alternative techniques should be assessed in advance of further investment.

If this is not done, aid donors will almost certainly bear some of the responsibility. Offers of cheap capital for sugar development make it harder for the Kenya government to assess objectively costs and benefits of the different methods. The motives of donors are obvious; large-scale technology is the type that their countries' firms can supply – Bookers, for example, finding that the methods they knew were profitable, did not consider many other techniques. Aid in such circumstances is simply an export credit on very soft terms. There is nothing wrong with that unless it hinders development by seeming to undercut more genuinely profitable alternatives. In the case of sugar, there is just a possibility that it might, and donors genuinely interested in development rather than exports and monuments will investigate the possibility before acting. Unfortunately we suspect that most donors will submit to competition among themselves and rural Kenya may be one of the losers.

Other Considerations on Mumias as an Aid Project

Cost-benefit analysis of sugar projects in Kenya throws up several well-known problems associated with this sort of exercise. The first is that of uncertainty. If the output is to be valued at world prices on the grounds that these best represent the value of output to the economy, as the prices that would have to be paid in the absence of the investment, one is faced with the difficulty of guessing the average price that will rule over perhaps 25 years in a commodity market that is notoriously unstable. Alternatively one would have to guess the price at which Kenya could obtain sugar under bilateral deals. Bookers surmounted this problem in the case of Mumias by taking a highly conservative view of the value of output which made the project look unexciting in prospect. Sugar prices have varied over the life of Mumias so far to an extent that renders insignificant possible variations in assumptions about other variables such as technical coefficients. Future assessments will have to take more explicit account of possible world market trends.

A more difficult question concerns whether the output should be valued at world prices at all. If there were a boom in sugar prices which were passed on to the Kenyan consumer, the consumption of sugar would probably fall. In other words the world price of sugar during a boom almost certainly exceeds the marginal utility of sugar in domestic Kenyan consumption. Some would say that does not matter because (a) the government must value sugar at the world price to import it in such a situation and subsidise its consumption, or (b) if it does not, and behaves 'rationally', it would not subsidise consumption but would export the surplus sugar, so realising the world price anyway.

However, if the Kenya government were not to stop subsidising sugar or to export it, we would be in the familiar dilemma of wondering whether to recommend 'efficient' production in the sense of that which would yield best results if the government acted optimally, or whether to accept government policies as a constraint and go for a 'third best' policy.[21] To value sugar at the world price instead of at its marginal utility in domestic consumption in this situation is to underwrite the Kenya government's pricing policy; to say that as, for example, an aid donor, one considers that the political benefits to the Kenya government of maintaining a low sugar price are a worth-while return for one's tax-payers' money. That is a perfectly possible judgement but it ought to be recognised for what it is. It might be a way out to argue that the Kenya government would persist in this policy anyway, so that if a sugar project has a positive return one is reducing the cost to the economy of the government's policy. This gain has to balance against the effect of the project in helping the government to maintain a wasteful policy. To call it such does not conflict with the notion of consumer sovereignty which entails letting consumers buy as much as they like of something at a price that covers the opportunity cost of production. Consumer sovereignty does not entail subsidisation. Our recommendation to a donor would be to look askance at any sugar project in Kenya whose social cost-benefit analysis did not have a positive estimated net present value, valuing output at the price the Kenya government proposes to pay for it. If such a rule encourages the government to let the price reflect possible world scarcity, so much the better. At present the Kenyan domestic price is much closer to the world price.

Mumias took place with practically no private commercial investment at all. Commercial companies were involved in putting up equity, but Bookers did so to obtain the management contract and the *quid pro quo* of Kenya Commercial Bank investment was that it obtained the company's banking business. The reason for commercial reticence was the controlled price regime that operates in Kenya with respect to sugar. The government lays down both the price paid for cane and the price paid to the factory for sugar. It can vitally affect profitability, therefore, at the stroke of a pen. Given that situation, aid funds played a role in getting a worth-while project under way. Now that Mumias has shown its profitability, however, paying a dividend in its first year of operation, there seems a less clear-cut case for aid money for further similar projects. It could be argued that certainly no more should be given than is necessary to launch a worth-while project; there seems little point in displacing commercial money. The only effect of that would be to facilitate a transfer of assets – from the potential investor to the Kenya government. Again that has a political point but it is reasonable for ODM to ask whether it is a political objective worthy of British tax-payers' money.

Perhaps this is the sort of quasi-commercial enterprise for which in some ways CDC is better fitted for a role than ODM. If a project is likely to be profitable and the profits will largely accrue to equity-holders rather than to the economy in a general way, to allow them to go to a recipient government is to admit it can probably put the money to better developmental use than HMG. That may well be so, but then why project-tie aid and evaluate projects at all? For consistency, therefore, this sort of quasi-commercial investment might be left to CDC which can put in equity and re-cycle dividends in the form of fresh aid to Kenya or some other country, whereas ODM cannot vary loan terms for particular projects. There seems to be a conflict of evidence on the question of whether CDC could have handled Mumias alone. But it seems unlikely in fact that it could have found sufficient funds quickly enough.

In the case of attractive projects like sugar factories such considerations tend to get swamped. Donors go ahead, as ODM did with Mumias, on the grounds that if they don't someone else will. The money spent does not finance a sugar factory at all therefore – that would have happened anyway – but the expenditures into which Kenyan, or more particularly, other donor funds were displaced.[22] This is satisfactory to the sugar-factory donor on export grounds if the other expenditures are less import-intensive.

Notes

1. Kenya Government, *Development Plan 1974-78*, p. 240.
2. An account of the Mumias project is given by J. A. Haynes, Director of Booker McConnell Ltd., in *Industry, Employment and the Developing World*, Overseas Development Institute, 1975.
3. CDC was asked to provide some £750,000 of loan. The request was later withdrawn but has since been reinstated, following the proposal to develop Mumias's capacity to 75,000 tons.
4. The controlled prices were changed when the factory began operation. At the end of 1974 they were K£61.5 a tonne of sugar and K£3.09 a tonne of cane. During 1975 they were increased again, to K£92 a tonne ex factory (after excise duty) and K£4.60 a tonne of cane.
5. 20s = K£1 = (approx.) £1.25 Sterling, at that time.
6. An interesting rationale for the Bookers' pricing is that traditionally the growing of subsistence crops was regarded as the work of women. There was no such stigma attached to growing the cash crop of cane, which therefore mobilised previously unused man-hours. Nevertheless, we doubt if this justifies a zero shadow price.
7. This ignores possible external benefits arising from improvements to the small holders' general agricultural practices. These were not considered in the report.
8. Prices for 1973 and 1974 from *FAO Commodity Review 1973-74*, pp. 111, 114; for 1975, newspaper reports. Deflated to 1970 prices: implicit price deflator index for Kenya, *UN Statistical and Economic Information Bulletin for Africa No. 6*, p. 40.
9. Registered output.
10. Sugar is a perennial crop which can be harvested after a variable growing period depending on conditions. The plant crop is the first harvest taken at Mumias about 22 months after planting. Subsequent crops – ratoons – are taken at 18-month intervals from the same planting. Yields of sugar per acre fall with each subsequent ratoon until eventually, after perhaps 5 years, it becomes worthwhile to replant.
11. A. H. Barclay, 'Aspects of Social and Economic Change relating to the Mumias Sugar Project', IDS, Nairobi, mimeo., 1974.
12. Wives could be regarded as an agricultural investment good given the labour shortage. As they are in inelastic supply, however, their acquisition for bride money is an asset transfer and the final destination of the money is unclear. As marriages are frequently accompanied by parties, some people have suggested that East African Breweries are the eventual beneficiaries.
13. This failure was, of course, purely local. Elsewhere in Kenya coffee has been the miracle crop to small holders that sugar is in Mumias.
14. These pressures were foreseen and were one reason why MSC wanted an outgrowers company, to take over the selection of outgrowers, subject to technical considerations specified by MSC.

15. Malcolm Harper, 'Sugar and Maize Meal – Cases in Inappropriate Technology', IDS, Nairobi, Working Paper No. 170, p. 3.
16. Ibid., p. 12; C. G. Baron, *Sugar Processing Techniques in India*, Geneva, ILO; *Industry, Employment and the Developing World*, op. cit.
17. *Khandsari* was the name of the product of traditional cottage plants; it was powdery in texture. We also use it for the more crystalline product of contemporary small-scale plants.
18. Results vary with location and these figures are approximate. Baron, op. cit., gives slightly different ones.
19. See Deepak Lal, *Appraising Foreign Investment in Developing Countries*, London, Heinemann, 1975, pp. 61-6.
20. This fact seems to be a complete answer to those who argue that Mumias was a poor investment on grounds of its inappropriate technology. Speed in execution was important, as it happened, and this was achieved by using more tried techniques.
21. This problem is lucidly discussed in I. M. D. Little and J. A. Mirrlees, *Project Appraisal and Planning for Developing Countries*, London, Heinemann, 1974, Chapter XIX. Also see A. K. Sen, 'Control Areas and Accounting Prices: An Approach to Economic Evaluation', *Economic Journal*, Vol. 82, March 1972.
22. An instance of the aid fungibility problem discussed in Chapter Six.

Part Three: The Special Rural Development Programme

Promoting rural development is seen by many concerned people as the greatest task facing the Kenya government. Virtually all the important aid donors have come around to this view, and all of them pay lip service at least to the need to direct aid to help in that area. The objective reasons are clear enough and were set out both in the ILO report and in successive World Bank reports on the Kenyan economy. The overwhelming majority of Kenyans, nearly 90 per cent, live in rural areas and they are very poor; the higher incomes earned by some in urban areas have led to migration into towns but the rate of growth of productive employment in urban areas has failed to keep pace. The ILO report[1] estimated that 20 per cent of the men in Nairobi and an even higher proportion of the women were without work or in very low-paid casual occupations. This situation is breeding slums, crime and social unrest. Given an overall population growth rate of over 3 per cent and the much faster increase of urban populations, it is difficult to see how industrial employment can ever hope to keep pace. The policy of encouraging import-substituting manufacturing industries has increased manufacturing output but, starting from a low base, employment has grown more slowly, owing to improvements in labour productivity.[2]

Rural development is regarded as essential, therefore, because it will affect areas where the mass of poor people live; it will reduce the imbalance of urban-rural incomes, directly alleviating some social problems, and by concentrating economic growth on agricultural and other processes that are labour-intensive it should expand employment along with output. That in turn will have a beneficial effect on income distribution. An investment in agriculture and related agro-industry might be less import- and capital-intensive than that in concentrated urban industry, so faster growth might be consistent with balance of payments equilibrium. Rural development is seen therefore as a key to long-run economic growth as well as to greater equity by the reduction of wealth inequalities within as well as between areas. The Kenya government in its Development Plan for 1974-78 stresses the primacy of rural development: 'The 1970-1974 Development Plan stated that the key strategy for this Plan is to direct an increasing share of the total resources available to the nation towards rural areas. That strategy will be continued and indeed reinforced during this Plan.'[3]

This is the situation that has lent importance to the Special Rural Development Programme (SRDP) which has been supported by five bilateral donor agencies including Britain as well as the FAO. Quantitatively, it is a relatively minor British aid project – some £250,000 in capital aid and a couple of technical assistance appointments over a number of years. Yet in view of ODM's commitment to rural development the lessons of SRDP have an obvious importance.

The idea for SRDP was born at a conference at Kericho in 1966 on education, employment and rural development.[4] Donor representatives at the conference expressed interest in considering Kenyan government proposals[5] in the field of rural development and this may have been the reason for continued activity on the subject within the then Ministry of Planning.[6] It was decided to select a number of areas for pilot experiments in rural development, and the Institute for Development Studies (IDS) at the University of Nairobi was called in to help formulate a programme. The major proposals of its report[7] were the following:

(i) The carrying out of a base-line survey of existing rural conditions;
(ii) that pilot projects must be designed for replicability;
(iii) that a central co-ordinating national body be set up;
(iv) that donors be utilised but made to understand that this was an extraordinary programme demanding flexibility on their part;
(v) that the programme be handled through the existing machinery of government, and that one of the prime goals of the entire exercise be to enhance Kenyan capabilities in every aspect of rural development planning and implementation.

ODM offered a central co-ordinator who arrived in Kenya in March 1968. A joint government-IDS working party was formed and selected fourteen areas of the country which were then surveyed for information on actual conditions and existing government programmes. At the beginning of 1969 a National Rural Development Committee was formed to co-ordinate the programme and negotiate external assistance for it. Its members were the Permanent Secretaries of the most important ministries concerned with the programme. Six areas were chosen for the first phase of the programme[8] and the preparation of detailed costed plans for these areas, with outline five-year programmes and the annual budget for the first year's operations, took up to the middle of 1970.

The aims of the programme were established as: 'The primary objective is to increase rural incomes and employment opportunities. The secondary objective is to establish procedures and techniques for accelerated and self generating rural development which can be repeated in other similar areas and, in particular, to improve the developmental capacity of Kenya Government officials in this field.'[9]

During 1970, discussions also went on with donors over finance. The Kenyan idea was simply to have a rural development fund to which donors would contribute. This, however, violated the entrenched donor prejudice for the results of their aid to be identifiable. Some donors were also loath to break rules against supporting local and recurrent costs. This situation led eventually to the identification of each SRDP area with a single donor who reimbursed the Kenyans for SRDP expenditure in 'his' district. Even that took some time to accomplish and the programme was held up for six months while the Treasury refused to allocate funds to SRDP in the 1970/71 budget despite its inclusion in the 1970-74 Development Plan. The reasons for this reluctance are unclear but it has been suggested that it was symptomatic of a general lack of enthusiasm for SRDP on the part of some officials.[10]

As it was to prove so critical, the coolness of influential people in the Kenya government towards SRDP stands analysis. It was perhaps to the disadvantage of SRDP that its National Rural Development Co-ordinating Committee was established in the Ministry of Planning.[11] Some officials in operational ministries feared that their autonomy was endangered by the planners whom they characterised as paper-pushers. This inter-ministry jealousy was aggravated when the University of Nairobi became involved in the planning of SRDP. There has at various times been tension between senior civil servants and senior academics in Kenya. The former do not always regard the criticisms of the latter as being offered in a constructive spirit. The conjunction of the Ministry of Planning and the University was enough to alienate some senior bureaucrats in operational ministries and the alienation was increased when an energetic expatriate took over SRDP co-ordination at the national level. The operational ministries also regarded SRDP projects as an additional administrative burden on top of their routine sectoral programmes, which were, of course, nearer to their collective hearts. The Treasury took a sceptical view because as far as it could see SRDP expenditures were recurrent in nature, and could be classified as consumption rather than investment. It was not entirely happy about authorising them even if they were covered by promises of aid, partly perhaps because of a reluctance to finance consumption out of repayable loans.

The programme received a fillip when the Norwegians announced in August 1970 that they would fund all expenditure in the Mbere division. Norwegian aid takes the form of grants. Other donors gradually followed suit.[12] The Norwegian decision had an important effect in strengthening Kenya-based representatives of donor agencies in appeals to their national headquarters to fund local and recurrent costs on an unprecedented scale.

ODM was the last donor agency to provide capital funds for SRDP but was relatively innocent of attempts to change its nature. Of the 1970 UK loan commitment, some £250,000 had been earmarked for rural development and when asked if this could be put into a common SRDP pool ODM said it would not rule that out if other donors agreed. After other donors had begun to support individual areas it was the Kenyans who in February 1971 proposed to spend the £250,000 on SRDP and suggested that the UK government might wish to have this contribution identified with a particular project area. After considering Tetu, ODM finally decided to support the Kwale area on the disinterested developmental grounds that it was much the more backward of the two. The other areas were already associated with foreign donors.

Donor preferences had other effects, however, beyond changing and complicating financial procedures. Once donors had 'their' areas many began to want to put in their own personnel as full-time technical assistance. This had obvious dangers, because the whole point of the programme was to try out management procedures as well as physical projects relying as far as possible on Kenyan resources and the Kenyan administration so that any successes in promoting development could be replicated elsewhere in the country. The Kenyans were unable to resist[13] the pressure for local-level technical assistance involvement. The pro-SRDP group in the Kenya government, located in the Ministry of Planning, was not all-powerful, and donor interest and leverage had been essential to it in getting things moving at all. ODM, starting with its project a year later than other donors, was aware that both the USAID approach in Vihiga and that of the Swedes and FAO in Migori, of providing a number of advisers and carrying out extensive planning, had come in for criticism. So it opted for providing just one 'project adviser' who would work in Kwale attached to the Ministry of Finance. It seems, however, that this was seen as a point of diplomacy rather than a point of substance. Other donors were regarded as having been tactless rather than wrong-headed. The British project adviser would in fact be a project director, but he would be unobtrusive and lead from behind. He could be supplemented by other experts or consultants on a short-term basis. Perhaps attitudes can be summarised as follows. The pro-SRDP group in the Kenya government needed donor backing to make any headway against high-level opponents of SRDP, particularly in the Treasury and Ministry of Agriculture; this made it vulnerable to donor pressures. Many Kenyan administrators regarded SRDP as an 'expatriate show' which they would not allow to interfere with their own departmental policies; its usefulness to them was as a device for getting aid donors to commit untied funds. Rural development experts in donor agencies wanted an involvement in SRDP because of the lessons it might yield them, as well as the Kenyans, about rural development, and no doubt they found it hard to resist the expert's suspicion that he is indispensable. Donor administrators had already had the bracing experience of committing untied funds to no clearly defined project and were keen to insert technical assistance as a means of regaining some control over the expenditure that was being incurred in their name. Although more aware of Kenyan sensitivities than other donor agencies, ODM by and large shared these attitudes.[14]

The need for technical assistance in rural development, what form it should take and what its role should be, we regard as very open questions. A lot depends on the details of the situation and the personalities involved. The constellation of attitudes described above, however, indicates that cases were unlikely to be treated on their merits. There was a systematic donor bias in favour of employing expatriate technical assistance on a full-time basis.

The programme began on the basis of plans that had been largely drawn up for each area at the centre. The plan for Kwale was almost entirely an exercise in planning from Nairobi by the Ministry of Finance and Planning. IDS monitored progress in SRDP areas during the first year of the programme's life and in 1973 published an overall evaluation of SRDP.[15] At that time very little had happened at Kwale. The programme there had started later as it was not clear which donor, if any, would provide support for the area during most of the Kenyan financial year 1971/72.

The IDS evaluation was rather critical of SRDP in general. It re-emphasised the experimental nature of the exercise and the requirement that experiments should be aimed at achieving replicative processes. In fact, it argued, a lot of the planning had been concerned with putting in more resources to obtain rapid results with the probable outcome that benefits would end with the particular projects, and long-standing bottlenecks to development had not been overcome.[16] Apart from excessive haste another factor making for failure was lack of success in involving local people and tapping local abilities and knowledge. District Development Committees, for example, are largely instruments of the government. The evaluation also noted the lack of authority which SRDP enjoyed at the centre and recommended a top Kenyan of at least Deputy Secretary level to be in charge of it.

External planning without local involvement led to one or two well-publicised failures, notably an attempt to get farmers in Mbere to grow cotton because it appeared technically suitable. It transpired, however, taking risks into account, that cotton was not an economic crop in the area and the farmers' resistance was entirely rational. A credit programme in Vihiga to get farmers to concentrate on hybrid maize production was also unpopular with local farmers for substantial reasons.[17]

That is not to say that SRDP had been a total failure. A number at least of the 123 sub-programmes under way in the six areas represented interesting experiments in the areas of agricultural extension and training, credit provision, and supply of other services. Supporters of SRDP claim that perhaps its greatest achievement then and later was in 'beginning to get to grips with the fundamental organisational bottlenecks which so often hinder effective rural development. The decision taken at the outset to work through existing government machinery had important beneficial results.'[18] Experience led to the development of prototype management systems. The most significant, Programming Implementation Management (PIM) for the government machine, was built around the appointment of 'area co-ordinators' who were established in the Office of the President and had the task of co-ordinating the development work of other ministries. PIM provided procedures for monitoring the work of field staff and focusing attention on bottlenecks within the administration in implementing programmes.[19]

In 1975, IDS prepared another report on the progress of SRDP. We shall be concerned in the remainder of this chapter with the experience of the SRDP in Kwale, and that of ODM as an aid donor, merely fortifying conclusions where possible by drawing parallels with experience in other SRDP areas. Here, therefore, we give a list of the main IDS conclusions classed into favourable (A) and unfavourable (B) as background to our own discussion:

(A) SRDP has demonstrated area-based plans can be prepared and implemented by local staff.

Infrastructure, especially of roads and water supply, has been developed in SRDP areas.

Management and reporting systems have been developed with varying degrees of success.

Some useful lessons have been learned about specific problems, notably about operating credit schemes for small holders and using labour-intensive methods in road construction.

(B) The major weakness has been, despite the emphasis on experiment, that very few new strategies have been developed.

Money has been spent on the obvious social services and infrastructure needs so that SRDP has emerged as another form of area development on a weak agricultural base. Although the areas are now more fortunate than average there is little sign of self-sustaining indigenous development.

There has been disproportionately heavy expenditure on recurrent costs and social services. In the first two and a half years, 75 per cent of spending was on salaries, housing and vehicles and only 25 per cent on capital formation.[20]

The principle of replicability has not been adhered to. One demonstration is that when SRDP concludes, as it is now scheduled to do after five years (January 1976), the Kenya government will be liable to recurrent costs of £K1m. generated by the programme. The total cost of SRDP programmes was under £K4m.

SRDP in Kwale

Kwale district is on the Kenya coast south of Mombasa. The SRDP area, some 417 square miles, did not for a long time include the whole district but only the southern part of it, taking in coast and hinterland. It was extended in 1974. The area is not densely populated. The 1969 census recorded 53,000 people, one to five acres. However, population is increasing rapidly not only through net reproduction proceeding at least as quickly as the high Kenyan average, but also because of migration into the area. The indigenous tribes, the Digo and the Duruma, are Moslem-animist. They are not intensive agriculturalists; the Digo rely largely on tree-cropping (principally coconuts and cashew) and the Duruma on animal husbandry. The attitude of the elders of these societies to change appears to be more than usually conservative. The migrants are mainly Kamba, who are generally Christian and more progressive farmers. Many of them hold land as a result of transactions with the Digo, but in a not unparalleled fashion, the nature of the transaction, whether for freehold or leasehold, is disputed. This tribal interaction, accompanied by a good deal of bad feeling, is one of the outstanding facts of social and political life in the district.[21]

The area falls into three basic regions. The coastal croplands are a narrow strip some 25 miles deep, with high rainfall (over 50 inches yearly) and good soils. Population here is relatively dense and tree crops and cassava are the main crops. The marginal lands are further inland where rainfall falls off sharply and is less reliable. The ranching lands are further inland still, where the rainfall is inadequate for any other enterprise.

The district is not untypical in climate, physical features, and economic activity of many other areas in Coast Province and that Province, in general, is not among Kenya's more developed areas. Experience in Kwale therefore could have relevance to pressing problems of development.

The plan laid down for Kwale SRDP, issued in January 1971, was written by Ministry of Planning personnel in Nairobi and was largely an exercise in planning from above. Existing projects in the area were supposed to be integrated with SRDP. These included a rural water project, financed by the Swedish aid agency, SIDA, and plans supported by IDA and HMG funds for a Development Centre incorporating a demonstration farm and facilities for courses in agriculture and adult education. The constraints to further development were identified as lack of water, roads and transport, and an overstretched agricultural extension service. A number of directly productive projects were planned. These included establishing sugar outgrowers to supply an Asian-owned factory running below capacity; setting up tree-crop and cassava nurseries; building cattle dips as part of an animal disease control programme and instituting a commercial ranch on the basis of co-operative ownership. There were also more general supporting programmes. Land adjudication was already proceeding in the area, supported by British funds; a programme of grading tracks to make roads providing access to the interior was started and various community development campaigns, including women's courses and functional literacy courses, were planned. The latter were necessary as census returns indicated 79 per cent of the population had received no formal education.

The implementation of the parts of this programme, in Kwale as in other SRDP areas, was in the hands of the operational ministries concerned.[22] Co-ordination was in the hands of the District Development

Committee. There was also a District Development Advisory Committee to include people not in the administration, like MPs and local self-help leaders. SRDP was expected to revitalise these committees. Early experience in other SRDPs also led to the appointment of an area co-ordinator, who was a sort of district planning officer charged with co-ordinating the work of the different ministries. This had to be done by cajolery as he had no authority over them and no access to funds. The area co-ordinator arrived in post in Kwale in January 1972. Each ministry in Nairobi had 'linkmen' who were supposed to liaise over SRDP at headquarters level.

The funds for SRDP activities were voted to the ministries within whose normal area of responsibility the activities fell. The area co-ordinator had to apply to the appropriate operational ministry for authority to incur expenditure falling within its ambit. In the case of projects involving more than one ministry, each had to be approached for authorisation and approval. Given even ordinary bureaucratic delays this could cause problems in the timing of projects but given the indifference or hostility to SRDP within some ministries, severe problems were encountered which the National Rural Development Committee failed to overcome. Even after authorisation to incur expenditure had been granted, no cheques could be signed by officers of the administration below provincial level[23] which led to further delays in spending voted funds. Authorisation delays led to some funds which had been voted being lost and returned to the Treasury at the end of financial years.

Many of the projects have been dogged by failure from the start. The Matuga Development Centre was to be multidepartmental with a farmer training centre incorporating a demonstration farm, and provision for public health and literacy courses. Some of the funds were voted to the Ministry of Agriculture and some to the Ministry of Education. Disputes arose over who was responsible for financing and running the centre. It was delayed owing to the inability of the Ministry of Works to provide adequate plans. It has only just been built and may not be in use before the end of SRDP in 1976.

Seed nurseries were quickly set up but half of a 26-acre sugar cane nursery was destroyed by arson ascribed to local jealousies; only 15 acres of a planned 100-acre nursery could be planted with seed-cane owing to shortages of it. Some 15,000 coconut seedlings were planted in another nursery but arson occurred again and 13,000 were destroyed.

All did not go smoothly with the ranching plans. There was considerable opposition to the idea from the Duruma despite *barazas* (public meetings) and a seminar at which an attempt was made to sell it to them. Even when their approval in principle had been won, it was difficult to reconcile the interests of everyone in the ranching area as some people were cattle-minders, not cattle-owners. It was decided to set up a central herd, but drought and opposition meant that by the end of 1974 only 100 animals had been pledged to it. A number of dams were planned for the ranching area but there was a delay over receiving plans for them from the Ministry of Agriculture, despite repeated requests. When plans arrived there was a further delay in authorising expenditure. Authorisation was finally received so late that building had to be rushed through, so expenditure could be incurred before the end of the financial year. A local contractor was employed and not adequately supervised. The dams were badly sited and poorly built and further expenditure will be necessary to make them serviceable.

Cattle dips were planned but authorisation was received for only two. These were built partly using self-help labour but one was caught by the end of a financial year and left half-finished. The local people who had promised to provide finance for dipping fluid failed to do so and the dips are unused.

A health centre was nearing completion at the end of 1974. It has, however, come in for criticism as being too elaborate – it is capable of dealing with 400 outpatients in a single day. On the other hand it is not clear whether there will be enough trained staff to match the building. There are not enough to go into outlying areas effectively and in any case they have no transport to do so.

Functional literacy courses and women's clubs have been started although the former are behind schedule. In addition social difficulties have been encountered. The Digo and Duruma are more reticent than the Kamba about attending – and this applies strongly to their womenfolk where Moslem mores have impeded participation.

On the other hand the provision of some other infrastructure has gone well. The SIDA water project, after early difficulties, is working. And the road programme was carried out quickly and at very low cost by the Ministry of Works which simply graded the most used tracks rather than planning new roads *ab initio*. Some 94km has been laid.

A number of common threads can be traced through many of the failures. One is that co-ordination between ministries has not been adequate, despite the efforts of the area co-ordinator and the National Rural Development Committee. One example is the Matuga Development Centre, which is not strictly part of SRDP, but it points a general pattern. The failures of co-ordination are a symptom of the second, deeper problem, that many ministries are indifferent to SRDP and give its expenditures no priority. An example of this is related below, but the fact, combined with the absence of financial delegation, led to the failure of the dips and dams. This indifference of the ministries is confined to the Provincial and Nairobi level. Local staff are usually glad enough of the opportunities and money that SRDP (eventually) brings.

A third problem is the failure to involve the local people adequately in SRDP project planning and implementation. The evidence of this is scattered but widespread: the arson, the slow progress with ranching, the dips not being supported, the low attendance at courses. A contrary sign is that farmers are said to be responding to the stepped-up agricultural extension effort in the area.

There are a number of reasons for this lack of local involvement. One may be a faulty government strategy to start with. The criticism that locals were not sufficiently involved in the planning of SRDP was noted and countered with the proposition that their support would come quickly enough when they saw a demonstration that the government was making a real input – roads and water – and then it could be hoped that in time the people would 'become involved in the developmental processes, especially the entrepreneurs, the better farmers and the younger generation . . .'. The involvement was thus seen as responding to governmental initiatives. One such initiative was to persuade herdsmen in the hinterland to stop milk production and switch to ranching. Milk production was to be concentrated nearer the coast. This radical change was 'planned' without consultation. More recently it has been suggested that tsetse fly control will not be as easy as once thought and might hamper ranch developments. On the other hand, milk might, after all, be a good cash product if more roads were built so that its producers could get it to market. In general it is a bad idea to attempt to implement radical and risky plans without taking the 'plannees' along with each step of the planning process.

Another problem is that government officers are usually from cultures that are quite alien to the local tribes, as the Kenya government tends to post officers away from their home areas. Many of the administrative and agricultural officers we met in Kwale were Luo whose homeland is about as far as it is possible to get from Kwale without leaving the country. Being Christian they have more in common with the immigrant Kamba than the Digo or Duruma, which is itself enough to create suspicion. There has been a tendency for government officers and extension workers to try to introduce agricultural techniques, for example, that are suitable for other parts of Kenya, but not for the coast, sometimes in response to national ministerial directives. An area like Kwale has a humid and debilitating climate and enervating diseases such as bilharzia are endemic among the population. On the other hand the land and sea have provided people with subsistence without their having to work very hard. Increasing population pressure will make this more difficult, but the local response is more likely to be hostility to immigrants than a desire to start working harder. Development can be seen in such circumstances as something that makes invasion of one's land possible rather than something to benefit one's family. Therefore it was particularly desirable to relate projects as far as possible to the local people's perception of their needs rather than trying out the bright ideas of outsiders.

A further problem is that not only do government staff represent outsiders but they are seldom in place long enough for personal relations to build up. Rapid turnover of local-level staff is a ubiquitous problem in Kenya, and Kwale is no exception. Practically no post is held by the same man now as it was when SRDP started and that is true of the area co-ordinator and the District Commissioner as well as less important officers. The lack of continuity increases the risk that government staff will be unaware of local constraints to the policies they are trying to implement.

Quite apart from the problems of Kwale SRDP as an area development project, the IDS report on SRDP in 1973 had pointed out that there was nothing 'special' or experimental in many of the developmental programmes under way. In Kwale the extra finance made available through SRDP was used to employ more staff by the ministries, so that more livestock and health officers, for example, were in the district but they were pursuing standard departmental programmes using standard techniques. SRDP crop programmes using small agricultural demonstration trials were normal extension activities pursued on a piecemeal basis without reference to any crop rotation or system. The British project adviser who arrived in post in September 1972 therefore pressed for SRDP money to be used for an intensive extension experiment. By his energy and persuasiveness he got this SRDP demonstration farm concept accepted by the local officers. The strategy was based on the belief that farmers needed to be convinced that they could reproduce the same results as those obtained on Department of Agriculture trial and demonstration plots and that the return justified the expenditure. This could only be achieved and farming practices modernised, it was thought, by physically demonstrating entire farming systems on the farmers' own land. The idea was for field staff of the Department of Agriculture to plan the farm layout and then work alongside the farmer every day during an initial on-farm training period. A number of small and large willing farmers, adjacent to one another, would be chosen, at first in areas where soil maps were available, adjudication complete, piped water on, access roads opened up, a farmers' co-operative established, and crops proven by trial. At a later stage a number of farmers in the marginal lands would get the same treatment when a system had been developed for such districts. All SRDP Agricultural Assistants, Animal Husbandry Assistants, and sub-staff were to be assigned full-time to the chosen blocks. Once modern farming was established, the extension staff would move on to another area.

Some data were available as a basis for farm planning; there was a semi-detailed soil survey covering part of the district, rainfall figures were available, and some crop trials had been conducted by FAO. Requests were forwarded to the Planning Unit in the Ministry of Agriculture for profitability studies to be made of possible crop rotations and for an extension of the coverage of the soil survey. Given the Planning Unit's inability to cope with its existing work, leading, as noted, to long delays in preparing major project submissions to aid donors, there was no chance of these studies being done. And given the Ministry's indifference to SRDP it was predictable that the requests would not be used to obtain technical assistance for the job. After waiting for eight months the project adviser began to do the planning himself for non-tree crops, coming up with a proposed rotation based on maize, sim sim, groundnuts, pigeon peas, chillies, and sunflower. He was an experienced man and the work was thorough: the crops were largely familiar to local farmers and the project adviser took account of the labour requirements of each and their seasonal distribution; he included the cost of labour and took the profitability aspect of farm planning into account.

When it was proposed to get the local resources of the Ministry of Agriculture devoted to the programme, as well as channelling credit to selected farmers, the project stalled again. The Ministry of Agriculture had recently decided on a policy of district-wide extension and refused to authorise its staff to go against that directive. Eventually the deadlock was broken but not until the second half of 1974 – three and a half years after the Kwale plan was issued, and two years after the arrival of the project adviser. Thirteen farmers were then selected, although the Ministry had still not issued any instructions to the Agricultural Finance Corporation about credit. Clearly, the experiment is most unlikely to have yielded any useful results before the end of the SRDP period.

The Ministry's actions were not simple obstructiveness or inefficiency. As a general policy the project adviser's approach was subject to a number of objections. The spread effects of which he was confident have often failed to materialise when intensive extension has been applied elsewhere.[24] In other SRDPs, experiments were being conducted to widen extension coverage with given resources, on the reasonable grounds that if some farmers are given an advantage over their fellows there is no reason to expect them to work hard at throwing it away by educating the others.[25] In the absence of spread effects, if the farm plans were successful the effect would be to increase inequality especially as the farmers chosen would be the enterprising ones with access to inputs like water and roads. It may well be politically unacceptable to concentrate government resources to achieve such an effect, especially in Kwale.

The sociological background in Kwale did not, *a priori*, look too good for the concentrated approach. Initial success could simply lead to more arson. In addition the approach could not be said to be economical in its use of skilled man-hours. We do not know what sort of farm plans local staff in Kwale could have drawn up but we do know that the Ministry of Agriculture does not have the capacity to prepare worth-while detailed farm plans on demand for the different districts of Kenya. Doubtless any plan adopted would require modifications in the light of experience, and who would make them, as junior field staff are often timorous about departing from plans they have been told to implement? These questions put in doubt the scheme's replicability without a continued technical assistance input. The Ministry of Agriculture no doubt feared this was a case of 'over-sophisticated techniques which generate shock-waves of demands for sophisticated information that only more planners can provide.'[26] In short the drearily familiar phenomenon of technical assistance generating the need for more technical assistance.

The justification for the project adviser's approach was that it was experimental. By using rural growth centres it sought not simply to effect marginal improvements in agricultural practices but to 'rationalise' farming in the area, revolutionising the outlook of a few farmers at a time, and preparing their entry into the monetary economy. It was clearly ambitious, perhaps excessively so, but it is a pity it did not get off the ground earlier. Although it was risky, risk expenditure, even if classed as recurrent, is what SRDP was supposed to be about. Experiment can only consist of trying out various ideas, and failures can be as instructive as successes.

Yet it must be said that the episode illustrates the dangers of technical assistance proposing plans that contradict a departmental policy. So much time is spent in in-fighting that none is left for the implementation of any policy. In the final analysis plans have to be evaluated not in isolation but in the political and administrative environment for which they are proposed. It is a pity both that the Ministry was not more flexible and that the project adviser did not plan taking into account the fact that it was not.

The Lessons of SRDP for Aid Donors

It is our conclusion that technical assistance is unlikely to be productive in area planning at the local level in Kenya. In the first place, in areas as undeveloped as Kwale we suspect that extensive resource studies leading to a master plan for development are a waste of time. In our view experience of SRDP, including Kwale, bears out some remarks of Chambers:

> The resource use strategy approach . . . much espoused and advocated by perfectionist planners, has a powerful appeal. While the forms it may take vary, it may be designed to include resource inventory and appraisal, determination of objectives and criteria for choice between alternatives, a search for and formulation of alternatives, and then choice between them and strategy design, with various forms of iteration between these. Ideally, of course, it should lead through to the working up of projects, budgets and action programmes and then to implementation. In practice the bitter and repeated experience has been that the process is slow, ponderous, given to premature elephantiasis, and exceedingly difficult to push through to implementation. The most common outcome is a large mimeographed document which presents much data about an area and sometimes suggestions of development strategy, but no detailed realistic of costed action proposals.[27]

Chambers concludes that such an approach leads to excessive data collection,[28] delays in processing, an absence of action proposals, domination by expatriate advisers, and low involvement of local-level staff.[29] He might have added low involvement of local population too.

If this approach is no good in a pilot rural development scheme, what are the alternatives? We believe a more gradualistic approach is called for, accepting by and large the choice of crops of the more progressive farmers at least and testing extension methods to get the techniques of all farmers up to the best local practice level, combining this with experiment in minimising the cost of providing services like roads, water, and agricultural inputs. The great spread in level of technique found among farmers in rural Kenya implies considerable gains in output if the average is merely raised to the level of the current best.[30] More ambitious project proposals could grow out of such an approach if improved two-way communication could be developed between government staff and the local people, and between field-level and headquarters-level staff. This entails appointing local staff with local knowledge and/or leaving them in post longer and improving management techniques within ministries. Even then we are not starry-eyed about local staff generating experimental project ideas. One of the great supporters of SRDP concluded: 'It was found . . . that field officials could not even after two years produce good project plans let alone comprehensive area plans without a great deal of direction and guidance from wider-looking, more experienced, centrally based officers.'[31] It is difficult to get the balance right; nevertheless, in common with many observers, we believe that the balance of initiative and power lies too much with the centre at present.

Our conclusion is that any technical assistance is best posted at Provincial level or higher where it can be called in by District staff to give specific technical advice as and when required, or better, help in the training of planning officers. Technical assistance at a lower level is often able to give salutary advice, but ultimately the role of an adviser not involved in implementation is difficult to sustain. When planning, without the responsibility to see to implementation, there is always the temptation to assume that an efficient administration is waiting to receive and act on one's quasi-optimal plan which will thus be implemented irrespective of whose political or administrative nose may be put out of joint. That is not true of any administration in the world. Yet it is only people who have to carry plans out who are likely to take such tedious constraints into account and whose plans are likely to have more than pedagogical value.[32]

That is why the experience of technical assistance in SRDP was almost uniformly unhappy. It either moved into implementation, as in Vihiga, or planned without implementation, as in Kwale. In Migori, things only began to happen when the original SIDA/FAO team moved out.[33]

ODM was aware of the dangers that a large-scale technical assistance input would, through the internal logic of the situation, tend to take over implementation and destroy replicability, so why did it put in technical assistance at all at local level? In fact it does not seem to have considered not doing so. One function which a project adviser could have – and has had – is that of helping local officers to train themselves, but this is not the whole story. British aid is in general underadministered. There are too few FCO or ODM officials on the ground to monitor projects or keep adequately in touch with British technical assistance personnel. Technical assistance can thus be given in an attempt to control projects by proxy in the belief that yet another expatriate will keep his eye on things and make sure 'British' money is being well spent. As Kwale cannot be described as a success, either as a development project or as an experiment, it is clear that this technique did not work. It was not the project adviser's fault. There can be no doubt that the greatest bottlenecks to SRDP were not at Kwale but in Nairobi. A project adviser attached to the Ministry of Finance and Planning and stationed in Kwale was not in a position to do anything about them.

Yet at the Nairobi level HMG entirely failed to use any leverage at all to support the pro-SRDP group in the Kenya government. Its negative reaction to a US initiative to tackle the Kenya government about its lack of support for SRDP has been referred to.[34] This incident occurred at about the time that the National Rural Development Committee co-ordinator, supplied by ODM, finished his contract, having been told, to his surprise, that the Kenyans were not applying for a further term of his services. Although the reason given was that the job could be done by a Kenyan, no appointment was made for five months and then a very junior officer was appointed. The co-ordinator was quite clear after leaving that SRDP had failed to realise its potential because of lack of institutional support at the centre. His conclusions are now accepted by some British officials with local experience and were indeed admitted by a very senior official of the Ministry of Finance and Planning at a staff seminar on rural development at the Kenya Institute of Administration in January 1975, who said support in key ministries had been less than he hoped. This danger was clear at the end of 1972.

Rather than putting in full-time technical assistance at Kwale, which was always likely to damage replicability and did not in fact much speed up the project, ODM would have been well advised to employ another adviser in the East African Development Division, Nairobi. Meetings with SRDP field staff and the SRDP central co-ordinator would have persuaded an adviser of the importance of backing the US initiative. The Kenyans could have been flatly told in 1973 that unless there was more co-operation and faster release of funds (if not financial delegation) by Nairobi ministries, no more money would be forthcoming for SRDP. Some ministries might have been annoyed but elements in the Ministry of Planning would have been grateful to ODM for this drive. The Kenya government is not monolithic, and in any case there are pleasant as well as unpleasant ways of telling someone you are going to pull the rug out unless he stands up.

Leverage could also usefully have been exerted, or at least suggestions made, at Nairobi level on details instead of leaving a project adviser to tell field staff who, without influence, then had to transmit the message up blocked ministerial channels. In this way representations could have been made about the rate of staff turnover, for example. Such pressure might have resulted in requests for technical assistance to do specific short-term tasks and relieve specific bottlenecks – perhaps carry out dam survey and designs. Requests from field staff carried no weight. It was up to British aid advisers and administrators.

We are not entirely confident leverage would have been successful. Perhaps the political basis of SRDP was after all so friable that it would have fallen apart, so to speak, around the lever. At worst ODM would then have saved some money.

SRDP and District Development

The Kenya government has decided after 1976 to phase SRDP expenditure into the general budget. It now proposes District Planning instead. District Development Committees consisting of the former bodies of that name and the old District Development Advisory Committees will be charged with preparing plans. A District Development Officer, trained in development planning and project preparation, will be posted to each district to assist. Provincial Development Committees will assist with professional guidance. Plans are to be forwarded to Nairobi and any projects not fitting into ministry programmes may be financed by District Development Grants. An average of £K25,000 a year for each district on this basis was set in the current Development Plan,[35] now increased to £K50,000; Forty District Development officers are to be posted by June 1976.

The justification offered for passing from SRDP to general District Development Planning has been that substantial political pressure is being exerted for a more general programme, and great concentration in SRDP provided a politically vulnerable target. It is also argued that SRDP has already demonstrated the potential for area-based planning and further experimentation is unnecessary. However this, in our view, is by no means conclusive. Certainly, to be successful District Development Planning would require adequate co-ordinatory units in Nairobi with full-time responsibility for district planning, headed by adequate influential and senior staffs, able to make swift decisions. Absence of this has led to many of the failures of SRDP. Lack of high-level support in both policy-backing and day-to-day administration must be overcome if District Development Planning is to work. The adequacy of the existing administrative machinery is open to doubt in view of the pace of implementation of projects. Several government departments are heavily committed to ongoing sectoral programmes, and staff and facilities are barely adequate to meet present needs. It could prove difficult to reconcile specific district requirements with sectoral priorities.

Most detailed write-ups for SRDP projects were done at provincial level or in Nairobi, and the same is true to date of district plans. Few spontaneous proposals from field staffs are received and there is very limited feedback even when they are asked to implement proposals that are inappropriate. Acceptance of the decisions of senior staff is strongly ingrained in the system and leads to a tacit acceptance of instructions that had just been passed down to the field.[36] Where grass-roots proposals are made, they are usually requests for infrastructure or social service spending rather than pointing opportunities for directly productive investment.

The Kenyans wish to get donors to subscribe to a Rural Development Fund. So far the Dutch, Swedes and Danes have accepted the idea in principle and agreed to contribute. The UK, using the excuse of the 100 per cent local-cost content required for district development funds, has demurred. The ODM feeling appears to be once-bitten at Kwale twice-shy over District Planning, and it is better to stick to discrete projects, although technical assistance might be provided.[37] That seems a pity. Any technical assistance given other than for training is likely to be a waste of money. On the other hand the usefulness of District Development Planning in generating proposals for development projects will depend on management procedures, including the arrangements for financial devolution and the willingness of the centre to give up some authority and some able personnel. This is a worth-while area for ODM to hold discussions with the Kenyans, in conjunction with other donors. Needless to say, capital aid should be given only if the details of the operation of District Development Planning and its financial control are satisfactorily worked out, the political adherence of the centre is established, and adequate District Development Officers can be made available. ODM experts may well have an important contribution to make to such discussions, and an entrée could be bought by the offer of a few hundred thousand pounds. The returns are likely to be greater than dropping some hapless technical assistance officers into a local situation. Some devolution is necessary in Kenya if local people are to be involved in development and it may eventually be a way of breaking the current bottleneck in project identification, if not preparation. District Planning is therefore an important initiative. What is in doubt is the extent to which the Kenya government takes it seriously. Some £K8m. is all that has been allocated – not enough to make the Treasury wince. SRDP, *inter alia*, was a device to get donors to commit untied funds, and no doubt District Planning is the same. In our view the correct response is not to shun it but to play back at the Kenyans by taking them at their word. Offer money on the condition that District Planning is made a reality. Such leverage involves taking a position in Kenyan politics, supporting the devolvers against the centralisers, but if

ODM does not like such an involvement it had better just hand over money and have done with it, as the involvement is implicit in any attempt to influence the use of aid. Of course supporting District Planning means British projects will not be identifiable enough to have plaques attached, the aid will not help British exporters much in the short run, and much of the expenditure may be recurrent. These should be unimportant considerations anyway. There is a deep ambivalence within ODM about such things. For example, ODM is understood to regard the health centre being built at Kwale as rather elaborate and to consider that more staff and transport might have been a better use of funds. On the other hand they appear somewhat alarmed by the fact that 75 per cent of SRDP expenditure was recurrent. You cannot have it both ways.

Notes

1. ILO, op. cit., p. 10.
2. See Chapter Two.
3. *Development Plan for 1974-78*, Nairobi, Government Printer, 1974, p. 109.
4. See James R. Sheffield (ed.), *Education, Employment and Rural Development: Report of the Kericho Conference*, Nairobi, East African Publishing House, 1967.
5. Rasmus Rasmusson, *Kenyan Rural Development and Aid*, Uppsala, Nordiska Afrika Institutet, 1972, p. 10.
6. J. W. Leach, 'The Kenyan Special Rural Development Programme', *Journal of Administration Overseas*, Vol. XIII, No. 2, April 1974, p. 358.
7. IDS, 'Pilot Projects in Rural Areas', Nairobi.
8. Subsequently it was decided to confine the programme to the six first-phase areas.
9. Leach, op. cit., p. 359.
10. Ibid., p. 360.
11. The Ministry was later joined with the Treasury and both became distinct departments of a single Ministry of Finance and Planning.
12. The final line-up was: Migori (Nyanza Province), SIDA/FAO; Vihiga (Western Province), USA; Mbere (Eastern Province), Norway; Kapenguria (Rift Valley Province), Netherlands; Kwale (Coast Province), UK; Tetu (Central Province), Kenya government.
13. ILO, op. cit., pp. 576-7.
14. A polar case was that of USAID. Having once bought the project they threw themselves into it with typical energy. In Washington, Vihiga SRDP came to be regarded as a showpiece – a pilot project of general importance for future USAID policy and, given the competitive element introduced by each donor adopting an area, a chance for USAID to show what it could do compared to other agencies. USAID's Kenya representative had to reconcile this intense interest in Washington with a good deal of indifference shown in Nairobi.
15. IDS, 'An Overall Evaluation of SRDP', Occasional Paper No. 8, Nairobi, 1973.
16. This was to some extent a political necessity. The pro-SRDP group had to have something to show high-level Kenya government sceptics quickly; aid donors had to have 'results' to justify untied aid and get good marks in the inter-donor competition implicit in the arrangements; the local people whose co-operation had been elicited with promises of development also had to be kept

agreeable.

17. IDS, op. cit., pp. 27, 920.
18. Leach, op. cit., p. 361.
19. For a description of the management techniques and how they came to be adopted following IDS research, largely in Mbere, see Robert Chambers, *Managing Rural Development*, Uppsala, Scandinavian Institute of African Studies, 1974.
20. We do not accept this point entirely. In our view, recurrent expenditure and capital formation can easily be the same thing. The fact that much money went to increase the routine extension activities of various ministries simply illustrates that these were undercapitalised for the task of reaching the rural masses. It may be true, however, that too much money went into the social services instead of more directly productive activities.
21. For some discussion of the tribes' social structures and the impact of immigration, see G. Mutiso in IDS, op. cit., pp. B7-B11, B23-B28.
22. In some areas donor representatives took an active role in project implementation. This was not so in Kwale.
23. As in the British colonial administration District Officers are subordinate to a District Commissioner who is subordinate to the Provincial Commissioner. All these officers are attached to the Office of the President.
24. In SRDP Migori for example, where a 'Master Farmer' scheme was proposed, of concentrating inputs on the 'best' farmers to make them into models for the rest. An expatriate team there made implementation possible.
25. See N. Roling, F. Chege, and J. Ashcroft, 'Rapid Development for Kenya's Small Farms', IDS Discussion Paper 173, Nairobi, 1973, for a description of techniques employed in Tetu, and Schonherr and Mbugua, 'New Extension Methods to Speed up Diffusion of Agricultural Innovations', IDS Discussion Paper 200, which analyses extension techniques in terms of innovation theory.
26. Chambers, op. cit., p. 117.
27. Ibid., p. 142.
28. In Kwale the data collection still failed to keep pace with requests for more data. While the project adviser was requesting extension of the soil survey, none of the local agricultural officers had seen the original, and it was not mentioned in the Kwale plan.
29. Chambers, op. cit., p. 144.
30. See R. M. Mbithi, 'Innovation in Rural Development', IDS Discussion Paper No. 158, Nairobi, 1972.
31. Leach, op. cit., p. 361.
32. The dangers are greater in the case of expatriates who often do not know the political constraints. And as their advantage over locals is likely to be in technical expertise they are likely to employ it even when inappropriate.
33. IDS, op. cit., p. D37.
34. See Chapter Four, p. 94.
35. *Development Plan 1974-1978*, pp. 111-13.
36. For discussion of these points see C. Trapman, *Change in Administrative Structures*, ODI, London, 1974.
37. Another, perhaps better justification for continuing this policy is that there is some doubt whether the Kenyans will spend all the funds now committed.

6 THE INFLUENCE OF AID

In the case studies of the last chapter we have tried to illuminate some of British aid's micro effects. We approach a tracing of the effects of aid in this chapter as follows: first we shall discuss the implications of fungibility and project-tying; then we look at the macro-level effects of aid on the Kenyan political economy. It will be difficult to single out the peculiar effects of British aid in this, except where particular British aid flows have characteristics which enable them to be distinguished. As official aid is given between governments, the recipient government is the interface between the donors and Kenyan society. In assessing the influence of aid, therefore, we focus on the Kenya government and move from the particular to the general. We shall assess aid's impact firstly on public finance in a narrow sense, then on other government policies, then on the style and pattern of government administration. Then we shall have to say something about aid's putative effects on the political nature of the Kenya government. In these discussions we shall distinguish capital aid and technical assistance on an *ad hoc* basis, where the distinction is relevant. Finally we shall give our conclusions based on this and the previous chapter about the influence of aid on income levels and income equality in Kenya.

Fungibility

Fungibility has sometimes been seen as providing recipients with the opportunity to use aid to finance projects that do not appeal to donors. So funds negotiated to build a hospital might release domestic resources for the construction of a presidential palace. The shunting of funds between discrete projects like that, however, is only one instance of a more general problem. After aid a recipient may be able to increase the salaries of civil servants or to cut taxes while maintaining an expenditure programme. Fungibility embraces consumption as well as investment, private as well as public spending.

Where there is more than one aid donor the possibilities are multiplied. British aid for a project in Kenya might displace the funds of another donor whose disbursements to Kenya may fall in consequence. So, for example, HMG loans to Mumias may have led to there being different West German aid projects elsewhere in Africa, or may perhaps simply have led to a swelling of the West German foreign exchange reserves. Faced with such vertiginous prospects it is no wonder that many donors avert their gaze. They continue to tie aid, taking it as an article of faith that 'their' aid finances 'their' projects and, as project appraisal is a large part of the business of an aid agency, they continue to evaluate the projects. Such evaluation can have useful effects even given fungibility. It might improve the micro-level effects of aid, it might have value in demonstrating rational methods of planning and appraisal and inducing the recipient to adopt them, and it might serve a cosmetic purpose with public opinion in the donor country. We shall return to the question of project-tying.

Apart from being tied to end-use, aid can be tied to purchase of goods from specified sources, usually the donor country. Fungibility, in this context sometimes known as 'switching', then means that the aid can be spent without increasing imports from the donor country by the full amount of the tied aid. If such imports are increased by the amount of the tied aid, unless the marginal propensity to import from the donor is one, the presumption is that it was not fully fungible and was consequently worth less than its nominal equivalent in free foreign exchange.[1] Here we are concerned with fungibility's effects on the composition of total spending rather than on the source of imports, hence with 'internal' rather than 'external' fungibility. We should, however, clarify the relation between the two. If aid is extremely fungible, although procurement-tied it will lead to additional imports from the donor only to the extent of the recipient's normal marginal propensity to import from that source. For it to be externally fungible it must be internally fungible too, but the reverse is not the case. Suppose aid is procurement-tied and tied to a project that in its absence would have taken place anyway, using other resources. The project, if unaided, might or might not have used imports from the donor country. If not, the aid increases the donor's exports by substituting them for those of a competitor. However, it releases to other uses the foreign exchange that would have been used to import for the project. It releases resources equal to the cost of the goods it has replaced, rather than to its own nominal value. As these goods were originally preferred, the aid may well be worth less than its nominal value but, for what it is worth, it has swelled general resources. It was therefore internally but not externally fungible. If the aid is tied to a project that would have used donor imports anyway, it is both externally and internally fungible.

If, however, aid is tied to a project that would not have taken place in the absence of aid, the project is additional and clearly imports for it are additional too. You cannot have external without internal fungibility. Therefore internal fungibility is necessary but not sufficient for external fungibility. From now on we consider the former.

There is a temptation to say that, in the presence of fungibility, an aid disbursement does not finance what we might call the target project, but a marginal expenditure – that which would not occur without the aid. This formulation can however lead to paradox.[2] In a sense every pound of anyone's income always finances the marginal expenditure, because (tautologically) it is that expenditure which would not be undertaken if any pound were withdrawn. To put the responsibility for the Kenya government's marginal expenditure (or revenue-releasing) decisions in each financial year at the door of British aid would be unreasonable. That presupposes the total of all other aid is fixed and invariant to the British aid decision, and can be known in advance. The essence of fungibility is that where it applies it does not always make much sense to say any particular aid tranche financed any particular project.[3] Those who would use a marginal expenditure formulation are in any case lost as soon as account is taken of time. The reaction of the administrator and accountant is to divide up time into financial years. But this year's marginal expenditure may be promoted to the middle of the order next year so someone 'really' financing it this year by courtesy of shunting, is 'really' financing not it but next year's marginal project. And so on *ad infinitum*. Can, for example, British finance for the Nairobi-Mombasa road really be said to have financed any one of every project of lower priority since, and any one of all those lower-priority projects still to come?

An aid disbursement causes a change in the time-stream of receipts and expenditures of the recipient government. The pure no-fungibility case is the one where the expenditure streams with and without aid would differ only by the addition to the aided stream of the 'target' project. The simple-shunting case is the one where another project,[4] not the target one, is added to the aided stream compared to the hypothetical unaided stream. Both are unlikely special cases. A number of projects may appear and disappear as a result of aid because of the repercussions on government spending and resource mobilisation and the actions of other donors. Or there may be no change at all in the inventory of projects appearing in the time-stream; the same projects may occur simply displaced in time.

Policy makers cannot be concerned, however, with the infinite ramifications of their decisions and have to confine themselves to proximate effects. The practical question which emerges is under what conditions will project-tying of aid make its effects more predictable and controllable? We are also concerned with whether past project-tying has made British aid's effects distinguishable from those of aid in general.

A necessary condition for project-tying to be effective is that expenditure on the project would not have been undertaken anyway by the recipient government. This is not however a sufficient condition because of the presence of other donors who may have supported the project. If the target project were favoured by other donors, the donor could not even be sure he was adding it to the expenditure stream. And then additions to the expenditure stream would depend not simply on the preferences of the recipient government but also on those of other donors who had some say in what, if anything, would be done with their 'displaced' funds. That sort of fungibility would not matter so much if donors cooperated and had compatible priorities with each other. Even without other donors there may be problems not usually considered under the heading of fungibility. Even if project-tying secures the genuine addition (or a considerable advancement in time) of the target project to the expenditure-stream, it could thereby give rise to other effects which might be neither predictable nor desirable. There is no reason to suppose that the priorities in projects of a recipient government remain unchanged whichever projects are undertaken, so to say, out of order. Projects can compete by sector or by geographical area. Push through a project in a deserving sector in a poor area and you may demote another project in the same sector or the same area. There really is no way the donor can be confident that there will be no ramifications of this kind.[5]

If the project would have been undertaken anyway and aid swelled the recipient government's revenue for other purposes, that is one type of failure which we call shunting; if the project would not have been done, but with its execution sets up other changes in government policy of which the donor disapproves, it is a second type of failure which we call shuffling.[6] Now we can review the conditions in which project-tying is said to be effective.

Fungibility is said to be reduced or eliminated if the recipient is not aware of it. Unawareness does not eliminate shunting. It means the recipient Treasury will be surprised at finding 'free' finance was greater than it expected and will consequently be slower to put through its own unaided projects. That eliminates crude, conscious shunting between projects but means either more private sector activity is permitted or the recipient's foreign exchange reserves are higher, at least until the Treasury wakes up. As domestic borrowing or credit creation by government tends to be residual it will probably be reduced. Unawareness does not eliminate shuffling either. Governments do not have to be aware of fungibility in order to, for example, change their mind about preferences when faced with new constraints.

Lack of preference-ordering of projects is said to reduce or eliminate fungibility. As long as there was a good probability of the donor's target project being carried out by whatever random selection method would have been used, this does not eliminate shunting, although project-tying can then be seen as a sort of insurance which may be useful in replacing the probability that a project will take place with a certainty. This situation might seem to rule out shuffling; if the recipient does not mind much what is done, he won't change his lack of mind because something has been done. If, however, there is a need to balance competing claims for resources in different ministries and in different regions, while there was no corporate set of priorities initially (conditions which seem to be true in Kenya), the execution of certain projects may set up political pressures for some other projects to be carried out before their alternatives. Therefore shuffling is still possible.

Fungibility, it is argued, can be exorcised by binding resource constraints on the recipient. So, for example, if the recipient has no domestic funds at all, or all of those he has are pre-empted as counterpart funds for projects promoted by donors, he cannot shunt or shuffle finances to advantage. That is true. This position is however entirely theoretical as far as Kenya is concerned, and if it applied anywhere, did so to only very small territories for a period immediately after independence. A more interesting variation of this argument, however, is to point to possible administrative and skill constraints on the part of the recipient. Even if he has foreign exchange reserves, it may be that his limited number of planners and administrators are fully occupied once he accepts aid and cannot find time to work up the other projects which donors would not approve. Although that obviates project-shunting, the result is likely to be increased government consumption spending, or reduced resource mobilisation by government. Another possibility, observable in Kenya, is for funds to be on-lent to parastatals or for equity to be taken in private enterprise so that central government expertise is not strained. This certainly imposes some limits on fungibility in that it prevents the use of additional resources in administration-intensive activities. If the project priorities of the donor and recipient are very different, the donor gets his way to a certain extent in that he influences the recipient government investment programmes. He does not, however, limit recipient government consumption or private sector spending, which he may or may not prefer to the public investment he has squeezed out. If he does not prefer it, he might improve matters by giving technical assistance. It is only sensible for the recipient government to accept aid, when constrained in this way, if it prefers a deformed investment programme with more consumption to its original investment programme with less consumption. In the real world, however, and certainly in Kenya, there is often no one to take that sort of decision and aid offers are taken up willy-nilly. If the donor has tied aid to projects that would have been carried out anyway, even with an administrative constraint, this is a classic shunting case. There is increased consumption or private sector investment. Provision of technical assistance would not obviate the shunting. It would merely enable the recipient to shunt resources into public sector investment as well as, or instead of, consumption or private investment.

This analysis has tended to the conclusion that project-tying of aid can only influence the macro-economic allocation of resources if the aid is tied to a project that would not have been carried out in the absence of the aid. Neither indifference nor ignorance nor shortage of skilled personnel on the part of the recipient necessarily makes tying effective. It possibly means that more consumption, not different investment takes place. If the recipient's indifference is considerable, project-tying can be a form of insurance. Even then, however, compensating resource shifts, what we have called shuffling, are possible.

The only qualification to this conclusion is based on the vagueness of the notion of a project, which also means that our division of aid's effects into the macro and the micro is a convenient classification, not a complete description of reality. In addition, the vagueness of 'project' means aid can be partly fungible rather than simply fungible or otherwise. A road project, for example, which a recipient government was going to undertake in the absence of aid might have been for a single lane of gravel. The donor may use leverage to insist on a tarmac dual carriageway. In that case only part of the aid was fungible, enough to finance the gravel; the rest was not fungible. Hence micro-effects can become so large as to qualify as macro-effects. In this example (not appropriate to Kenya now, although it might have been ten years ago) the donor has increased the proportion of the recipient's public expenditure going to road-building. It could, of course, work in reverse; the donor by imposing economies on projects to which his aid is tied could reduce spending in that area and release more resources than the nominal amount of his aid.

Project-tying, therefore, is not always pointless. The donor may want to ensure that the recipient undertakes certain projects which he suspects may be marginal in the eyes of the recipient. And he may make the judgement that the chances, and magnitude, of other effects arising from shuffling are relatively small. Perhaps most important, he may think micro-effects reaching the status of macro-effects are possible. It is true, nonetheless, that these reasons are probably inadequate to explain the great popularity of project-tying among donors. Apart from the other reasons for it already noted,[7] which have some developmental legitimacy, there are three other reasons less creditable. One is what has been called the 'strange vanity' of aid agencies that there should be monuments to their efforts (although this cannot be entirely separated from the donor public opinion argument); a second is the organisational interests of the aid agency itself – Parkinsonian growth is facilitated by the requirements of manpower and expertise that project evaluations entail; a third is that project-tying greatly enhances the effectiveness of procurement-tying so that there can be strong commercial reasons for it.

In case this should be thought too cynical, one observation is apposite. Whatever the scope for the shunting of aid funds as a whole by the recipient – and in the case of Kenya we shall argue there is not great fungibility between Kenya funds and aid *en bloc* – the aid of any single donor is much more fungible. We should say that in the case of Kenya the views of a single donor in influencing Kenyan resource allocation are not worth much unless shared by other donors, when they can become very powerful. If the point of project-tying were seriously to influence resource allocation, this fact would put a very high premium on donor co-operation. Such co-operation is emerging in some areas and is certainly more conspicuous than it used to be. But donor competition is still common and it reflects badly on the developmental pretensions of project-tying.

Public Finance

The Kenya government's domestic sources of finance are substitutes for the aid it receives from abroad. For any given level of expenditure the government can obtain the necessary resources by various combinations of aid, foreign and domestic borrowing, taxation, and charges for the services of the state. The revenue-raising and expenditure decisions are not of course independent. Expenditure plans partially determine what efforts will be made to raise revenue, and the constraints on revenue-raising influence expenditure plans. Attempts to formalise this interaction have been made by specifying a 'utility function' for governments with the usual diminishing marginal utilities for each policy objective. The government can then be thought of as a rational agent seeking to maximise its own utility subject to the constraints of its budget. As a literal description of what happens in Kenya (and indeed in most countries) that is not accurate. Expenditure decisions are in fact the outcome of a bargaining process between individual ministries and the Treasury and are partly determined by successes and failures in Treasury control and by factors outside the control of the bureaucracy altogether. Agents who can rock the boat include the President and perhaps a few other political heavyweights in a position to insist that certain things are done, the Kenya public where its desires are so strong and general as to threaten political stability if not met (the proliferation of schools is an example), and aid donors. Total expenditure is nothing but the sum of all the individual decisions made under these pressures. How far the utility function approach can serve as a useful metaphor or model we shall not go into here, but as long as there is some interaction between government objectives in revenue-raising and expenditure it is reasonable to suppose that aid tends to increase spending, while acting as a partial substitute for domestic resources.

We cannot go from there with any confidence to give a quantitative estimate of what proportion of each aid tranche to Kenya has brought about extra government spending and what proportion has gone in reduced domestic resource mobilisation.

An interesting attempt at such measurement has been made by Dr Peter Heller, who computed that for a sample of Anglophone African countries, bilateral aid flows at the margin increased expenditure by only 18 per cent of the aid; 55 per cent went in reduced domestic borrowing and 26 per cent in reduced taxation.[8] Heller's model, which relies on the utility function approach, is very interesting, but not much confidence can be put in the actual figures it yields because of the large standard errors of the estimates.[9] The figures, anyway, would be averages for all the countries in the sample,[10] and would not necessarily apply to Kenya alone. However the financial sector in Kenya is at least as developed as that in most of the other countries, so *a priori* one would not expect domestic borrowing to be less important in Kenya than for Heller's sample as a whole.

Table 17 shows the importance of domestic borrowing in financing Kenya government expenditure. The other significant domestic source of finance, taxation, is more important. In the period 1969-74, for example, taxation accounted for an average of 92.7 per cent of 'recurrent revenue'.

In the early post-independence years, except for 1965/66, the government easily covered the borrowing requirement with long-term borrowing. In fact in 1966/67 and 1967/68 long-term borrowing exceeded the deficit and government cash balances rose.[11] Short-term borrowing has been used in subsequent years, mainly through the issue of Treasury Bills. In 1969/70 and 1970/71, the government borrowed directly from the central bank. Since then, while short-term borrowing has remained a feature of the government's finance, long-term borrowing has kept pace with the total borrowing requirement. It was 62 per cent of the requirement in 1971/72, 80 per cent in 1972/73, and 79 per cent in 1973/74.[12]

It seems clear that there was scope for more domestic borrowing by the government than occurred in the ten years after independence. That is not because the Kenyan banks by-and-large had ample liquid balances so increased borrowing would not have upset financial markets. That is true but not the point. We have to consider what the effect would have been on real markets and there we believe both that the government could have obtained more resources from the private sector by long-term borrowing and that it could have afforded to borrow more short-term and create credit. Furthermore we believe that with less capital aid but the same technical assistance it would have done so. The effect of a larger government deficit partly financed by short-term borrowing and credit creation, even if it mobilised some resources that would otherwise have been unemployed, would eventually have been reflected in the balance of payments. In most years since independence, Kenya has had a modest surplus on the balance of payments, and foreign exchange reserves have risen from £K42m. in 1966 to £K82m. at the end of 1973. The increase in reserves represented an average annual growth rate of 10 per cent, comfortably faster than that of imports at current prices. Import price inflation began to exceed 10 per cent only in 1972. In 1970 the reserves were enough for four and a half months' imports compared with three months' in 1966. For most of the post-independence period, therefore, the government could have run the economy at nearer full throttle than it did, and reductions in aid would not have needed to be matched pound-for-pound by expenditure cuts. This was in fact accepted in the 1974-78 Development Plan – written before the oil crisis developed – which pointed out that the government had drawn little on the banking system for short-term credit but stated it intended to do so more in future.[13] There are, of course, dangers to such a policy. Fine tuning of the level of demand is no more possible in a country like Kenya than

Table 17: Kenya government expenditure and finance

	K£'000								
	1965/66	*1966/67*	*1967/68*	*1968/69*	*1969/70*	*1970/71*	*1971/72*	*1972/73*	*1973/74*
Recurrent revenue	56355	65996	77077	84703	97927	123983	141628	148999	187243
Recurrent expenditure	63267	68529	74991	80515	91136	111317	128670	139578	166203
Recurrent surplus	−6912	−2533	+ 2086	+ 4188	+ 6791	+ 12666	+ 12958	+ 9421	+ 21040
Net development expenditure[a]	8059	9333	11356	13645	18898	29354	39341	44169	69470
Total deficit	−20647	−11866	−9270	−9457	−12107	−16688	−26383	−34748	−48430
Investment expenditure[b]	5676	6614	7356	10177	11030	15757	12087	17053	
Deficit	−14971	−18480	−16626	−19634	−23137	−32445	−38469	−51801	−48430
Financing of the deficit									
External loans	9427	7839	7831	7115	10774	10941	11489	24657	20000
External grants to development	5098	3474	1902	974	1440	824	1794	521	4357
Total external finance[c]	14525	11313	9733	8089	12215	11765	13283	25178	24357
Domestic borrowing[d]	6122	7167	6893	11545	10992	20680	25186	26623	24073

a Net of development project earnings and other receipts (almost negligible).

b Largely purchase of equity, and loans to private and public corporations. Loans to public corporations were the most important in each year except 1970/71 when equity purchases were higher. These loans average 74 per cent of total investment expenditure.

c Almost entirely supplied on concessionary terms. Grants have been for both recurrent and development account with the latter becoming more important. Loans have been mostly for development account; recurrent account loans have been nil since 1970/71 and were negligible after 1967/68.

d Long- and short-term borrowing and changes in government's cash balances. This is the difference between the total deficit and total external finance.

Source: Kenya government, *Economic Survey 1974*, p. 165.

in a country like Britain, and we cannot say how much extra government expenditure (or unrequited aid reductions) would have been consistent with a tolerable net drain on the balance of payments of say £K25-30m. over seven years, without accelerating inflation. Clearly, however, some slack existed.

The government could also have obtained more resources without inflation, either by long-term borrowing or by the combination of short-term borrowing with quantitative credit controls on the banks, a policy it adopted in 1971 in response to a temporary balance of payments deterioration. Either course represents the channelling of resources from the private sector with no necessary increase in demand. Long-term borrowing does so through the voluntary saving and lending of the public. Borrowing from the banks and imposing credit controls does it by a form of implicit taxation on the banks, forcing them to lend to the government rather than other customers. Either policy could be disadvantageous to the banks; the former might well reduce their deposits, as bank deposits are one of the few substitute assets for government securities in a country like Kenya with rudimentary capital markets, and the latter would reduce their profitability directly.

There does not seem to be any reason why the Kenya government should have been concerned with moderate falls in banks' profits, as they were not likely to quit the country, so all it had to consider was from whom it would have diverted resources by increasing its own borrowing. In 1967 Africans and African farm enterprises received only 2.6 per cent of total commercial bank loans and advances.[14] Recent Kenya central bank figures give the following breakdown by province of commercial bank advances, loans and discounts:

Table 18: Distribution of commercial bank lending

(percentages)

Nyanza	Western Province	Rift Valley	Central Province
5.0	0.6	7.1	5.7
Eastern Province	**Coast**	**North-eastern Province**	**Nairobi**
1.9	14.8	0.03	65.3

Not all large-scale business or expatriate business is in Nairobi, of course, but there is no doubt that the great preponderance of lending in Nairobi, followed a long way behind by the Coast and Rift Valley, reflects a continued bias in favour of established modern sector business. There is nothing sinister in this and the commercial common-sense reasons are plain enough. It is still an issue of considerable political sensitivity in

Kenya where politicians and district administrators have claimed that while the geographical distribution of bank deposits is heavily skewed it is not quite so uneven as that for advances, so the banks are in effect channelling funds from rural to urban areas. African businessmen also claim that British banks still discriminate against them.[15] Of course, because the average bank borrower in the private sector is a businessman, often urban and often expatriate, it does not follow that the marginal borrower is. A public borrowing squeeze on bank lending could hit the small up-country borrower rather than more favoured customers. It is doubtful, however, how many such there are. We are probably safe in concluding that any big expansion of public borrowing would have largely hit modern sector business.

Exchange control regulations now limit local bank overdrafts to a proportion of a company's foreign long-term liability. Where more than 60 per cent of the equity is foreign-owned, overdrafts are limited to 20 per cent of that liability; for foreign holdings of 51-60 per cent, a sum equal to 40 per cent of the foreign equity can be borrowed locally; and if 50 per cent or less is held by foreigners 60 per cent of their holding can be borrowed. Historically, foreign private investment in Kenya has made great use of local savings. B. Herman, in an examination of foreign investment, computed the 'degree of use' of local savings as private plus public local debt divided by private foreign equity.[16] All the enterprises he examined – 81 set up over 11 years – had a ratio of local funds to foreign equity of more than one.[17] For British firms the ratio was a startling 4.4, much higher than that for firms of other countries of origin. The figures are somewhat misleading in not taking account of inflation or, more importantly, the companies' retained earnings as part of the foreign equity. Considering retained earnings would reduce the apparent dependence of British firms on local capital both absolutely and relatively, because as they had on average been in existence longer than the firms of other foreign investors, their total retained earnings would be greater. Nevertheless, Herman's hypotheses that foreign investors extensively use local savings and that British investors find it particularly easy to do so because the banks are British, probably have a good deal of truth.[18]

We are not arguing that the Kenyan government would or should have followed a policy of forced borrowing and reckless credit expansion. It seems clear, however, that while building up foreign exchange reserves may have been a good policy, given the aid flows into Kenya, if those flows had been significantly lower it is doubtful whether the build-up would have been preferred to various forms of government expenditure. More government borrowing would therefore have resulted if aid had been lower. If the government attempted to borrow without inflation the burden would have fallen on Kenya's banks and/or modern sector business, significantly involving British interests. One effect of aid has therefore been to maintain liquidity in the economy and so help those interests.

That could have been good for private investment, but it could also mean that aid has been a substitute for private capital flows. Even if it did increase private investment, by artificially cheapening capital for larger firms, aid could have distorted the investment in a labour-saving direction, although it is doubtful whether the size of such an effect was significant, even if it occurred.

An examination of taxation leads to similar conclusions. Kenyan tax revenues have not been particularly buoyant and without periodic changes to tax rates, allowances, and bases, revenue would have grown more slowly than GDP since independence.[19] Owing to the general rise in money incomes, the proportion of direct tax receipts in total revenue from taxation rose from 36 per cent in 1963/64 to a peak of 47 per cent in 1972/73 and then declined to 37 per cent following the introduction of a sales tax on both imports and local manufactured goods. In its first full year of collection the sales tax netted about a third of indirect tax receipts and a fifth of all tax receipts and was responsible for the recovery in the government's recurrent surplus (see Table 17). If the government had been faced with the necessity of raising more revenue earlier it seems probable that it would have been done by the same technique, namely an increase in indirect taxation. There is scope for a tightening up of assessment and collection of income tax but that is expensive in skilled manpower (although we have little doubt it is worth doing in Kenya).[20] In any case the Kenyan direct tax structure is not very progressive, although reforms in 1973 made it more so, and it may be that this accords with the government philosophy towards development. It is noticeable that the current Development Plan, for example, defines progressivity as a situation in which the rich pay more tax than the poor![21] It seems likely, therefore, that an increase in indirect taxation would have resulted from aid reductions, probably involving, as subsequently happened, a sales tax on luxury goods,[22] and perhaps increased excise duties. The burden of a sales tax would fall on the consumers and producers of locally manufactured goods, again the modern, largely expatriate, business sector.

Beer, cigarettes and sugar yield most excise tax revenue. The first two are produced by monopolistic firms, one a wholly-owned subsidiary of a British company, the other a Kenyan company in which there are substantial British equity interests. As their products are price-inelastic, the (mostly African) consumers would have paid most of any duty increases. The commodity yielding most import duty since independence is fuel, which is an important part of the costs of any modern firm.

Altogether we can say that the provision of aid has alleviated a competition for domestic Kenyan resources of capital, and perhaps manpower, that would have been carried on between the government, faced with political demands, and the modern sector of the economy, in which expatriate business has a dominant interest. It is very difficult to know what the extent of competition would have been and what its effects would have been on tax rates, interest rates, the 'diffused difficulty of borrowing', and the level of foreign investment. There is, however, no reason to suppose that aid has permitted an increase in the average propensity to consume of the Kenyan economy. Resources for which the government might have competed have been released to the private sector but they could well have gone into private investment. And while we have argued that aid must have reduced government resource mobilisation we have not said what its effect has been on the balance of public sector consumption and investment within total government expenditure. To government expenditure we now turn.

The Kenya government divides its expenditure into recurrent and development. This distinction is not exactly the same as that between consumption and investment. The division is based on the following principles:

> Recurrent Estimates include estimates of personnel costs, other recurrent expenditures, small items of equipment, including vehicles, maintenance and cash transfers;
>
> Development Estimates include estimates of expenditure for major equipment items, buildings, construction works and land; investments, grants and loans to other sectors and purchases of equity. All equipment items relating to new projects and financed partly by external grants or loans are included in the Development Estimates. Similarly, any expenditures on personnel or other items, normally regarded as Recurrent, which are financed from external sources are included in the Development Estimates.[24]

The classification depends partly, therefore, on whether a particular project is new or not. Salaries and vehicles for a team to carry out a tsetse fly control exercise would be development if the team were new and financed by aid, recurrent if it were already in existence. Many recurrent expenditures are not consumption, but capital replacement or maintenance, or working capital for existing projects. Some development expenditures are not investment but 'placement' – the acquisition by government of claims on existing capital assets.

Even if development equalled investment and recurrent equalled consumption, however, the fact would be largely without normative significance. Without getting involved in semantics we can note that much expenditure that would be classified as consumption in a developed country can raise future output more than expenditure that would be classed as investment. Education and health expenditures among an illiterate population suffering from endemic diseases could be more productive than a four-lane highway or a large factory doomed to run at

20 per cent of capacity.

It is necessary to make these familiar points because in Kenya both the Treasury and donors have tended to venerate 'investment' above 'consumption', and by illicit extension 'development' above 'recurrent' spending. No doubt, partly to blame are the emotive names applied to these categories which the accountants find convenient. If rational men wish to retain the categories it might be better to rename them the lumpy budget and the smooth budget.

At any rate it is not the case in Kenya that a chief effect of aid has been to enable the government to expand its recurrent expenditure or consumption. Table 17 shows recurrent expenditure at current prices rose by less than three times between 1965 and 1974, an average annual growth rate of 13 per cent. Development expenditures, excluding investment expenditure, went up over eight and a half times in the same period, a growth rate of almost 31 per cent a year. In Chapter Two we noted that while public sector consumption remained a constant proportion of monetary GDP between 1964 and 1973 (about 20 per cent of resources available), public investment greatly increased its share. All gross investment rose from 16 per cent of GDP in 1964 to 29 per cent in 1973 at current prices, and the public sector's share in fixed capital formation went up from 28 per cent to 46 per cent. It is possible, logically, that the figures might have shown even more dramatic increases without aid but that is implausible. The reverse is probably true: aid increased government expenditure absolutely, although by less – perhaps much less – than the amount of the aid, and it raised the proportion of government expenditure that could be classified as either development or investment. This latter effect may have been so strong in fact that aid actually squeezed government consumption and tended to reduce it absolutely.

That was certainly the finding of Heller's econometric analysis.[25] Although we do not regard that result as self-sufficient, for the reasons given,[26] there are ready explanations for it in the case of Kenya.

First is the tendency for donors to provide loan finance for part but not all of a project. The Kenya Treasury adopts a conservative approach to life. That was the view of foreign donor personnel and Kenyan civil servants in operational ministries, and as noted in Chapter Four, was one reason why the Swedes give advance disbursements.[27] We have noted two cases of the Treasury's reluctance to authorise recurrent expenditure even though loans had been promised to cover it.[28] In other words the Treasury does not regard loan funds as fully fungible and is reluctant to use them to finance consumption. Their acceptance means that an attempt is made to increase investment and where this is impossible, resource mobilisation is reduced. Loans tend to be matched to investment projects but they rarely fully finance them, so that Kenyan counterpart funds are drawn in too.

Second, donors exert a good deal of pressure on the Kenya government to show it is doing its best in resource mobilisation and the main concrete evidence of this is taken to be the surplus on recurrent account. So the Kenyans believe, with reason, that they can generate more aid by having a larger recurrent surplus to provide part of the funding for more development projects and then appealing to donors to finance the balance. Aid has to be obtained that way because the donors frequently agree to support only part of discrete development projects. This fact fundamentally alters the return the Kenyan money earns in marginal investment projects because the concessionary element of aid becomes one of the benefits of such projects. It is no wonder then if Kenyan funds are drawn into such projects by the existence of aid. Of course they do not have to be drawn from government consumption but could come from other projects or increased resource mobilisation. It is our judgement that the funds were diverted from government consumption in the sense that this would certainly have been a higher proportion of government expenditure and might conceivably have been absolutely greater without aid.

If this is so, one thing follows immediately: donors, as a bloc, were financing the marginal projects and there was only limited fungibility of aid. If the donors had only been providing aid conditional on the execution of projects that were top priority for the Kenyans (believing they were financing them), Kenyan money would have been released and the Kenyans would have had an unconstrained choice between marginal investment projects and consumption. There would thus have been no tendency for money to be drawn from consumption into investment by aid. If, however, the Kenyans carried out their own top priority projects and donors offered to partly fund the more marginal ones, that would change the attractiveness of the marginal projects relative to other ways of using resources, and pressure on government consumption would result.

We believe that was the case and that aid as a whole was not much shunted between investment projects. But the aid of any single donor, from the mid-1960s on as the number of donors increased, was in a sense fungible, as most assisted projects would have been undertaken by other donors.

There is a third and even more compelling reason for believing that aid increased saving and investment propensities, as conventionally defined, in the Kenyan economy. Through most of the post-independence period the Kenya administration has not had the capacity to plan, execute and run an investment programme of large projects on the scale that the supply of capital would have allowed. That is the view of all aid donors to whom we spoke, and evidence of it is Kenya's consistent underspending of project-tied aid commitments. The public sector project list which the Kenya government presented to donors at their Consultative Group meeting in Paris in 1974 showed that the Kenyans themselves thought technical assistance was 'required' for a high proportion of the projects they proposed. When road projects, which the Ministry of Works can handle perfectly well, were excluded along with routine extensions to institutions like hospitals, the proportion of projects for which technical assistance was required became very high.

Technical assistance has failed to close the gap between the administratively-constrained level of investment activity and what finance alone would have made possible, given that financial aid was also available. Yet expatriates have played a significant, often crucial, role in practically every major investment project in Kenya. Two, if not all three, of the projects we examined in Chapter Five were conceived by expatriates and two were largely executed by expatriates in their early stages. They are not untypical. Furthermore, not only are many large projects, especially the bigger ones, planned, prepared and largely carried out by expatriates, but as pointed out in Chapter Four[29] the Kenya Treasury surrenders the selection of all but a few projects to donors. It lacks the capacity and the political authority to vet and rank projects so the *sine qua non* of its approval becomes the promise of aid. If no technical assistance had been forthcoming, could the Kenyan administration have arrived at decisions and invested the 50-60 per cent of the Development Budget available from Kenyan resources? We believe that some of those resources would have gone to recurrent expenditure, or other expenditures requiring less planning than large projects.

There is evidence that not only has aid increased government investment relative to government consumption, but that it has done so excessively. Many donor civil servants take the view that the provisions for recurrent expenditure by some ministries in the Development Plan for 1974-78 are inadequate to service the capital in existence, let alone that implied by the Plan's level of development expenditures. The main work in this area has again been done by Peter Heller, who, from an analysis of projects, calculated the percentage of development expenditure in each sector which would be required as an annual recurrent allocation, if projects were to run at the planned level of efficiency.[30]

He found that on any reasonable assumptions about capital-output ratios, aid flows, etc., the 'fiscally consistent' level of investment the Kenya government could undertake if its recurrent expenditures were to be adequate to service capital was below the target investment level of the 1970-74 Development Plan. Whereas the target for government development expenditure was about 6.1 per cent of GDP, the recurrent financial capacity of the government was sufficient at the planned growth rate to finance investments of the composition laid down in the Plan at about two-thirds of that level. With planned aid inflows of 50 per cent of total investment the government could afford to invest only 3.8 per cent of GDP. Higher investment levels, unless made possible by higher-than-expected growth rates of government revenues, entail falls in the recurrent financing of projects.

The experience of SRDP[31] showed that when it came to rural development the felt needs were for more recurrent expenditure. Kenya is by no means Nkrumah's Ghana but it has some expensive aided projects with a distinct whiff of the white elephant about them – the Russian-built hospital in Kisumu, the Cyprus bins for grain storage supplied by Britain – while many an agricultural or health extension worker would do better with a bicycle, a larger petrol allowance, or rather more training. It is difficult to substantiate that statement beyond saying that we met many such in rural Kenya when researching for Chapter Five.

This behaviour of boosting investment may, of course, be quite rational for the Kenya government which has to consider whether the loss of efficiency and output from any project owing to a lack of recurrent finance (e.g. the school with fewer teachers or less qualified ones) exceeds the gains from a new project subsidised by donors. Historic costs should not influence its decision. It is hard to see, however, that the action of donors is rational in insisting on new projects. And as a matter of fact we do not think the Kenya government pays enough attention to the problem. While donors, including Britain, are guilty of distorting government expenditures, it is only fair to say that they often seem to be pushing an open door and the Kenyan government has its own appetite for the grandiose. The fine modern buildings in Nairobi housing government departments and parastatals, the KANU conference centre, extensions to Nairobi airport, to Mombasa airport (financed by a Japanese loan) and plans to extend Malindi airport (so far refused assistance by at least two donors) may all be examples of this. Once involved with a project, ODM tends, in fact, to be a restraining influence on the Kenyans, who may also be trying to spend aid promised to them by inflating the expenditure on individual projects. The case of Kenyatta Hospital has been noted and there are others involving, for example, educational establishments. Unfortunately it is all rather late. The emphasis of donors on 'projects' and 'investment' offering between them more money for these things than can usefully be spent has fortified the illusion in Kenya that capital is cheap for such purposes and has fed the appetite for grand symbols of modernity which is frequently present among the elite of a new state. Having helped to establish such an atmosphere the more responsible donors, who include ODM, have to wrestle with its manifestations in individual projects. Others, including notoriously the IBRD, have sometimes accepted ludicrously high specifications for roads etc., and financed them regardless. The resistance of even the most responsible donor can be sapped by other considerations. It is easier to resist a prestige building or road requiring local labour and materials than airport or television installations involving substantial export orders.

Other Government Policies

Clearly one area where donors might be thought to have influenced the

Kenya government is via its investment programme, affecting both the sectoral and geographical distribution. This could have occurred in two ways, by the provision of experts who gave influential advice to administrators and by leverage in the giving of capital aid, even if only the negative leverage of refusing to finance what one doesn't like. It is difficult to discern any consistent tendencies in the investment policies of the government which can be attributed to the influence of technical assistance personnel, who vary widely in competence and political leanings. We shall say more about technical assistance in discussing the impact of aid on the style of Kenyan administration and concentrate here on capital aid.

We have argued above that donors appeared explicitly to finance the marginal projects in the government's plans, which suggests fungibility may be limited. The 1974/75 Development Estimates reveal that the development projects in which donors have no involvement are the minority. Some ministries got no external aid by virtue of the kind of activities they carry out. These include the Judicial Ministry, Information and Broadcasting, Labour, Defence, and Vice President's Office and the Office of the President.[32] Together these accounted for 6.1 per cent of proposed development spending of £K88.3m. in 1974/75. Housing is an unfashionable ministry with donors and also received no aid, but accounted for another 6.8 per cent of development spending. Housing may be an exception, but the expenditure of the other unaided ministries can probably be regarded as high priority which would go ahead whether the Kenyans received aid or not. Of the expenditure of the remaining ministries, aid accounted for some 38 per cent. That is lower than in an average year, which fact will merely fortify our points. In Agriculture, aid was expected to account for 43 per cent of total expenditure. Projects with no capital aid input at all accounted for 30 per cent of the total. Capital aid was therefore involved in 70 per cent by value of the Ministry's expenditures – the 43 per cent of finance that was aid tied up another 27 per cent of the total. In the Ministry of Works, estimates were for projects totalling £K20m., but only £K5m. – 25 per cent – seemed to be wholly Kenyan-financed. Here £K6.9m. of aid tied up local funds of £K8m. In those ministries where a higher proportion of the funds were wholly disposed of by the Kenyans their use is revealing. In the Ministry of Finance and Planning, for example, some £K4.35m., out of a vote of £K4.95m., was on wholly Kenyan enterprises, but £K3.54m. was capital subscriptions, loans to public and private enterprise and other share purchases. Similarly the Ministry of Commerce and Industry received little aid towards its development budget of £K2.92m., but £K2.27m. of that was for loans or grants to other bodies, including funds for ICDC to purchase equities.

These figures might seem to reinforce the view that Kenyan resources of finance, and more particularly skilled manpower and administrative cohesion, are inadequate to allow much shunting of aid funds as a whole between government investment projects. It does not quite follow from this, however, that donor preferences have dominated or determined the pattern of public sector investment in Kenya, simply because there are many donors and the Kenyans can play them off against each other. It is in the organisational interest of the highest-minded aid agency to spend money in a country once a certain sum has been allocated to it. And representatives of donor governments are conscious that they are *inter alia* involved in a competition with each other for commercial and political preferment by the recipient. Donors therefore sometimes finance projects pressed on them by recipients even though they are against the better judgement of development-minded technicians in aid agencies. In the case of ODM we have already mentioned Mombasa television. Another example may have been the Naivasha-Suswa pipeline to take water from Lake Naivasha to range areas in the Rift Valley at a final cost to HMG of £465,000 (the initial estimate was £150,000). The project seemed a very marginal one, on the basis of cost-benefit analysis. Its social benefits also depended critically on the Ministry of Agriculture controlling range management strictly and inducing Masai herdsmen to prevent environmental damage by moving to rotational grazing – an outcome in which no one could have much confidence. However as the Masai were very poor, ODM authorised the project. One of the features of the scheme, however, which may or may not have been widely known in HMG, was that it benefited several large ranches owned by important people and people with important connections. No doubt the Masai would be flattered to know this was one project the Kenya Treasury submitted for tender before aid funds had been secured – the tender notices were published in the newspapers long before ODM's authorisation date. Ironically, however, the project's completion is now held up because ODM wants higher charges for the water than the Kenyans are willing to impose.

Nevertheless, donors as a group do have considerable influence over public investment in Kenya because there are not all that many aid projects about which the Kenyans feel so strongly. For the most part donors select projects from a list that is not ranked for priority by the Kenya government. Not having their own ranking, the Kenyans allow donors to choose in order to maximise aid.

The question of how to maximise aid is an interesting one, and it does not follow that the recipient necessarily succeeds in doing so by offering donors projects they like. That is likely to be true when dealing with donors like USAID and the Germans, who negotiate the amount of aid they will give at the same time as they discuss which projects they will support. In the case of donors like ODM and Sweden, however, who agree a fixed sum in advance of project discussions, a different technique may be best. If the donor has already committed, say, two-thirds of an agreed aid allocation to projects he likes, he may cavil at marginal-to-donor projects then offered. If, however, he has managed to commit nothing in the first year or two of an aid agreement he may in desperation take those marginal projects. After he has aided these he can be offered the glamorous one. The Kenyans do not play this game in a very sophisticated way, but they certainly play it.[33]

It seems, however, that donors as a whole have had an important influence over that part of the public investment programme which requires detailed planning. They have had little influence over politically important projects on which the Kenyans were determined, as the Kenyans had enough money to finance these and, up to a point, could obtain technical expertise at commercial terms. Donor competition is, in any case, usually sufficient for the Kenyans to obtain aid finance for such projects once their political importance becomes known. These projects are, however, a minority.

Donor influence does not seem to extend over government recurrent spending, beyond a tendency to restrict it by swelling the development budget. This is indicated by the record of the Ministry of Agriculture. Half of its development expenditure is financed by aid, more than the average for Kenyan ministries, and 20 per cent of all capital aid to Kenya has gone to it. Yet agriculture's share of total public sector spending, including recurrent spending, has fallen from 21.2 per cent in 1963/64 to 8.4 per cent in 1970/71. In the 1974-78 Development Plan the share of recurrent expenditure going to agriculture is projected to fall, while that for education is projected to rise; tendencies that fly in the face of much that is written in the Plan. There is, of course, a strong flywheel effect operating, and much of the educational expenditure is forced by past spending. But the fall in agriculture's share cannot be explained, as some observers have attempted to do, by the difficulty of preparing projects in the agricultural sector, a problem which would restrict development rather than recurrent spending. The motivation for these allocations is largely a matter of domestic Kenyan politics. In other words the donors get their way to some extent in the sectoral distribution of development spending, but their writ does not run so far where the recurrent budget is concerned.

It is clear, however, that the influence of an individual donor, even Britain, the largest one, is negligible unless its views are shared by the other donors. If a project is attractive to other donors, or they can at least be induced to do it, it does not matter whether one donor aids it or not. There is, however, some tendency for donors to be cagey of projects which they know other donors have turned down. Quite a good way to kill a project therefore may be to say one is considering it. If one then rejects the project, the others may be shy of it. The Kenyan Treasury suspects the British of adopting this technique, but ODM denies it. We are inclined to take ODM's word for that and to put delays down to normal bureaucratic difficulties. In any case, the technique does not always work; other donors can step in and take a project over, as the West Germans did with the Mombasa Polytechnic which ODM thought it would be aiding. (It is fair to point out that there has been as much delay in prosecuting the project since the Germans took it on as there was when it was a British 'possible'.)

We conclude, therefore, that there has been considerable, but by no means total, donor influence over the sectoral pattern of public investment in Kenya, owing largely to a lack of overall policy by the Kenyans and their readiness to accept aid offers which tie up their own resources. The influence is moderated by competition between donors and is generally insufficient to kill those few projects for which there is considerable Kenyan political pressure. As the Kenyans lack expertise in project preparation, the influence of donors has been considerable over the details of projects. There is, however, little or no evidence of donor influence over the pattern of Kenya government recurrent expenditures although we believe aid has tended to keep these down – probably too much so, if one believes they would have gone where they were needed.

We could find no evidence that donors' influence had any marked effect on the geographical distribution of public investment. It is almost universally believed in Kenya that economic development has proceeded very unevenly with Nairobi and Central Province growing much faster than other areas, particularly Nyanza and Western Province. ODM appears to share this belief and to look kindly on projects in areas that are thought to lag. It chose Kwale not Tetu for its SRDP area, and its currently favoured projects of rural access roads and livestock marketing facilities are essentially rural enterprises focused on areas outside Central Province. While rapid urbanisation is a serious problem and Nairobi is growing very quickly, there is less evidence that Central Province as a whole is developing faster than many other areas of Kenya since the spurt some years ago owing to the dissemination of small-holder coffee. We approached the sales managers of a number of firms producing mass consumption goods for a regional breakdown of their sales figures. Each subscribed to the general view that development continued to be lopsided, but no set of figures when produced bore out the belief. In nearly every case there was an enormous disparity in levels with a very high proportion of sales being in Nairobi and Central Province (which is reason enough for public policy to favour other areas) but the proportions appeared to have been roughly constant for several years.[34] This in no way constituted a scientific survey, however, and we had no information on, for example, the income elasticity of demand for the goods in question.

In one case British aid can be said unequivocally to have helped Western Kenya relative to other areas. The National Agricultural Research Station in Kitale, which has received British and other technical assistance on a large scale, has developed the hybrid strains of maize that have undoubtedly had a considerable effect on Kenyan maize production.[35] The hybrid maize development also received CD&W funds during the period 1955-65.

Being sited in Kitale, the station developed first of all hybrids suitable for Western Kenya and the Rift Valley and so increased the relative importance of those areas in maize production. The Katumani, or dry-land, maize which helps Eastern Province areas has had rather less dramatic success. As more strains are developed and introduced, it may be that other areas will catch up. Quite apart from its geographical impact, the maize breeding programme has been one of aid's biggest successes. Some 86 per cent of hybrid maize in 1973 was on small-scale holdings, and the social returns to the expense involved (less than £1m.) are enormous.

On the wider range of government policies, economic and social, we could find little evidence of aid having any effect at all. Most donors seemed well-disposed to the East African Community, for example, and both HMG and IBRD have aided it substantially. The Kenyans, on the other hand, have seemed to regard it as very much an 'optional extra', and if donors have been concerned to promote its well-being, they have failed. As noted, over Mumias ODM felt unable to resist Kenya's desire for its own sugar factory despite the implications for Uganda.

There has tended to be a donor consensus on the correct economic policy for Kenya, which follows the lines of successive IBRD analyses. These in turn tend to reflect the prevailing orthodoxy in development economics. So in the early years of Kenyan independence, industrialisation via import substitution seemed a reasonable policy. Now that is out of style and the accent is on rural development, encouraging manufacturing industries to export, reducing and rationalising the structure of protective tariffs, and devaluing as and when necessary. All of these things have found their way into the current Development Plan. However, as we have noted, the Plan is largely written by expatriates and, the cynical would say, for expatriates. Just as the distribution of recurrent expenditure does not reflect that of development expenditure, neither reflects the statements in the Plan all that well. The expenditure on rural development hardly matches the importance the Plan says that it has. And we have heard of negotiations to afford trade protection to firms in flat contradiction to the policy of the Plan for reducing protection.[36] Foreign investment, even where it yields negligible social benefits, affords substantial pecuniary opportunities for well-placed Kenyans in a position to render it services. That makes it difficult, in the absence of a strong and coherent government policy, for foreign investment to be controlled. It is an error, however, to assume that aid agencies are merely handmaidens of every private firm from their country that wants to set up in Kenya. There is precious little contact between the British High Commission in Nairobi and most British businessmen in Kenya and practically none at all between them and the East African Development Division. In so far as British aid can be seen at all as a means to support private enterprise in Kenya, it does so in a much longer-term way than trying to influence Kenya government policies to the short-term advantage of British firms. In fact if the current fashions in development economics, which ODM professes, were really taken to heart by the Kenya government, many British enterprises would lose protection and have a harder time of it.

Sometimes donors have attempted directly to influence policy in certain sectors. One example is the IBRD and USAID support for birth control. An IDA credit of about £5.5m. in 1972/74 was given for a national family planning clinic, a health education centre, five nurse-training schools, and 27 rural health training centres. The Kenyans accept the family planning element as part of a larger health scheme, but for the most part they cannot be persuaded to give birth control the sort of priority that the North Americans think it deserves. Even references to population in the Development Plan,[37] where donor opinions tend to be courted, are muted.

The British have attempted to improve Kenyan educational policy. Supported by an enormous groundswell of popular feeling, education expenditures in Kenya, especially on secondary education, appear to be out of control. The demand for school places, leading, it is hoped, to paper qualifications and a lucrative modern sector job, is so intense that the government seems powerless to resist. Where it does not build secondary schools itself, villagers construct their own *Harambee* schools and it becomes the test of the local MP or other leader that he should obtain government finance for the schools. A secondary school with a fifth form or higher is a great status symbol, so there is also a tendency for the smallest schools to attempt to provide training right up to sixth-form level. Thus resources of teachers and other inputs are increasingly stretched and the result is declining examination pass rates and an increasing output of arts students, as the smaller schools rarely have the trained teachers or equipment to teach science adequately. Many of the classes thus created cannot be filled with pupils with reasonable qualifications. One outcome is the production of more arts specialists than can be accommodated in higher education or than can be employed. There is now an excess of Kenyan non-graduate teachers in all arts subjects except English and French. As a very important supplier of secondary school teachers under the OSAS agreement, Britain might be thought to have some influence over this. It has attempted to use that influence in a number of ways. It has deliberately run down the number of teachers supplied to Kenya, phasing out all arts teachers except those teaching English; it has restricted its teachers to approved educational establishments, keeping them out of the smaller schools.[38] Its manpower planning reviews with the Kenyans have occasionally become heated as the British insist on reducing the number of teachers faster than the Kenyans would prefer. (To some extent, the battle has been beside the point as ODM has been unable to recruit the planned numbers anyway, owing to inadequate salary supplementation.) ODM also insists on projections of the number of students and the employment requirements for them when considering capital aid for higher education establishments. It did this, for example, when proposing to aid the Kenyatta University College expecting it would train science teachers which was a priority, especially as OSAS was running down. The result has been four years of delay in getting the project moving as there is some opinion in the Kenya government that the college should be a second separate university and this opinion cannot be justified with figures satisfactory to ODM. Technical assistance was also given for the Planning Unit of the Ministry of Education in order to improve the Ministry's planning.

This pressure has been largely, although not entirely, in vain. Secondary schools have proliferated in spite of it all. A withdrawal of British teachers would not halt the process which goes on in response to political imperatives. The political nature of the expansion is shown by the fact that where schools have gone is correlated with political influence, with Central Province being specially favoured. One of the difficulties is that the consumers of education in rural Kenya do not have any well-formed expectations about the quality of the education they are getting. They are fatalistic about the fact that some schools are better than others. An argument that a school should be closed and merged with one a mile away, or even that top classes should be merged, falls on deaf ears even if it would undoubtedly be educationally better for the children. As one civil servant despairingly put it: 'closing a school or taking away a fifth form is taking away "development", and is always bad, and that is that'.[39] The scope for British leverage then is strictly limited. In collaboration with other donors ODM can stall the construction of over-elaborate university buildings. It may have had something to do with the Development Plan commitment to manpower planning in education and the concentration of upper secondary teaching into fifth- and sixth-form colleges. These remain paper plans, however, and ODM has been unable to do anything about the mushrooming secondary schools or recurrent expenditure. The problem will probably only be 'solved' by an increase in school graduate unemployment leading the public to re-evaluate formal education.[40] This may be beginning to happen. The growth of *Harambee* schools has peaked and is down since 1970.

HMG has also attempted to influence the Kenyans towards a consistent grain policy. The Kenya government decided that a strategic grain reserve was necessary following the harvest failures of 1965. ODM made a loan and Cyprus bins were installed at two points in the country in 1966 at a cost of over £150,000, but they were made redundant by normal weather conditions and the development of hybrid maize varieties which greatly increased production. The bins were large, hermetically sealed structures, in groups of about thirty, designed for a strategic reserve and not easily adapted for rapid handling as part of the country's normal storage facilities. They were also badly installed and began to develop cracks and other faults. Faced with apparent over-supply of cereals, the Kenyans decided on a policy of being self-sufficient in wheat and exporting maize, and requested aid for storage facilities. IBRD was interested in financing a large grain silo at Mombasa, but would only do so if the Kenyans would guarantee a certain volume of exports. Bad weather in the early 1970s and rising domestic demand, especially for wheat, then put the export policy at risk again and, in response to political pressure from MPs, a new policy of siting grain stores up-country in consumer areas was proposed. HMG was keen to aid grain storage for a number of reasons. One, it was a worthwhile expenditure given the losses to pests which occur when a grain harvest is badly stored; two, the equipment would be British, beating off an Australian challenge to British companies for the supply of grain storage and handling equipment; three, the British were embarrassed about the Cyprus bins and were anxious to renovate them and install handling equipment so they could be usefully integrated into the country's storage capacity. The aid remained undisbursed, however, because the Kenyans did not develop a consistent policy towards grain production and storage that would enable planning of the siting of the storage facilities to be carried out. Another minor difficulty was that they did not want to spend any more money on the Cyprus bins, which they regarded as pouring good money after bad. The British, on the other hand, did not give the Kenyans credit for realising that historic costs should not influence current decisions, but were determined to relieve their embarrassment by improving the Cyprus bins and getting them into the Kenyan national storage policy – a clear case of a donor wanting its monuments to be seen to be successful.

It is difficult to know why over nearly five years the Kenyans have not been able to settle on a grain policy that would enable them to make a detailed submission for aid. One problem was the volatility of national policy in response to climatic fluctuations changing the size of harvests. In addition, cereal prices, particularly the maize price, can be something of a political football with the maize farmers importuning the government, especially the President, for higher prices, but with the government anxious to keep food prices down for the urban consumer. Another problem was the rapid staff turnover within the Ministry of Agriculture. This tended to mean that a grain storage policy lasted as long as the incumbent of an office; when he moved, someone else took over, called for another report on grain storage, and the cycle started again. ODM supplied one team to prepare a report; there has been at least one Ministry of Agriculture report and in 1974 expatriate advisers at the Maize Board prepared yet another, this time proposing a conversion to storing grain in bulk instead of in bags. At the time of writing, however, no policy has crystallised. Meanwhile, while ODM was poised to spend £1m. on grain storage as soon as the Ministry of Agriculture produced a policy and a request, Denmark stepped in and gave £K350,000 worth of grain-drying equipment to be installed on an *ad hoc* basis at existing storage facilities.

British ambitions in this area were modest, and the tactics were gentle. The idea was simply to dangle a large sum of money in front of the Kenyans to be handed over when they came up with a national plan for grain storage that made sense against the background of an agreed grain production policy. Up to date this tactic has not worked. It is not simply that ODM was unable to influence Kenyan policy, but that it was unable even to influence the Kenyans to agree on their own policy, despite technical assistance as well as promises of capital aid.

The influence of foreigners on Kenyan government policies appears to be extensive. Foreign investors, aid donors and technical assistance personnel are all important. The influence, however, is largely uncoordinated and in some cases (e.g. over rates of tariff protection) self-cancelling. Aid donors have influence as a group over the composition of the public investment programme and individual donors can influence the detailed specifications of individual projects. Practically all attempts by them to influence sectoral policies have been failures, however: birth control and education are examples. We could find no evidence of donors influencing wider policies in practice, although plenty of evidence of them influencing the contents of the Development Plan. It may be that much the greatest donor influence comes through the activities of technical assistance personnel within the Kenya government machine, but it is extraordinarily difficult to assess this.

Administration

The existence of aid has profoundly affected the Kenyan administration. In the early years of independence, the presence of OSAS personnel ensured a continuity of government services and of the style in which they were administered. We cannot doubt that this was of inestimable benefit to Kenya. Whatever view one takes of the record of colonialism in Kenya and elsewhere, a precipitate and total withdrawal of the colonialists has usually been disastrous. The events in the Congo and more recently in Angola are examples. Most colonialists have been guilty of considering only very late in the history of colonialism, and then perhaps inadequately, the development of the indigenous people they ruled. But, having committed that crime, simply to clear out when indigenous opposition makes the game unprofitable is to compound the offence. In our view, some form of post-colonial involvement, although it runs the risk of becoming neo-colonialism and the much greater risk of being called neo-colonialism, is a responsibility.

At independence, Kenya inherited a relatively efficient civil service. In some ways, it was not adapted to the task of delivering developmental services to the mass of the people. Agricultural marketing boards and some services of the Ministry of Agriculture, for example, largely served the expatriate farmers with extensive landholdings, although the Swynnerton

Plan was an exception to the point. The provincial civil service was more concerned with its judicial functions and the maintenance of law and order,[41] especially between ethnic groups, than with development *per se*, although it, too, became concerned with land adjudication and enclosure measures having developmental implications. At all events a relatively efficient and corruption-free machinery existed, and it is rather easier to adapt and reform such a structure than to build one from nothing. That was especially so in a country where few indigenous people were experienced in administration, where loyalty was principally to sub-national ethnic groupings rather than to a geographical entity that was the product of colonialism, and where there was no more political unanimity than in any diverse society, despite rhetoric about development and building the nation. There were shortfalls in government expenditure in the early days of independence owing to constraints of administrative and executive capacity as many experienced expatriate civil servants left anyway.[42] OSAS enabled some to stay. Yet the important point is not that many OSAS personnel carried out tasks more efficiently than any Kenyans who could have replaced them, so their absence would have led to an even greater fall in efficiency, rather that their presence preserved traditions, conventions, ways of doing things, and a collective memory that was no doubt highly defective for many of the tasks it had to discharge, but at least worked. Kenyans could come in, inherit this, take it over and change it.

It is possible to argue that such gradualism leads to acculturisation and resistance to necessary changes by the new elite and a desire to emulate their predecessors in unfortunate ways. Perhaps the most important of these is the example expatriates set their successors in the matter of standard of living. The continuation of expatriates in government at independence and the gradual movement of Africans into their positions involved the taking over of colonial salary scales. Now, OSAS personnel receiving supplementation and wholly-funded technical assistance personnel being paid by foreign governments can be paid more. This in turn can arouse envy and provide a pattern which Kenyan civil servants strive to emulate by fair means or foul. It is the right of Kenyan civil servants to engage in business and many of them, especially the senior ones, take advantage of it.[43] The task of keeping entirely separate one's functions as a businessman and as a bureaucrat with access to state power is a superhuman one and the people in question are only human. Technical assistance is only one very small element in a welter of foreign and domestic influences making for acquisitiveness in Kenyan society,[44] and it would be nonsense to blame the existence of technical assistance for the high living of some Kenyan bureaucrats. Nevertheless, the existence of highly-paid expatriates, many of them understandably eager to enjoy their time in Kenya to the full, cannot help in encouraging the indigenous civil service in the matter of restraint.

At any rate, there has been, by all accounts, some increase in corruption in recent years. There is anyway a stronger temptation for people in a privileged position in a poor country to take mercenary advantage than was true of colonial civil servants who are part of a career structure stretching back to London. Corruption is not simply of the venal kind, however. There is also the practice of giving illegitimate preference in jobs or contracts to people of the 'right' ethnic or regional background, with or without any pecuniary inducement. Increasing corruption is a fact of life in most African states, no doubt for general sociological reasons, some of which apply in Kenya. By continental standards, the Kenya civil service does not appear to have done badly in maintaining high standards of rectitude.

Now that ODM is running OSAS down, it finds, to its surprise, no urgency about Kenyanisation in many ministries. Teaching is the area of greatest disagreement, but other OSAS officers are maintained at skill levels where one would suppose competent Kenyans were available. A few OSAS officers have converted to advisers under SCAAP, but ODM resists this kind of concession in general.

It is sometimes argued that donors and technical assistance personnel are responsible for persistent use of expatriates when adequate locals are available. Certainly unsolicited offers of aid, including technical assistance, are made. Apart from budgetary reasons – fully-financed foreigners are cheaper than locals – there are domestic political reasons for the phenomenon too. These have nothing to do with so-called psychological dependency, a supposed relic of colonialism which we failed to observe. Expatriates have the important attribute in Kenya of not owing special loyalty to any of the country's ethnic groupings. In terms of the balance of posts within a ministry, for example, an expatriate may be regarded as preferable to the commitment of the post to a Luo or Kikuyu or whatever. In addition, expatriates are not suspected of being politically ambitious. This is very important where high officials in a ministry may have risen to their position in a very few years. However able, they must be short of experience and prone to make errors or ask questions which reveal that. To confide in or otherwise reveal this to fellow Kenyans is to make a possibly damaging admission of vulnerability. An experienced expatriate can answer the questions such an official is not supposed to need to ask without risk to the position or authority of the superior. He has no interest in plotting because he has no political ambitions, ethnic or personal.[45] Having expatriates in positions is also a sort of saving – their jobs, it has been suggested, represent unused opportunities for the exercise of patronage which help to keep juniors in line. Therefore having political neuters around can be useful and when Kenyanisation reached a certain level, the political pressures for more were balanced with those against it. Many donors at present, quite apart from the British, observe that there appears to be little steam behind the Kenyanisation issue in the civil service.

Expatriates can cause resentment, especially among middle-level staff who might regard them as a bar to advancement, but they do assist higher-level staff in the ways mentioned. It is difficult to say what the net effect is on morale and efficiency of having expatriates around, especially in view of the obvious difficulty of expatriate researchers in getting frank reactions on the issue.

The use by some expatriates of rational problem-oriented management techniques also has some demonstration effect. This is the aspect of their work that most expatriates stress. Each time a report is ignored, or in the case of those in established posts, each time a decison is overturned, on what they regard as improper political or venal grounds, they console themselves with the thought that someone has observed their approach and perhaps some converts have been made. Now this is doubtless true and important; the difficulty is that it provides a convenient justification for any expatriate who realises that little substantive is coming of his work.

This might seem to beg the question of whether the techniques and approaches which expatriates use are always appropriate. Clearly they are not always so. Some expatriates do import cultural presumptions or are excessively attracted to planning techniques requiring information that does not exist. It is extraordinarily difficult to generalise here; some do and some don't. In a diverse country like Kenya, expatriates – at least those with overseas experience – are sometimes more flexible about problems than Kenyan nationals but, of course, so they should be. One does not import people simply to improve the quality of one's mistakes.

Perhaps the errors are more likely to occur where there are a large number of expatriates to get together and insulate each other from the surrounding reality. When that happens it also reduces any educative effect that technical assistance could have on Kenyan civil servants. In Kenya, however, aggregations of expatriates have occurred to the point where they become practically a separate estate of the realm. The UK shows its greater experience over other donors here and is relatively guiltless. Other donors make initial proposals and put in quite large teams to staff planning units, for example, in the Treasury and other ministries. ODM generally waits to be asked. When discussing aid projects in the early stages, donor representatives may talk to these technical assistance personnel and perhaps no Kenyan is present. Another possibility, which has happened, is that a donor holds talks with an operational ministry about a project and the Treasury representative present is an expatriate. If the ministry's plans are too expensive the donor and the Treasury may concur in opposition, but the confrontation takes on racial overtones and the legitimacy of the Treasury representative is compromised.

The most glaring example of technical assistance as a separate estate is in economic planning and particularly in the preparation of the

Development Plan. It is no secret that large sections of all Plans since independence, as in many new countries, have been written by expatriates. The Ministry of Finance and Planning is very conscious of the Plan's function in attracting aid and the Plan often reflects donor opinions. That is not as a result of cynical dissimulation, however. The expatriates who write the Plan sections genuinely share these opinions, and the control of the Ministry of Finance and Planning over their Plan is much better than it is over the actual spending and policies of other ministries. The Plan does not necessarily represent the agreed view of the Kenyan government therefore. The notion of collective responsibility is weak; ministries only fight for their policies to appear as such in the Plan up to a point. Beyond that point they concentrate on ignoring the Plan if it does not suit them. The fact that only certain expenditures are budgeted in the Plan can act as a powerful constraint on a ministry (although within their budget ministries can change policies how they like), but the Plan should be seen therefore not as the outcome of a battle for resources, but merely as a shot in it. Pumping in expatriates to the Planning Units of 'weak' ministries can certainly lead to better paper planning (i.e. a Development Plan that coincides better with donor views), but at the risk of making the Plan deviate further from any kind of description of a political consensus. What donors frequently diagnose as a technical failure ('inability to draw up adequate sectoral plans') for which they prescribe technical assistance is in fact a political failure. Priorities in development or clashes between ministries over policies or for resources are all too rarely resolved in Kenya by Cabinet decision. Cabinet meetings for that kind of business are rare. A sub-committee of the Cabinet, the Development Committee, used to fulfil the role but it was wound up in 1967 and its replacement, the Committee of Economic Ministers, has failed to fill the gap. Hence some political decisions are taken at administrative level and more are not taken at all. If a powerful Permanent Secretary does not like a policy, he may simply not implement it, unless it is one of those few policies handed down by the President, as for example, when he announced free primary education. The announcement, made without consultation, held up the publication of the Development Plan while it was hastily written into the section on education. The announcement was interpreted so as to water it down and restrict it to the first four years, but it still left the Treasury wondering where the finance was to come from. No Cabinet decision was taken, however, on what expenditure should be cut to allow the extra spending. Instead some things just failed to happen owing to the Treasury failing to find money for projects in an essentially haphazard way. The same applied, to a lesser extent (some attempt at re-planning was made and given up), to the oil crisis.

This lack of political direction is why the Kenya Treasury does not rank development projects. That, too, is wrongly viewed by some donors as a technical failure. But no government ever really decided on priorities by establishing parameters for cost-benefit analysis of projects in different sectors and then ranking them all by their net present value at a Treasury-determined accounting interest rate. It is true that the Kenya Treasury does not even have an accounting interest rate, but that is the least of its worries. More importantly, it does not have Cabinet decisions saying this ministry's baby before that one. Without that, each ministry is a semi-independent fief of its top officials called to render particular service now and then when the President speaks. And that is why donors can determine collectively much of the shape of the government investment programme. Technical assistance cannot solve this basic problem and, in fact, may make it worse. It can strengthen the cost-conscious elements in the government who are in favour of rational forward planning on the basis of minimising costs to achieve given ends. But it can lead to a concentration on just that sort of problem at the expense of concentrating on developing agreement on what the ends are. The resulting plans are then just weapons in the battle to decide what the ends are in the absence of inter-ministerial agreement. The battle is fought within the Kenyan administration with project plans, unilateral policy statements, promises of financial aid from donors, and appeals to public opinion (the last being the particular trump card of the Ministry of Education). Some observers claim, of course, that technical assistance is not supposed to help but to make it even easier for donors to control recipient government policies. That is not true of British aid at any rate. As noted, there is no contact between ODM and technical assistance personnel, and while the British are more permissive about supply of personnel under SCAAP than they are about capital aid, they are relatively diffident about thrusting them at Kenya.

It is clear that ldcs, including Kenya, have an absorptive capacity for technical assistance that is as limited as that for finance. The fact is not widely realised because, unlike finance, the technical assistance is taken up whether it can be usefully employed or not, if the recipient thinks doing so is a condition for receiving more capital aid. We believe technical assistance is at saturation point in the planning nexus of the Kenya government. It may be so in other areas too.

While one can guess that, at the margin, any shift in the supply of technical assistance should be down rather than up, it is almost impossible to generalise validly about the overall impact of technical assistance on the Kenya administration at the present time. We should guess it is positive and to advocate dispensing with all of it would be pushing the baby down the plughole in advance of the water. That was certainly true at independence, though probably much less so now. At any rate, the ODM policy of introducing a manpower review and seeking to scale down OSAS commitments is timely. ODM's relative forbearance in the matter of proposing technical assistance projects to the Kenyans is also to be applauded. Indeed, there is still a case for offering assistance with specific technical skills to do specific work in the preparation of specific projects on a short-term basis. There can rarely be a case for offering anything other than that. When donors do offer technical assistance to an operational ministry, there are two different procedures for the offer to be accepted. In the case of wholly-funded personnel – in the British case, advisers supplied under the SCAAP agreement – the request goes to the appropriate division in the Ministry of Finance and Planning for appraisal. In the case of partly-funded personnel who will have an established post in the Kenya civil service – in the British case OSAS personnel – the application goes to the Directorate of Personnel.[46] This control, however, is partly annulled by donor practices in extending capital aid.

It is easier to generalise about the effects of capital aid on the Kenya administration. On balance, the effects have been bad, but the British again have been less guilty than most other donors. In principle, requests for a budgetary allocation for a new project or any sort of financial request are supposed to be forwarded in the first place from an operational ministry to the Ministry of Finance and Planning. New projects are supposed to go to the Planning Division and routine matters to the Finance Division. Proposals should be considered by the Estimates Working Group which has both Treasury and Planning representatives. The External Aid Division are also represented, as are people from the operational ministry, on the Group. If a project is passed by the Estimates Working Group, it is included in the operational ministry's budget and then sent to the External Aid Division for a donor to be found. Otherwise, it may be rejected or referred back. When the Plan is being written, Development Plan working groups deal with sectoral plans as the Estimates Working Group does with projects. So much for the theory. In practice, operational ministries after initial talks with a donor, at which the Treasury may or may not be represented, often pass proposals to the External Aid Division for forwarding 'officially' to the donor without the Planning Division being told at all. This means there is not even an adequate central projects registry. The project planning unit at the Ministry of Finance and Planning (supported as a technical assistance project by the Canadians) has no procedure even to be informed as to what projects are in prospect.

Once the donor has agreed funds it becomes very hard for the Treasury to refuse a budgetary allocation for the project, which is a *fait accompli*. There is a rule that Treasury officers should always be present for negotiations on revenue and finance between an operational ministry and the donor. Even if this obligation is carried out, there is no ruling that Treasury representatives have to be present for technical talks. More-or-less technical talks may be the important early ones, however. In any case, the technical talks always have enormous implications for finance. This is a situation in which the Treasury finds it extremely difficult to exert any inter-sectoral control. In order to be able to meet obligations which it may be confronted with, the Treasury is reluctant to make a budgetary allocation for any project unless there is a prospective donor. Donors therefore not only have enormous influence, as noted, on the inter-sectoral balance of Kenya development spending, they also undermine the functions of the Treasury and Planning Division. Operational ministries do not have to go to the Treasury and compete for funds on any rational basis. If they try that, however technically good a project may be, they are unlikely to get a cent. The first step therefore is usually to find a donor.

As we noted in Chapter Four, the British scrupulously attempted to follow the procedures of always dealing with the External Aid Division of the Treasury, with the effect that their disbursements were very slow. Now they are increasingly making more informal contacts with operational ministries. That is understandable, and it is difficult to see what else to do if one wants to spend money. Some donors confine themselves to making approaches on the basis of the Development Plan, but others, such as the USAID, do not even so confine themselves.[47] The situation has led to a condition among Kenya bureaucrats satirically referred to as aid-happiness. Sufferers from the condition may be recognised from their habit of approaching their ministerial tasks not with the question, what needs to be done, but with the question, what can we get aid for?

The answer tends to be for something big. All donors prefer to support large projects if only because of the saving on administrative overheads that implies. This preference generates the need for more technical assistance.[48] It is largely beyond the capacity of the Kenya administration to assemble and present data to justify many very large projects. Consultants or technical assistance teams have to be used, and there is no question of these people having local counterparts – an example is the British technical assistance team largely staffing the Tana River Development Authority. The Kenya government machine can cope reasonably well with small projects. That is clearly shown by the fact that the aid it has such trouble getting through is only 12-15 per cent of total government spending. Some 35 per cent of the projects in the current Development Budget are of less than £50,000 and include most of the wholly-Kenyan ones. Fewer than a quarter cost more than £0.25m. In this area, too, the British used to be more flexible than other donors and were prepared to finance very small projects but that is no longer so.

Capital aid has therefore had deleterious effects on Kenyan administration by undermining central control of the development budgets of operational ministries. The accent on large discrete projects has put the staff of these ministries under a burden which they cannot bear and led to a greater felt need for technical assistance. While central control of applications for technical assistance is tighter, the need for it, to which the centre accedes, is a result partly of the desire of donors to spend capital aid on large projects, and partly of the desire of the Kenyans to receive foreign exchange. In fairness we must repeat here an observation of Chapter Four that Kenyan civil servants in the Treasury do not seem too concerned about the pattern that has evolved. Donors remove the need for them to make choices in the absence of political leadership, and the procedure facilitates the spending of money. Our judgement, however, is that the situation is regrettable.

Political Economy

The way that aid has weakened the Kenya administration and has resulted, in effect, in the organisation of the investment budget by aid donors, has been possible only because there has been a lack of political leadership for development in Kenya. Some donors, including ODM, would be happy to see such leadership, and indeed some ODM practices in the past have been based on the incorrect assumption that it existed. This leads to the question, whatever aid agency professionals believe, does aid have any effect on the political nature of the Kenya government? In weighing the probabilities we shall describe briefly Kenya's political system.

Formally, this is one of parliamentary democracy. There is only one political party, but there are no laws under the Constitution against the formation of others, although they must be registered under the Societies Act which gives considerable discretionary powers to the government. There are few restrictions on citizens joining the existing party, KANU, and standing as parliamentary candidates. The House of Assembly and the British House of Commons work similarly, in theory, in retaining financial control of government expenditure, and the executive is supposed to retain the support of the majority in Parliament to pass legislation and indeed to remain in office. The President is elected by universal adult suffrage directly, but he must also be a member of Parliament to which he must be elected in the usual way. At least one textbook writer has stated[49] that this formal political system is in fact subordinate to the bureaucracy in Kenya. Governmental control is exercised and policy executed through the provincial administrations, directly responsible to the Office of the President. The influence of the political party, KANU, and its functionaries is not great and neither is that of the typical back-bench MP. While the system has democratic elements, therefore, it is sometimes represented as being managerial or bureaucratic with the collective interests of the bureaucracy as a class being most influential in the running of the country. Certainly a number of senior and, more especially, middle-level civil servants to whom we spoke declared that the civil service was running the country, that there was a lack of strong political direction and influence. The view was expressed that this may be no bad thing. The bureaucracy was interested in efficient management for development rather than the demagogic considerations that influenced politicians and furthermore it had, if not a monpoly, at least much of the management expertise available in Kenya.

We must stress that in our view this picture is inaccurate and does not adequately describe the situation in Kenya. The formal political system may appear to lack power if not animation, but as in many, perhaps most, countries, the loci of political power are not what a study of the Constitution or of textbooks would lead an observer to expect. In fact what might be termed political considerations, as opposed to managerial ones, are dominant in the running of many departments of state and in the allocation of economic resources except, partly, those that are allocated in the development budget. This is so although critical decisions are not made as part of the operation of the formal political system.

There is an identifiable power elite in Kenya. It is grouped around the person and authority of the President and members of the Kikuyu ethnic group are prominent in it.[50] The President enjoys widespread authority in Kenya both for his symbolic role in the independence struggle, and because subsequently he has come to represent national unity in a society with strong centrifugal tendencies. Nevertheless one important basis of his political power and that of his attendant power elite is ethnic. Kenya is a plural society with considerable regional and tribal loyalties and rivalries. In the past, leaders of clans have been able to maintain their position by appeals to clan solidarity in the face of the rivalry of other groups. The position of such ethnic leaders in the Kenyan power elite is now enormously reinforced by the group's access to the resources of the state. Political supporters can be rewarded and opponents deprived. The importance of the bureaucracy in distributing resources also means that tribalism cannot be dismissed as false consciousness. It really does help if members of one's clan are on the selection committee, so it is in one's interests to keep them there. The elite's position has depended therefore on a combination of presidential prestige, traditional authority, ethnic solidarity and the power of patronage. Outright coercion and, many believe, occasional assassination have been employed as well as electoral malpractices – certain candidates are prevented from standing or, if allowed to stand, from holding meetings. Overt repression has, however, been rare in Kenya compared to many European and most African states. Obviously it may be that the relative importance of these different pillars is shifting, and that a distinct socio-economic class is emerging under the umbrella of the regime, whose loyalty has been cemented by patronage and who are losing any autonomous tribal base. The general perception, however, remains that Kenya is still a reasonably, if precariously, liberal society, and the Kikuyu as an ethnic group have a dominant importance in the system.

The reasons for this eminence have been discussed by other writers.[51] In maintaining their position in the polity as a whole, the Kikuyu hierarchy employ similar means to those used in the intra-tribal context. Coalitions are made with acknowledged leaders of other tribal groups. Some of the Kalenjin have recently been in a coalition with the ruling Kikuyu against more disaffected groups such as the Luo. The line-up was different at independence with the Luo and Kikuyu in alliance in KANU against the other, mostly smaller, tribes of KADU.[52] The coalitions are dynamic, and there are tensions and shifting allegiances even within the Kikuyu. Tribal allies are cemented to the elite by the power of a patronage that is both personal and collective. Certain government expenditures can be directed to the areas that are the natural constituency of the allied leaders, thus establishing their value as political leaders by demonstrating their own, derived, power of patronage. And opportunities are afforded to them to thrive in business via the direction of both private and public money.

While there may well be an elite group which holds general political views or at least loyalties based on common economic interests, it does not seem that this class consciousness has spread to the people as a whole, with the possible exception only of some unionised urban workers.[53] Certainly people do not vote for politicians to represent distinct views on economics and politics, and the government does not consist necessarily of people with very similar views on matters of economic and social policy. Politics in Kenya is not about policies at all in that sense. At the grass-roots level groups still identify themselves on the basis of tribal parochial affiliation rather than economic or class interest and they vote for the people who will maximise their access to the pork barrel – certain resources at the disposal of the state. This is demonstrated by the nature of the appeal that politicians attempted to exert in the 1974 elections.[54] It is probably inevitable for two reasons. One is the ethnically heterogeneous nature of Kenyan society; the other is the uninformed position of the general public about what can be expected of the quality of government services. For example, the electorate does not vote for the man with the most persuasive transport or education policy and hope to enjoy its share of the fruits of a national improvement; it has no views on such matters. It votes for the man most likely to get a road or a school for its particular constituency. It scarcely matters whether the road is the best possible, or what the examination pass rate of the school is. People in general have few expectations on such matters and are unaware of the possibilities for improving the quality of the contents of the pork barrel. They are simply concerned that their man should bring home his share of the bacon. The power of grass-roots aspirations is often considerable, as shown by the growth of the *Harambee* movement. In some areas, and education is the most obvious, the peasants make themselves felt and the centre has to make provision for their feelings. In general, however, political power in Kenya runs largely downwards, from the President and that group of people who have his ear or who are very important in the intra- and inter-tribal balancing act.

To describe the system is to reveal immediately that there are considerable 'political' constraints on planning or the rational allocation of economic resources to maximise some objective function such as the growth of GNP per head.[55] Actors and agents in the informal (but real) political system, and their political constituencies, have to get their pay-off. Leaders of important marginal tribal groups have to be given positions of access to certain state resources (ministries etc.) if stability is to be preserved. Such claims take precedence and any 'economic' plan that ignores them is waste paper.

This raises the question of what, apart from maintaining and strengthening this *status quo*, are the objectives of the power elite. The answer is that they appear to have few apart from the desire to accumulate wealth. The wealth accumulation by prominent people is a matter of near public comment.[56] The Ndegwa Report[57] merely legitimised an existing situation in which senior civil servants devoted considerable time and energy to the development of their personal business interests. In case this appears to be painting too dark a picture, it should be stressed that the system has the virtues of its defects. There is no overwhelming politicisation of Kenyan life. Kenyan society is relatively liberal and has enjoyed, for example, significant freedom of speech. Indeed, those civil servants who, out of *esprit de corps*, wish to plan for rapid economic development are free to do so. As we have pointed out, there is not much political dynamism in support of many of their efforts, but as long as these are not inconsistent with the political balancing act and the desire of the elite to accumulate wealth, and as long as they do not require much co-ordination between ministries, they can, and do, go ahead.

The extent to which 'rational' development planning is possible in a ministry depends on the political importance of the ministry's services. Education and land are the most coveted commodities in Kenya, and this is reflected in the course of educational policy and land adjudication, which both have their own dynamic. On the other hand, with the replacement of large-scale expatriate farmers by African small holders, the services of the Ministry of Agriculture have become less valued (though not less valuable). Consequently, the Ministry has declined in both influence and efficiency. Politically less important ministries are much more open to donor influence, which is expressed largely by the pattern of development expenditure.

It should not be assumed that the importance of a ministry is adequately indicated by the apparent prestige and power of the Minister. The Kenyan elite spreads across the conventional lines separating the formal politician from the bureaucrat. And the political operator and disinterested administrator may be the same person at different times. The Minister or civil servant who attempts, via a Cabinet or Civil Service Committee, to restrict the expenditure of, say, the Ministry of Works, in the interests of optimal allocation of resources, may be the same man who pulls strings in the informal political system to get a tar road built in his 'constituency' or just past his front door.[58]

This is clearly a system in which inequalities of wealth and of access to the means of wealth – political office, credit, land and education – are not likely to diminish and may well grow. Up to now, however, sufficient material improvement has been diffused through the system to maintain its stability without comprehensive repression, despite plenty of grumbling by out-groups. As long as the elite does not become too acquisitive, but allows some resources to flow to areas where it has no direct interest, this may persist, although many people have expressed fears that acquisitiveness has become too conspicuous and, once the personal charismatic authority of the President is removed by his death, the system will have lost a possibly critical stabilising factor. An increase in obvious acquisitiveness and a crackdown on parliamentary opponents of the regime have occurred recently.[59] Some academic opponents of the Kenya regime have, for some time, prophesied increased repression by the Kenya government as a tendency somehow inherent in the system, although there has been less repression in the past than in most surrounding states. Recent developments may still simply reflect the ageing of the President and an attempt by his immediate associates to secure the succession.

The attitude of the main Western donor nations to the system in general has been largely predictable. They have had no quarrel with it. It has provided a stable climate in which foreign commercial enterprises may prosper. It is true that the foreign manufacturer may be pressured into appointing a Kikuyu wholesaler rather than a Kenyan of his choice, and he may have to pay to get favourable decisions out of civil servants about regulations that affect his business. Businessmen, however, are used to dealing with the price system and this is just another form of corporation tax. From an elite dedicated to the acquisition of private wealth, talk of nationalisation and expropriation is not to be feared.[60] Indeed, foreign enterprise is to be welcomed for the additional resources it brings in and 'taxes' it can pay.

So far, we do not think many observers would quarrel with this account. Disagreement arises about whether the situation is to be regarded as exceptionally bad, what are the reasons for it, and what is to be done. Marxists will be inclined to see this situation as arising from the machinations of international capitalism and to view the Kenyan elite as its creatures.[61] There is in fact little evidence for this. Britain, for example, had few expectations of an independent Kenya and foreign investment fell heavily after independence. The KANU government was allowed to take office as the only group that seemed likely to command popular support and maintain some kind of stability. Little more was expected of it. The causal origins of the individualistic acquisitive ethic evinced by the Kikuyu elite today are doubtless complex. We are not competent to say what are the relative importances of colonialism and longer-lived indigenous cultural factors in its development. It may, however, be a form of inverted racialism to assume that every attitude evinced by an African government is the responsibility of white men.

Kenya does not occupy at present a militarily strategic position, nor are there scarce resources of vital minerals there. The effort which an optimising exploiter would put into keeping his heel on the country's neck would be strictly limited. Because 'international capitalism' takes advantage of a situation and donor states support it, we cannot conclude that it was created by external agencies. Furthermore, if as seems likely, the system has indigenous roots, it is not clear that aid donors are wrong to support it, even though it is a highly imperfect system. In supporting it, in fact, donors may be able to effect marginal improvements. The widespread support of donors for ILO-type proposals and the Kenya *Sessional Paper on Employment* suggests now that donors may be aware of possible limits to the system's stability and be concerned to broaden the base and legitimacy of the present elite by pressing for a more equal distribution of benefits. In so far as the Kenya elite does not keep pace with donor wishes in this regard, it appears that it is unable to transcend the short-run claims on resources described above in the interests of a securer future. In assessing the 'whiggish' approach of donors (which no doubt is in some donor country interests too), the crucial question is: what is the most likely alternative to the *status quo*? It would be nice to think it was an egalitarian commonwealth of free and progressive people (then donors could be condemned for postponing this consummation), but we find it difficult to believe that. If the pork barrel were smaller, the existing system might be less stable. But inspection of the regimes of poor, ethnically divided countries turns up few model democracies. Whatever the most probable alternative to a relatively liberal ethnically-based plutocracy in Kenya is, there seems little reason to assume that it would be an improvement.

Conclusion: Incomes and Income Equality

Aid has constituted a flow of resources to Kenya, and nothing that we have seen leads us to reject the common-sense conclusion that it has raised incomes in the country. One effect almost certainly was to release resources for the private sector that might otherwise have been obtained from a private capital inflow, but any such substitution was probably small. It is more probable that private investment would have been lower without aid. In some pathological cases of over-protection of industry that might have been a good thing, but, in general, investment must have increased domestic value added. Alternative patterns of industrialisation might be more appropriate but (if sugar is anything to go by) one cannot be confident that they would have evolved in the absence of foreign investment.

The activities of government, boosted by aid, have also by and large raised incomes via the provision of infrastructure and productive and social services. In the long run aid has perhaps been less effective in raising income than it might have been, by causing the government to emphasise discrete expenditures at the expense of recurrent ones and large expenditures at the expense of small. Having induced this bias, however, some donors, including ODM, have resisted some of its worse effects by scrutinising applications for projects and attempting to resist grandiosity.

ODM has kept up with current thinking in development. Obviously it would be unreasonable to blame an agency for not thinking more about appropriate technology and rural development in the intellectual climate of the early 1960s. Once a view has taken hold, however, ODM attempts to apply it in a fairly disinterested way. The sectoral preferences it has shown have by and large been appropriate therefore, as far as anyone can tell. In so far as they have been shared with other donors, they have had an effect on the pattern of public investment in Kenya. In general the sectoral preferences of the majority of donors now correspond with those of what we regard as the more enlightened and progressive elements in the Kenyan administration, so their influence is not bad in this particular. The techniques of giving capital aid, however, have weakened central control and the need for consensus in the Kenyan administration, and the benefits of technical assistance, while once overwhelmingly important, may no longer be making up for this. Aid as a contribution to resources may make some marginal continuing contribution to political stability, although we doubt it. The provision of large numbers of OSAS personnel in the early years of independence and the Land Transfer Programme did assist political continuity – the Land Programme not because the Kenya government could not have paid for the land without the capital sums (we believe it could, and indeed should, though at somewhat lower prices) but because it might not in fact have done so. That a different Kenya government might have been instrumental in raising its people's incomes on average by much more (or much less) than has occurred is pure supposition. Comparing Kenya's flawed and unequal progress to the continental average the best guess is perhaps that another government would have done worse.

Aid has probably increased economic inequality among Kenyans. It has done so partly as a simple by-product of raising incomes. In releasing resources for modern sector development, aid probably caused a relatively few highly-paid jobs to be created, so increasing inequality. All three of the projects we looked at in Chapter Five also had such an effect. The Land Transfer Programme financed by Britain transferred large areas of mixed farming land from European to African ownership. The land was sold to the new owners; it was not distributed free to the poorest of the poor, though the *Haraka* settlement might be thought to fall into this category. The benefits of this programme accrued to a minority (though large in absolute terms), and not a minority composed of the poorest. The benefits of the acquisition of land were multiplied by the large input of agricultural extension and other services into the settlement schemes, which had its origin in the plans of the colonial government to create a class of substantial small farmers. Britain may be thought, therefore, to have some responsibility for the growth in inequality among the African population that has resulted from the Land Transfer Programme. From another point of view, of course, land transfer must substantially have reduced inequality, because the numerically few European farmers were in general far richer than the numerous Africans to whom the land was transferred. It is to be remembered, in this connection, that half of the aid provided for land transfer was for settlement schemes, that is, for the subdivision of farms, and therefore must have financed the redistribution of wealth in an egalitarian direction. In addition to this form of land transfer, large farms have been transferred from Europeans to Africans as going concerns. This form of transfer may not greatly have affected the overall distribution of wealth, Africans having replaced Europeans, but it undoubtedly increased the inequality within the African community. Although it could be argued that British aid was not directly involved with most of these transfers, and cannot therefore be held directly responsible for their effects on the distribution of wealth, British aid provided funds for the Agricultural Finance Corporation and the Agricultural Development Corporation, which have been involved in the transfer of large farms. It could, of course, also be argued that the settlement schemes took the steam out of what would otherwise have developed into an irresistible movement for the seizure of land by the landless, and so made possible the transfer of other European farms to a new class of African large land-owners. It is not implausible that without substantial small-scale settlement, the remaining large farms could not have been kept intact, so that the maintenance of large farms in private ownership was dependent on the settlement programme. But although the absence of aid might very likely have meant that the farms were not purchased for settlement, in the way that they were in fact purchased, it would not necessarily have prevented the operation of enough settlement to take the steam out of the demands of the landless, and to enable some large farms to be transferred intact to would-be African large land-owners, so long as it was the policy of the Kenya government to encourage such large-scale farming. We have found no evidence to suggest that this policy is pursued by the Kenya government as a result of leverage exerted by Britain, or that the Kenya government would have discouraged large landholdings by Africans in the absence of aid for land transfer for settlement schemes. The interests of the rich and powerful in large-scale farming are too great to suggest that such a difference in policy was probable.

Of course, the maintenance of conditions under which the continuation of a private large-farm sector was possible is seen by some as the major beneficial contribution of aid to Kenya. The maintenance of 'law and order' and the absence of the disorderly and violent seizure of land could be considered as the great achievement of the Land Transfer Programme.

Our view is somewhat different, because we do not believe that settlement in much the same way as that undertaken would have been impossible without capital aid for land transfer. However, the purchase of the land, instead of a more or less open dispossession of the European farmers, as well as maintaining the productivity of the large-farm sector, is also likely to have had favourable effects on Kenya's international image and on her attractiveness for foreign business and investment. Nor do we think that a breakdown of law and order, if it had occurred, even though in the process of an egalitarian redistribution of land, would have been to the benefit of the poor and unprivileged.

In summary, then, it is our view that aid for land transfer and settlement can be criticised for contributing indirectly to the growth of inequality, by one who attaches little weight to the absence of major civil disorder and who sees no disadvantage in the creation of an economic and political climate which international business finds unfavourable. For those who rate the absence of violence highly, and who believe that it is possible (though not inevitable) for a poor country to benefit from the operations of international business, the indirect influence of British aid on the degree of inequality in Kenya may be seen as the price to be paid for other benefits.

The discussion of the Mumias Sugar Scheme in Chapter Five drew attention to the inequalities it has generated within the African population of the area. Those who were in a position, because of the location of their land, to be enrolled as outgrowers gained very greatly in income. The benefits have not so far spilled over very much to those who were unable to enrol, or who did not obtain wage employment with the company or with outgrowers. The gains were in the nature of an economic rent, unrelated to the supply price of the factors of production contributed by the outgrowers, who were protected by the structure of the scheme from the competitive erosion and wider distribution of their rents. It is certain, however, that with the further development of sugar-processing capacity the benefits will be spread more widely, and the inequities in that sense will diminish. It was suggested in Chapter Five that a differently designed scheme might have been practicable, which would have spread the benefits more widely from the start. But it was not the fact of aid that led to the problems of the scheme in the form in which it was introduced, let alone the fact of British aid. Indeed, a purely commercial scheme would have emphasised estate production more. Mumias is another scheme that would have been undertaken by some other donor, or even without aid, if Britain had stood aside. A design which might have led to a wider distribution of the benefits might have been possible if the Kenya government had been clear on what should have been done differently, and had insisted on such changes in the scheme. But it does not appear that the form of the scheme adopted reflected the intention of the Kenya government, the donors, or the commercial interests, deliberately to neglect the adverse distributional effects in their own interest. The scheme was innovational in its use of outgrowers to supply cane. It is not surprising, therefore, that it was desired to limit risks by supervising outgrowers closely and by adopting familiar, well-tried methods in other elements of the scheme, which would be easier to implement (and more certain of success) than if these also required new ideas, adaptation and experiment. It is easy enough to see, with hindsight, that a more beneficial scheme might have been implemented. A repetition of Mumias, without detailed examination of alternatives having more widespread benefits, could be more open to criticism, though investigation might well reveal that a Mumias-type scheme was best.

An examination of other British-aided projects leads to much the same conclusion about their effect on inequality. The improvement of the Mombasa-Nairobi road, with the replacement of the gravel surface by tarmac, carried out partly with British aid funds, had several disequalising effects within Kenya, as well as knocking a nail into the coffin of East African Railways. It did benefit the rich, who were able in consequence to drive in comfort and speed between Nairobi and the Coast. In fact, the expectation of this benefit was the main reason for the high priority given to the improvement by the Kenya government. The improvement made the transport of petroleum products by road feasible and, with the relaxation of licensing restrictions, opened opportunities for highly profitable investment in bulk-haulage vehicles by a few Kenyans. In these respects, the investment distinctly added to inequalities. But petroleum products were the railway's most profitable traffic, and the diminution of these profits as a result of road competition probably added further to inequalities by shifting the burden of charges on to goods consumed to a relatively greater extent by the poor. On the other hand, it must not be assumed that only the rich travel on the road; although the benefits of lower operating costs may not have been passed on to the passengers, the bus and taxi services between Nairobi and the Coast, much used by passengers of only modest means, must not be neglected. The improvement of the road did not benefit only the rich. And if it did, can aid be blamed? In this case, the availability of aid certainly did not divert resources from other projects which would have had beneficial effects on the distribution of income and wealth. In fact, the fungibility of the aid may have resulted in the financing of some project that could be judged as more socially beneficial than the road which was nominally financed. The improvement of the road was given high priority in high places in Kenya, and it is unlikely that it would have long remained unimproved, whatever the attitude of Britain and other donors. One might speculate on whether refusal of all aid from a large donor such as Britain – or perhaps the World Bank – if the project were carried out, might have deterred the Kenyans. But it was hardly so bad a project as to justify such extreme leverage; and in many ways it looked a very good project to aid donors at a time when more attention was being given to such easily planned and executed projects as trunk roads than is, in theory, now fashionable.

It is not only British aid projects which have contributed to inequality. Studies of other aid projects in Kenya have arrived at similar conclusions. An account of a Swedish artificial insemination programme showed that it benefited more progressive farmers, increasing their milk output, to the relative disadvantage of others.[62] A study of the industrial estates programme supported by West German aid[63] showed that the estates mostly benefited established industrialists, by subsidising their inputs, and failed to induce new entrepreneurs into operation.

We do not know what the effect would have been on income distribution if the Kenya government had spent more on maintaining existing projects and less on new ones, or, not knowing aid was correlated with bigness in projects, had gone in for smaller projects. Much depends, of course, on the details of what expenditure would have been incurred and that is unknowable. There must be some presupposition, however, that a large project is worse for income distribution than a number of small ones. An exception might be if the large project is in fact a programme consisting of many linked small projects. It is only recently, however, that donors have moved to such a concept. Whether one considers that aid is a force for inequality, above that which is inherent in growth, probably depends on the date at which aid is considered. It may be that aid was a force for inequality for the first ten years of independence and cemented the Kenya administration into certain practices. Now enlightened donors, by pushing rural development, may be a force for equality.

What has aid done for dependence? It depends whether integration into world trade counts as dependence or not. If so, CDC by increasing tea production has increased dependence while by increasing sugar production ODM has reduced it. In both cases there was considerable initial but subsequently declining dependence on outside experts. Clearly the dependence consideration can rapidly degenerate into semantics. For example by providing experts for the Tana River Development Authority, ODM may be bringing nearer a hydro-electric development that will substantially reduce Kenya's dependence on foreign oil. The authority itself, if the scheme comes to fruition, will undoubtedly have to be run largely by foreigners for the foreseeable future, this perhaps being one of those schemes that are worth undertaking although any conceivable technology for them is 'inappropriate'. Is this a net increase in dependence or not?

Perhaps increasing dependence could be defined as a situation in which a country becomes more dependent on the outside world at any level of income per head. That would appear to be a bad thing. One can, if one chooses, however, call dependence a situation in which a country becomes more dependent on the outside world (through, for example, trade specialisation) but income per head is increasing. That situation, however, which may apply to Kenya, cannot be inferred to be worse without further value judgements. It is a situation in which one can trade off one desideratum against another. Field Marshal Amin has made one choice and the Kenya government, hitherto, has made another.

Notes

1. See Chapter Three for an attempt to arrive at the true value of procurement-tied aid.
2. Consider two donors who prefer project A to project B. If donor one finances project A, he pre-empts donor two and pushes the latter's funds into project B. If we hold, with some, that donor one has therefore effectively financed project B, what has donor two financed? We are forced to conclude that they both effectively financed B and no one effectively financed A.
3. An exception might be where there is an historical causal connection, so the recipient Treasury was poised to give the go-ahead to some project as soon as a donor could be found to finance some other project. The marginal project was just waiting for the marginal donor. However this is unrealistic as the common scenario.
4. 'Project' is used loosely here – it encompasses any clearly defined expenditure or reduction in government receipts.
5. Perhaps the only way would be to find a project that required no counterpart funds from the recipient and no administrative input by the recipient, and was regarded by the recipient as so worthless that it did not affect his resource mobilisation or preference-ordering of other projects. That does not sound like a recipe for a successful project. There may be an iron law here: the more dissimilar are the preferences of donor and recipient, the more likely is project-tying to get a genuine addition to the expenditure-stream but the more likely is the recipient to arrange offsetting changes in his priorities and, anyway, the less likely is the project to be made to work well.
6. There is no reason in general to expect shunting to be worse than shuffling. Suppose, for example, the recipient wants to undertake projects 1 to 4 but can finance only three of them. The donor insists on financing project 5, regarded by the recipient as a substitute for 2. Consequently the recipient undertakes projects 1, 3, 4 and 5. We know the donor prefers 5 to 4 but we do not know that he prefers the above line-up to 1, 2, 3, 4.
7. See p. 185.
8. P. S. Heller, 'A Model of Public Fiscal Behavior in Developing Countries: Aid, Investment and Taxation', *American Economic Review*, Vol. 65, No. 3, June 1975.
9. Specifically, Heller estimates three structural equations of his model by two-stage least squares, but estimates of the co-efficients in one equation have to be used to construct variables in the other equations – and the estimates have large standard errors. Furthermore estimations of the three equations give structural parameters of the model, but to find the effects of aid, treated as exogenous, Heller needs to know the value of the co-efficients of the reduced form equations of the model (i.e. the equations expressing the endogenous variables as functions of exogenous variables only). These co-efficients are obviously functions of the structural parameters and are derived algebraically from them. Such derived co-efficients, however, would obviously have larger standard errors than the parameters directly estimated. Although this is much

the best attempt to date to estimate the effects of aid econometrically, therefore, the results are suggestive at most.

10. The countries were: Nigeria, Ghana, Kenya, Uganda, Tanzania, Malawi, Liberia and Ethiopia. The data were pooled cross-section and time series for the post-independence period. Whether Kenya differed significantly from the average could be ascertained by omitting it from the sample and conducting a 'Chow' test to see whether parameters changed. This was not done in view of the problems of the methods already noted.
11. This would tend to reduce the money supply, which, however, rose owing to secondary credit expansion by the banks and the effect of the balance of payments surplus.
12. Kenya government, *Economic Survey 1974*, p. 166.
13. *Development Plan 1974-78*, Nairobi, Government Printer, pp. 178 and 182.
14. D. Ndegwa (Governor), *Central Bank of Kenya 7th Annual Report* (year ending 30 June 1973), p. 63.
15. See 'Tribulations of an African Tycoon', *Financial Times*, London, 10 April 1974.
16. B. Herman, 'Some Basic Data for Analysing the Political Economy of Foreign Investment in Kenya', IDS Discussion Paper No. 112, Nairobi, 1971, mimeo.
17. There was a single exception – a short-lived Rhodesian firm.
18. The principal banks are Standard, Barclays, and the Kenya Commercial Bank, owned 60 per cent by the government and 40 per cent by the National Grindlays group. In 1973 these three banks held over 80 per cent of bank deposits in Kenya.
19. V. Diejomoah, 'Taxation and Government Savings in Kenya', *Eastern Africa Economic Review*, Vol. 2, No. 2, December 1970.
20. International Labour Office, *Employment, Incomes and Equality: A Strategy for Increasing Productive Employment in Kenya*, Geneva, 1971, p. 272.
21. *Development Plan 1974-78*, op. cit., p. 25.
22. The advantage of taxing luxury goods is not simply equity but having an income elasticity of more than one, the goods should yield a tax revenue growing faster than personal disposable income.
23. British American Tobacco and East African Breweries, respectively.
24. *Republic of Kenya Development Estimates 1974/75*, p. (i).
25. Heller, op. cit. For a marginal aid tranche, Heller calculated that 18 per cent of it went to increased government expenditure, but that was made up of an increase in investment of 34 per cent of the tranche and reductions in consumption of 16 per cent.
26. See note 9, p. 228.
27. See Chapter Four, pp. 88-9, and note 26, p. 102.
28. Chapter Four, p. 88 and Chapter Five, Part 3, p. 167.
29. See p. 93.
30. P. S. Heller, 'Public Investment in LDCs with Recurrent Cost Constraint: The Kenyan Case', *Quarterly Journal of Economics*, Vol. 88, May 1974.
31. See Chapter Five, Part Three.
32. The Office of the President received some aid for SRDP personnel attached to it.
33. E.g. over Mumias, see Chapter Five, Part Two, pp. 147-8.
34. Almost all the firms asked for their anonymity to be preserved.
35. Hybrids usually outyield local maize by 40 per cent at least. If the 786,000 acres under hybrids in 1973 had been under local maize, production would have been down by about 2.6m. bags. Over the period 1963-73 hybrids have increased maize output by over 11m. bags. Without this development Kenya could have had severe food shortages in some years.
36. In fertiliser manufacture, for example. See *Development Plan 1974-78*, pp. 26-8.

37. Ibid., p. 6, para. 1.20.
38. Volunteers have, however, taught in such schools.
39. An example is a letter to *The Nation* headlined 'A backward step indeed', published 11 October 1974.
40. ILO, op. cit., Chapter 14 and pp. 517-28.
41. Law and order is a phrase sometimes used euphemistically by those in power when submission to unjust authority is what is really meant. The usage is reprehensible but the concept is not. Law and order is not sufficient for development, but it is quite certainly necessary.
42. M. L. O. Faber and D. Seers (eds.), *The Crisis in Planning*, London, Chatto and Windus, 1972, Part II, p. 132.
43. See Chapter Two, p. 36.
44. See Chapter Two, pp. 25-6 and p. 44.
45. Some expatriates do get involved in the hurly burly, take sides on all issues they detect, and proselytise. Our impression is that such people seldom last beyond their first contract period irrespective of the quality of their work.
46. A full description of the system is given by Laxman Bhandari, 'Technical Assistance Administration in Kenya' in *Technical Assistance Administration in East Africa*, Yashpal Tandon (ed.), Stockholm, Almqvist & Wiksell, 1973.
47. USAID attempts to maintain co-ordination by copying all correspondence with an operational ministry to various divisions in the Ministry of Finance and Planning.
48. At the time of writing, the World Bank was attempting to get a team of no fewer than eight expatriates into the Ministry of Agriculture to help them to spend money on large programmes in that sector in accordance with the current IBRD policy.
49. C. Gertzel, *The Politics of Independent Kenya*, London, Heinemann, 1970, especially p. 173; also J. R. Nellis, 'Is the Kenyan Bureaucracy Developmental?', IDS Staff Paper 103, Nairobi.
50. J. R. Nellis, 'The Ethnic Composition of Leading Kenyan Government Positions', *Scandinavian Institute of African Studies*, Research Report No. 24, 1974.
51. Gertzel, op. cit., p. 17. Nellis, IDS, op. cit., pp. 8, 21.
52. Gertzel, op. cit., pp. 9-10, 93-4, 120.
53. At the 1974 election, the General Secretary of the Kenyan TUC stood as a candidate in an urban Nairobi constituency. He could finish no better than third out of six candidates.
54. See 'The kind of MP voters want', by Horace Awori in *Joe, Election Review 1974*. A partial exception is the case of ethnic groups who regard themselves as out-groups, bound to be discriminated against by the government. They can vote for someone who personifies the group consciousness and opposes the government. An example is the support of the Nandi for Mr Seroney, now in detention.
55. See 'Systems Management and the Plan Implementation Process in Kenya' by Michael Chege in *African Review*, November 1973. Chege, in a perceptive article well worth reading, lists a number of presidential decrees obviously made on the basis of 'political' considerations. These decrees are unchallengeable.
56. See *Sunday Times*, London, 17 August 1975.
57. See Chapter Two.
58. Although his ministry had been involved in a struggle with the Ministry of Education to restrict the number of new secondary schools, the Finance Minister, Mr Kibaki, promised his Othaya constituents more such schools when a candidate in the 1974 election – *The Nation*, 29 September 1974.

59. The two most outspoken MPs, Mr Shikuku and Mr Seroney, were detained as a result of their questioning of the circumstances of the death by shooting of Mr J. M. Kariuki, a Kikuyu MP noted for his populist approach to land distribution.
60. Article 75 of the Constitution of Kenya expressly rules out compulsory acquisition without compensation. It is often joked by Kenyans that this will be the last part of the Constitution to be amended.
61. See, for example, Colin Leys, *Underdevelopment in Kenya: The Political Economy of Neo-Colonialism 1964-1971*, London, Heinemann, 1975.
62. M. Radetzki, *Aid and Development: A Handbook for Small Donors*, New York, Praeger Publishers, 1973, pp. 244-51.
63. Deepak Lal, *Appraising Foreign Investment in Developing Countries*, London, Heinemann, 1975, p. 254.

7 POLICY IMPLICATIONS FOR BRITISH AID

Our judgements about a number of issues have appeared in preceding chapters. Here we draw some of them together and bring out the implications for British aid policy in Kenya. How far these implications have validity elsewhere we leave to others' consideration. Our standpoint is that aid should have the purpose of raising incomes in the recipient country with particular emphasis on the incomes of the poorest. Inequality is acceptable in so far as it serves the purpose of raising the absolute level of income of the poorest, but in so far as it fails to do so, it is to be disapproved. Ideally policies should make a state more able to withstand external pressures and less reliant on external support. Sometimes this objective and that of raising material living standards go hand-in-hand but sometimes, we fear, they do not. Then choices have to be made by the legitimate government of the recipient country. In general terms our preference would be to emphasise living standards where people were very poor, but rarely to the point of sacrificing all freedom of action in any particular area of policy. Such general statements are, however, of little use to someone dealing with policy and confronted with specific trade-offs.

In offering policy prescriptions from such a standpoint, we are in effect stating that it is not inconsistent with the notion of development which is dominant in shaping ODM policy. In the past that notion was not clearly articulated and there was no equivalent of the Swedish policy declaration in favour of economic independence and equality. More recently, especially under the past Minister of Overseas Development, Mrs. Judith Hart, an attempt has been made to articulate policy, as in the 1975 White Paper.[1] This indicates a wish to focus aid both on the poorest countries and on the poor within those countries. More details of the ODM consensus can, however, be inferred from conversations with officials and the revealed project and sector preferences of the ministry. It is undeniable that ODM is faced with other non-developmental considerations owing to organisational interests within it and the interests of other government departments, notably the Treasury. However these do not seem to be critical, although they will doubtless continue to modify some decisions.

The attitude of mind into which a professional aid administrator tends to fall is to ask what are the problems of giving aid in any particular case. In Kenya one answer in the past would have been underspending. The next step may then be to say that the great task facing the administrator is to increase disbursement and eliminate underspending. In beginning this study, we too were tempted into that train of thought. On reflection, however, we believe it is a mistake. At the moment, Kenya undoubtedly faces balance of payments difficulties, hence the current ODM programme grant. In the past, however, that was not so and it may not be so in the future. In that case simply spending money is not a priority. More important is to achieve certain specific developmental objectives which entail ensuring that extra money is well spent – if that is possible.

It might be objected that a donor has no right to try to ensure aid is 'well' spent by his own criteria, implicitly putting these above the preferences of a recipient government. We take the view that the donor has such a right because it is his money, but that the recipient government should be equally at liberty to refuse aid offered on conditions it finds unacceptable. Then the donor does not elevate his notion of development above national sovereignty and self-determination, as he is not trying to subvert the recipient government, only offering it a free choice. Clearly, the offer of aid can influence policies but that is not a bad thing in itself.

Unfortunately, things are rarely so clear-cut. Energetic selling of aid, perhaps using known weaknesses of governments as bargaining points, and offering one thing in the guise of something else can look like dealing between two unconstrained parties, but can in fact amount to an infraction of sovereignty. We do not say that is always wrong – some values can take precedence over national sovereignty – but it places a heavy moral responsibility on the aid donor. One which, in general, we think he should be reluctant to bear. No country's motives are entirely unmixed in giving aid, so it is bad to set a precedent that could be used for non-developmental ends, and in any case, uncertainties and ignorance are so great in the area of 'development' that there are narrow limits on the confidence with which opinions should be held and the methods with which they should be advanced.

Our impression is that ODM has stayed well on the right side of the line between having legitimate preferences in the use of its aid and putting illegitimate pressure on a sovereign government. The effort to eliminate underspending will push the ministry nearer to that line, into an area already occupied by other donors. Already technical assistance personnel and donor agencies are too influential in shaping the Kenya government's development budget. Not only is that regrettable in itself, but it also sets up tensions between this aspect of the government's activities and others over which the Kenyans retain full control. Donors in general are more worried about the latter problem than that of Kenyan autonomy, hence the desire to increase the numbers of expatriate planners and to introduce sectoral loans as well as project loans[2] so that the micro-level influence of aid is being promoted from the project to the sector level. There are, of course, several sound reasons for doing this. The extended leverage which donors exert will, on the whole, probably be beneficial to the majority of Kenyans as long as donors continue to favour a moderately egalitarian and rural-oriented growth strategy. It will enable aid to be spent on sectoral programmes which will include many small items of expenditure, getting away from large discrete projects and perhaps increasing the local-cost content of aid disbursements. It may divert Kenyan manpower from detailed appraisal of narrow projects towards broader sectoral planning, which may be a better use of their skills. However, further penetration of the Kenyan administration and an extension of the area it surrenders to donor decision-making will create new tensions and may set up a xenophobic reaction if there is a change of political direction in Kenya.

Many of our suggestions can be seen as attempts to minimise the tension between spending aid, and spending it well, and elbowing excessively the people of the recipient country. Although not without dangers, the move towards sectoral programme support is on balance to be welcomed. It requires, however, a certain forbearance by donors if the dangers of excessive intervention are not be be realised. The aim should be to use leverage not to get an optimal plan from the donor viewpoint, but a self-consistent, feasible and (to the donor) tolerable plan. It is true that Kenyan planning capacity is strained by very large exercises but there comes a point where learning can only be by doing and a willingness by donors to accept slow disbursement and the risk of error is probably in order. The threat of no aid or slow aid should be a goad to the Kenyans to improve their planning and administrative capacity, using foreigners for training if necessary, not a blackmailing point to get them to surrender functions to expatriates. Unfortunately it is difficult for one donor to follow this advice if others do not.

For project aid, if ODM advisers on their travels spot possible projects, this could, of course, be put informally to Kenyan colleagues, but an approach should then be left to them to be routed via the Treasury. As noted, the Rural Development Fund could be viewed favourably because of the possible benefits to project identification from decentralised planning. If approaches for aid coming via the Treasury appear promising but half-baked, it is only realistic for Development Division officials then to have talks with the operational ministry and to assist with a re-submission – keeping all relevant sections of the Treasury informed. An early agreement to help in principle, followed by active involvement, also maximises the micro-level influence of aid over projects. If a great deal of preparatory work is required, consultants could be used or perhaps ODM headquarters staff seconded temporarily, rather than technical assistance personnel being put into the Kenyan ministry. Working with visitors in that way is likely to be at least as instructive for Kenyan officers as having expatriates in to do the work. There may be occasional exceptions to this policy – e.g., for high-technology projects like the Tana River development – but these ought to be extremely rare.

In our view, the whole philosophy of technical assistance ought to be reconsidered. The aim should be to make an input that can be 'amortised' rapidly, but which will continue to yield benefits thereafter. In other words, to achieve not a once and for all improvement in recipient government efficiency which collapses when the assistance is withdrawn, but permanent expansion in the technical capacity of the recipient. The training function of technical assistance personnel (as most of them stress) is therefore the most important aspect of their work. It has not been the only aspect. If the ha'porth of tar needed to complete an invaluable ship is an expatriate, it makes obvious sense to supply him, but twelve years after independence this ought to be a consideration of declining importance. Many things which, in a developed country, a good social democrat would regard as quite properly the function of the state, lie outside the competence of the state machine in a country like Kenya. This might include the setting up and manning of large public corporations to produce marketable goods and services, the provision of welfare services with complex rules for allocation, or certain kinds of centralised planning. Ideally, bureaucratic ambitions should not outstrip bureaucratic competence, and we do not see that it is necessarily a good thing for poor countries' administrations to be in a state of constant or even increasing 'personnel debt'. This can happen if they are encouraged to tackle enterprises by the offer of capital aid and then technical assistance is inserted to try to close the gap between competence and aspiration. Aid should assist the local administration to push at the borders of the currently possible, not provide foreigners to run the border out of sight.

Consequently, we applaud the ODM policy of running down OSAS and we doubt whether there should be any compromise on the issue. ODM's feeling that it is futile to check individual requests for SCAAP personnel is quite understandable. Even here, however, a general policy of scepticism should reign, and the Kenyans might be told that requests for support for training facilities will be looked on more favourably than requests for advisers or operational personnel. In some areas ODM has done this already. One example is an offer to support teacher training facilities while phasing out OSAS teachers.

Many professional skills are in short supply in Kenya. Apart from teachers, there are serious shortages of trained accountants, tax and revenue officers, investment analysts, as well as many sorts of technician. Devising and supporting basic professional training schemes for educated but unspecialised local people should be a top priority. An imaginative attempt in this area was a British Council-sponsored plan for teacher training colleges in the UK to second some of their best staff to Kenyan institutions with perhaps some return facility for Kenyans. Such devices would be preferable to full-time employment of contract personnel to work in Kenya. Sometimes excellent people can be obtained, but often they tend to be either relatively young and inexperienced in their profession, or else to be relatively unsuccessful. Manpower planning reviews should be exercises to identify training needs as much as specific personnel requirements.

The need for training is shown by the fact that while Kenya has a school-leaver unemployment and even an arts graduate unemployment problem, the Kenya government cannot recruit enough middle-level staff. Turnover rates and the 'brain drain' to the private sector are high. Some expatriate advisers believe technical assistance is popular because, net, it is cheaper to the Kenyan government than employing a local man. On this view, if donors untied their technical assistance the Kenya government would recruit more Kenyans, reducing the numbers of foreigners in public sector employment. ODM may be sceptical but then why not try it and see? Just as good, perhaps, would be more training to increase the supply and so perhaps reduce the cost of competent Kenyan administrators and professionals.

The past pattern of technical assistance, whereby an expatriate did a job and had a local 'counterpart' who picked it up from him as he went along, was an attempt to kill two birds with one stone. It bears a strong resemblance to 'apprenticeship' training schemes which have done such incalculable harm to British industry. The competence of the apprentice is postponed by not giving him structured training and, when he has acquired as much competence as he is likely to get without tackling the job himself, doubts about his competence keep him out of it. There is a further parallel: in British industry few want to be apprentices, and the Kenya government does not usually bother to provide counterparts for technical assistance personnel. Both systems thus perpetuate, rather than eliminate, shortages of skills. The invaluable training functions of technical assistance personnel should be discharged more directly at the expense, if need be, of other duties. These other duties are also best confined to the specific and the short-term. As noted, we cannot imagine that Kenya needs more expatriate planners, for example.

Some functions of technical assistance personnel would be better carried out by having more officials in ODM Development Divisions. That is so where technical assistance is given, in effect, to supervise the use of funds and proffer good advice rather than do a specific technical task. Such monitoring, observation and advising is more authoritative coming from a donor operative. That would not look good on paper, of course – reducing output of the aid programme in order to increase its overheads. However, we are sure in many cases – as was true of SRDP – it would pay. We have not studied the structure of ODM as a ministry but it may well be that it could discharge its duties even better with a different balance between overseas and London-based staff. There is certainly plenty of work to be done in East Africa, perhaps yielding higher returns than work now being done in London. In order to achieve a better geographical distribution of its manpower, perhaps ODM should obtain the authority to post staff abroad instead of relying on their volunteering, as at present.

An alternative might be a larger corps of experts directly employed by ODM to be sent to ldcs like Kenya to carry out specific short-term engagements at present done by people while on contract as technical assistance. Such a corps could also conduct *ex post* evaluations of aid projects. They could be financed by saving some money on longer-term contract technical assistance.

This bears some resemblance to suggestions for providing a career service for technical assistance personnel in order to improve the quality of workers in the field. This was suggested at least twelve years ago;[3] there were few good reasons against it then, and there are no more now. An argument sometimes presented is that the government cannot guarantee employment for people hired specifically to spend most of their time working in developing countries. It is inconceivable, however, that there will be no need for an aid programme during this century, so the argument has little force. At least ten years after it was advanced there are still well over a thousand publicly-financed British expatriates in Kenya. There would be a number of advantages from ODM employing people and using them, perhaps in groups, on technical assistance projects of months rather than years. The people would have career records and a known competence in particular fields so the risk of sending duffers would be reduced. Reporting and feedback on the operation of projects would be improved. It would be a more attractive job, perhaps, than that of a two-year expert with no job security and even sometimes no quotable references afterwards.

Our attitude to aid strategy then is that the aim should be to make Kenya as self-sufficient as possible in personnel as quickly as possible and to continue to exercise as much leverage as necessary over the use of capital aid from the outside, rather than by a 'fifth column' of technical assistance. That situation, in which everyone's interests and responsibilities are clear-cut, is likely to be less invidious in the long run.

That brings us on to the awkward matter of 'style' in aid administration. It is strange to find the impression abroad in the Kenyan administration of Britain as 'perfidious Albion'. Yet so it is. Many Kenyan administrators respect ODM for its greater knowledge and experience of local conditions. They acknowledge it is less likely to make mistakes than other donors, yet they find it unpredictable and suspect it of using deliberate delay to kill projects. We must regretfully conclude that, in general, the British are no good at diplomacy, so perhaps they should give it up. When they fondly imagine they are being diplomatic, they are often suspected of being merely sly. Excessive diplomacy is after all a way of being patronising. We are sure the situation is improving as Development Division officers make closer personal contacts with the Kenyans, but mistaken attitudes linger, as evidenced perhaps by an excessive secrecy in ODM's dealings. Evidence about style must be anecdotal. The unkindest word we heard used about British negotiating methods was 'squelchy', by an expatriate member of the Kenyan administration who related how a meeting over a project had dragged on with British officials being pleasant but faintly elusive. Afterwards one had confided to him: 'Of course, we could never really give a penny for any project in that form.' That is not an isolated story. Difficult as it may be for the British temperament to understand, the Kenyans, at least, prefer the downright dealing they get from USAID or the World Bank. It is hard to change the habits of a lifetime, but we strongly recommend greater openness in negotiating, in disbursement planning, and in divulging the contents of the CPP both to the Kenyans and to other donors. The latter would also have the advantage of making ODM articulate more of what it is trying to do and submit it to critical scrutiny.

There is another advantage to being blunter. It puts a premium on making sure that the things one is going to insist on are clearly sensible. Many of the conditions which ODM puts on its aid are eminently sensible. We can find little to criticise, for example, in its wish to control the end uses of its aid or in its sectoral preferences. Procurement-tying is, of course, a nuisance that is largely pointless when the pound is not overvalued, but our impression is that it is the fault of the British Treasury and ODM would be as glad as anyone else to see an end to it. Its one advantage might be that, as it makes the Crown Agents buying agents instead of leaving that to the Kenyan ministries, it might reduce the scope for corruption over contract tenders. There is no reason, however, why ODM should not appoint buying agents to consider tenders from anywhere, as the Crown Agents can when so authorised.

One rule that really is absurd, however, is the one against financing recurrent expenditure. We really think that if ODM had to operate a rule against financing either recurrent or development expenditure, the latter would be less damaging than the former. The Kenyan administration has shown itself capable of running sensible recurrent programmes, and it could administer expansions of them as long as these were on a modest scale. This organic growth of productive expenditures would not pose the administrative problems that the demand for projects and new large integrated programmes does, although it would impose others of control and supervision by donors.

Everyone should realise by now that recurrent expenditures can be as productive as investment expenditures. Furthermore, they do not imply an open-ended commitment by a donor. Any investment almost certainly implies continued recurrent expenditure when it is complete. In the case of, say, a bridge, the recurrent expenditure may be quite modest – painting and maintenance – in the case of a school it will be considerable, quickly outstripping the original investment sum. Projects consisting of recurrent expenditure have nothing unique about them at all in that regard. For the donor commitment not to be open-ended, all that is required is for a phased take-over of costs to be arranged at the outset. The Swedes already do this and have encountered no problems. The nature of the accounting conventions covering public expenditure should simply be ignored by ODM when assessing Kenyan proposals. The question to be asked is would this be done if we did not support it? If the answer is probably not, it does not matter how the Kenyans or anyone else classifies it.

Another rigidity which ought to go is the classification of the aid programme into separate funds. We have suggested a single sum in aid agreements for disbursement as capital or technical assistance. However, we would go further. If it is clear to both ODM and the Kenyans that a given agreement sum is not going to be disbursed within its terms, why not an arrangement to on-lend the balance to CDC to be invested in Kenya if opportunities exist? No doubt the Kenyan government would prefer to have the money, but a private sector use is better than no use at all from its point of view. Such a transfer could scarcely become a regular or perhaps sizeable feature of British aid because CDC might well have no project opportunities appearing in Kenya when ODM had spare cash, and the corporation is not geared to finding uses quickly for odd funds in particular countries. However, an awareness of the possibility of a match could be fruitful and if the money were lent, CDC could repay it to ODM for credit to Kenya after five, ten, or fifteen years. The point is that the British government wants to spend money on productive enterprises in Kenya and has various channels for doing so. It is pointless to have rules or accounting procedures that make that more difficult.

Despite the fact of fungibility, we would not advocate the abolition of all end-use-tying of aid to Kenya. Even if donors were less intrusive, Kenyan forming of priorities would probably remain haphazard to some extent, at least under the present regime. Granted that, however, the problem of fungibility has not been given enough consideration by ODM. In considering support for any project, capital or technical assistance, the first question to be asked is, will anyone else do it if ODM turns it down? If the answer is probably not, and the project is substantial, it then makes sense to ask the question of whether it is worth doing by carrying out full-scale appraisals and feasibility studies. If these lead to the conclusion that the project in some form is worth doing, a third question then needs to be asked, namely, given that no one else would have carried out the project, is there enough Kenyan political support and expertise for it to operate satisfactorily after ODM moves out?

If the answer to the first question – will anyone else do it? – is probably yes, the second question ODM ought to ask is – why should we do it? There may be good developmental answers to this question. ODM might believe itself to possess some particular expertise which the Kenyans and other donors could not match, or it might think that the micro-level influence it could exert would be different from, and preferable to, that of any other donor in that particular case. It is necessary to realise, however, what that influence would be costing. In order to exercise influence over the form of some project, ODM would be giving fungible resources, and with the scale of Kenya's importing from Britain, that practically amounts to free foreign exchange. In any particular case it should be simply considered whether the influence is worth it. This requires a slight reorientation of attitude by ODM staff. Aid agreements are not money already down the drain; they are pieces of paper. Subsequent disbursements are the real cost to Britain, and micro-level influence should be weighed against them. It may well be, of course, that ODM comes under pressure to aid a project with fungible resources for reasons that have nothing to do with development. The project may have a higher import content than any alternative project, or it may bring political kudos with the existing regime. It is idle to pretend that such considerations do not have some place in aid administration, but ODM pursues them only at risk to developmental considerations. In carrying out a project that some other donor would execute, it leaves to that other donor the greater macro-level influence over the allocation of resources. He then may operate in the region of the marginal projects, and his influence may actually be critical in seeing that one such project rather than another comes to pass. If his policies are like ODM's, no one may mind. In general, however, if donors are queueing up to carry out a project, ODM should consider letting them get on with it.

If, however, ODM decides there are sound developmental reasons for aiding a project which would have been done anyway, it is clearly quite pointless to insist on evaluations and appraisals before finally agreeing to aid. On the contrary, the whole point then is to agree immediately and tell the Kenyans the money is certainly earmarked. As much help as possible should then be given in the preparation and planning of the project, in order to achieve the micro-level influence which is presumably the whole point of the exercise. If ODM suspects for a moment that there may be any difficulty in exercising such influence (which would be unusual), there can be no developmental point whatever in aiding the project in question.

It would be quite unethical in our view to offer to aid a project that would be aided by another donor merely to delay its implementation or to emasculate it with economies.[4] There is an asymmetry in that one can offer to aid a project in order to put in more resources than would otherwise have been devoted to it. One cannot however 'aid' a project in order to eliminate or greatly reduce it without being guilty of improper interference. One can state to the recipient that a project is misguided or aid it believing that one can cut costs while maintaining 'output', but that is a different matter.

Assisting sectoral plans with sectoral programme aid means that fungibility is still a consideration but it is likely to be less of one than with project aid for two reasons. One is that a programme is more segmentable than a discrete project; some bits could be done without others. A sectoral grant, therefore, is quite likely to increase the scale of government spending in the area concerned, to bring it forward in time, and to protect it from economy cuts when these are required in government spending. The aid is likely to be only partly fungible. Secondly any micro-level influence which the donor can exert to improve a sectoral plan, in its own terms, is likely to be more important in terms of overall allocation of resources in the economy, than is the case with project aid.

There are a few activities which receive aid, which the Kenya government would undertake anyway even if there were not a donor in the world. Land adjudication and registration may well come into this category. It is a continuous exercise for which the Kenyans have all the necessary expertise. There are strong Parkinsonian bureaucratic reasons for it to go rolling on, and there is political push behind it too. It is largely a local-cost programme so UK aid for it is simply free foreign exchange. If ODM wants to extend some programme aid to Kenya as a token of good faith because it is difficult to spend all agreed aid on definite projects or programmes, we can see no great objection to doing so, but there is no reason for tying it to land adjudication. It is not even clear that in doing so, ODM is associating itself with a winner. We have made no special study of the programme and its effects, so we rely on the balance of informed opinion among agriculturalists and academics to whom we spoke. The consensus appears to be that the programme was useful in its early years in sorting out claims to land in densely populated areas. Its benefits were probably somewhat over-rated, as it was untrue that no one could get agricultural credit without land title – it was possible with other collateral – and it is untrue that anyone can get credit with land title – other collateral is still regarded as necessary by most lenders. So one of the claimed benefits for adjudication and individual freehold is a myth. Nevertheless, no doubt the programme has yielded other, perhaps psychological, benefits. But these must be declining as it is pushed into less and less densely populated areas where it will not change the methods of semi-nomadic pastoralists. Even in more densely populated areas, it appears the land register becomes rapidly out of date owing to unofficial transfers and subdivisions.

We conclude that support for the land adjudication programme has become simply a way of disbursing aid so that underspending does not reach too embarrassing a scale. We recommend an end to aid specifically for the programme. A modest amount of general programme aid as part of future aid agreements would be more suitable. That would not necessarily even mean that adjudication would be prejudiced but nor would it have the effect of fortifying the adjudicators, if other elements in the Kenyan administration ever decided to take a long hard look at the programme.

Would the Land Transfer Programme also continue without aid? We believe it might, at least under the present regime, although the prices offered for farms might well fall. We cannot see any sound developmental reason for maintaining the land price in Kenya. There may be good arguments for subdivision of holdings, but there are now many large Kenyan holdings which could be subdivided and there is no need to look exclusively to expatriate farms for land to be allocated to the poor.

The present tranche of aid for land transfer was supposed to be the last. In 1970 about 200 British citizens were thought to be still farming in Kenya, and 150 of them had landholdings that might qualify as mixed farms. It is in fact unlikely that the present tranche will be enough to buy out all those who want to sell. There are three reasons. First is an inflation of land prices; the tranche was worked out assuming a price in the region of £20 an acre, but £30 an acre is nearer the going rate. Second is the fact that some Kenyan citizens may opt to revert to British citizenship, as they have the right to do, and their farms then become eligible for transfer. No one really knows how many people are likely to do this, but as whites become more exposed in the Kenyan countryside and their post-colonial way of life changes with the departure of European neighbours it could become a frequent occurrence. The third reason hinges on the definition of mixed farm. It is an exceedingly complicated one that is execrated by British and Kenyan civil servants alike. Unfortunately a degree of mutual suspicion has so far prevented successful negotiation of a new definition. The existing one specifies that the farm must have more than 25 inches of rainfall a year, have more than 25 per cent of the land under cash crops, be 50 per cent arable land, and have not more than 50 acres or 25 per cent of the land under plantation crops. The Kenyans point out, with reason, that a lot of basically mixed farms do not fall under this definition, having too much coffee or a slightly higher proportion of pasture or arable land, but that if this definition had been applied from the first some 40 per cent of the Million-Acre Scheme land would not have been eligible! (Kinangop, for example, one of the most politically sensitive areas, was often less than 50 per cent arable.)

The British are loath to abandon the definition for fear of incurring an open-ended commitment to buy out all Europeans, including ranches and plantation owners. The Kenyans want the definition replaced with a clause simply stating that the farm is 'suitable for settlement'. Ideally they would like it left up to the Department of Settlement to decide whether a farm qualified, although it could be done by a joint committee of both sides, a procedure already used in the case of Compassionate Purchases. A difficulty here, however, is that while 'suitable for settlement' meant something when settlement implied subdivision, as the land had then to be sufficiently arable to support peasant small holdings, now with *Shirika* it can mean anything. Even ranches could be taken over and run on a co-operative basis.

Ranches, however, cannot usually support more people than are currently employed on them, and though some plantation crops such as tea and coffee have been successfully grown on small holdings, there is limited scope for making production of these crops more labour-intensive and increasing yields per acre. With current policies, at least, there does not seem to be much economic or social rationale for an extended programme.

ODM has long since surrendered any attempt at micro-level influence in land transfer; it was not consulted over the *Shirika* schemes, for example. Therefore we can see no developmental reason for the continuation of aid for this programme beyond the current aid agreement. It is simply transferring assets without much changing their economic use or contributing to political stability. That applies *a fortiori* to any extended programme to cover acquisition of ranches and plantations. We say that, having argued as strongly as anyone, in Chapter Five, that the Land Transfer Programme constituted extremely valuable aid to Kenya in the past. However, there is no longer the danger of a precipitate flight of most of the country's best farmers. There are, of course, non-developmental reasons for going on with the programme which HMG might think potent. People unable to take advantage of it because of the mixed farm definition, whose farms are mixed, could reasonably feel discriminated against, especially if a future Kenyan government expropriates expatriate landowners. However, those British farmers still in Kenya must surely have written off their original investment by now. Human problems are involved about which we have no wish to be callous, but further money for land transfer would be underwriting the assets of people who, by and large, have not done too badly. Apart from the human problems, there are political problems in stopping this sort of aid and HMG must search its conscience. All we would say is that further money for land transfer is without developmental merit. So there is no reason why any further sums should be a charge on the aid programme. As with adjudication, some of this money might in future be re-allocated to untied programme loans, accounting for some part of the total aid programme to Kenya.

There has been a considerable improvement in the area of donor co-operation over the past few years. However, it should be clear that many of the suggestions we make would be more effective if there were closer liaison between donors. Fungibility is largely a problem in Kenya of the substitutability of one donor's aid for another's. Some knowledge of each other's preferences and agreed areas of specialisation therefore greatly reduces the risk of it. There is also more point in ODM winding down its technical assistance commitment if it is confident that other donors will not unthinkingly replace British personnel with their own. Our suggestions for a more open administration of the aid programme apply to relations with other donors as much as to relations with the Kenyans. Greater openness would also reduce Kenyan suspicions of donor collusion. The traditional reasons for donor co-operation – elimination of duplication of effort and wasteful competition, and the opportunity to match complementary skills and inputs – apply with undiminished force. Perhaps the UK could seek to invigorate the East Africa Donor Consultative Committee.

Strangely enough, it is traditional for researchers to conclude reports by calling for more research. Without being too predictable one can point out that in Kenya some of aid's greatest successes have had a strong innovative element. Maize provides an example of successful research but there are also concrete programmes, such as CDC tea, which owe their achievements to the development of new techniques suitable to the local situation and factor endowments. Donors should, therefore, be willing to accept risks in financing applied research and innovation. They are often better placed to do this than either commercial concerns, out to minimise risk by following tried techniques, or recipient governments who may be highly risk-averse both because of poverty and the need to avoid providing 'hostages' to political opponents.

Notes

1. *The Changing Emphasis in British Aid Policies: More Help for the Poorest*, HMSO, Cmnd. 6270, October 1975.
2. The World Bank and USAID have already made sectoral loans, and Sweden and West Germany as well as ODM want to move in this direction.
3. See, for example, I. M. D. Little, *Aid to Africa*, London, ODI, 1964, p. 69.
4. We do not suggest that ODM has followed this course.

9 CONTROVERSIES OVER AID

The previous chapters analysed the effects of aid on Kenya and gave policy prescriptions. This final chapter presents our conclusions in a different context and examines some general propositions about the purpose and effect of aid in the light of the Kenyan experience. Views about aid range from the over-simple altruistic, that it is a straightforward act of charity, to the over-simple Machiavellian, that it is the pursuit of colonialism by other means. Despite its obvious appeal to the better instincts of the people of the rich countries, economic aid has been much attacked. Aid is unpopular with the extreme of both left and right. Even where there is no ideological viewpoint to generate hostility to aid, its failure to transform the state of the poor countries has caused disillusionment among some who underestimated the difficulties in the way of their economic progress.

The naive altruistic view of aid is inadequate because it ignores the mixture of motives in the donor country, assuming a single-minded benevolence, and ignores the possibility that aid can have detrimental effects on the recipient. The Machiavellian view of aid is inadequate because it ignores the mixture of motives in the donor country, assuming a single-minded and narrow self-interest, and excludes the possibility that the beneficial effects of aid will predominate. Curiously, this view also excludes the possibility that aid can benefit the recipient even though it also serves the interests of the donor. In reality, donor policies reflect the balance of diverse views and interests, and the effects of aid on the recipient reflect the balance of beneficial and adverse effects.

Both these over-simple views of aid policy are inadequate for another reason: they ignore the effect of ignorance and unintentional error. It is itself a great error to assume that the path to development is known and charted, and that it is simply a matter of the will and the means to travel along it. A donor may, indeed, pursue a particular policy for non-developmental reasons: it may tie aid, for instance, in an attempt to stimulate its exports. A recipient may also adopt a policy for non-developmental reasons: it may, for instance, decide on the location of a particular project because it benefits places of political importance, or even because it benefits influential individuals. But donor and recipient may take a different view about development policy, about the regional and sectoral distribution of investment, for instance, each for perfectly genuine developmental reasons. Either view, and indeed both, may be mistaken, and the policy implemented may be judged on balance to be detrimental. But it would be a mistake to attribute such failures to anti-developmental motives rather than to ignorance and error.

Our study of British aid to Kenya does not incline us to an extreme view of either the benefits or the burdens of aid for the recipient country. Nor has the fact that Kenya remains a poor country caused us to conclude that aid has been a failure.

Our judgement is that in British aid policy towards independent Kenya the developmental motive has increasingly predominated. When better policies could have been pursued, and better projects supported, it is easier with hindsight to see the better way than was possible at the time, and the deficiencies have been generally the result of faulty judgement, rather than of bad intention. On balance, in the effects of aid on Kenya, the benefits have vastly outweighed the costs.

One proposition about the allocation of aid is that it is given to compliant governments, those that follow the dictates and support the policies of the donor. Such a government receives aid because it is compliant, and is compliant because it receives aid. A difficulty in fitting the facts of aid to Kenya into the model of aid to a compliant state is that there are so many different donors whose interests and policies are not uniform. Can Kenya be compliant to them all? It is not as if donor co-operation were so close and strong that a single donor policy prevailed. It was suggested in Chapter Six that donor co-operation has been weak in fact, and there are still possibilities for Kenya to play off one against another. The theory of the compliant state does not stand up to investigation in terms of Kenya's domestic policies. It is even more difficult to fit Kenya's international policies into the model, and to demonstrate that Kenya is not only a compliant but also a client state. Where the international interests and policies of donors differ as widely as those of, say, Sweden and the United States, it is impossible to give credence to such an idea.

Of course, on some large issues donors agree. They might, for instance, unite in opposition to a wholesale expropriation of foreign capital, and the pursuit of such a policy by the Kenya government might reduce the aid allocated to Kenya. As an explanation of the allocation of aid, therefore, to that extent the theory of compliance has some basis. But the other leg of the proposition, that governments are compliant because they receive aid, does not follow. It does not follow that Kenya fails to expropriate foreign capital – to continue the example – because of the aid it receives. For one thing, there are too many private Kenyan interests, to which the government is sensitive, which would be adversely affected by such a move.[1] But it is not only a concern for particular Kenyan private interests which could justify the attitude of the Kenya government to private capital. It is perfectly possible that an objective assessment would lead to the conclusion that the benefits of foreign investment in Kenya outweigh the costs. It is a flaw in the compliance theory, when used as a criticism of aid policy, that donor policies are assumed necessarily to be against the social interest of the recipient.

The historical roots of British aid policy are far too deep and complex for a simple 'compliant state' explanation of aid to Kenya to withstand even the most superficial examination of the facts. It is true that the origins of the aid programme may be traced to the time when the extreme of compliance – colonial status – existed. It is also true that the Land Transfer Programme was instituted at a time when Kenya had not yet achieved independence, and when the acceptance of the programme by the African leaders cannot have been uninfluenced by their desire to ease the negotiation of independence. But Kenya has not sold herself for aid, nor has aid been given in the hope of buying her. Britain's aid to Kenya is the result of history and of a British interest, real or imagined, in the maintenance of law and order, and in Kenya's development. It has been argued that:

> part of the explanation why aid has not led to faster development is that it is not designed for this purposes. That is, the major purpose of aid is to further the interests of the donors rather than those of the recipients.[2]

That is not an adequate assessment if applied to Britain's policy in aiding Kenya. It would be even more of a caricature to present Britain's aid to Kenya as being 'from a metropole to a satellite' and as 'a way of safeguarding relationships with a client state'.[3] Such an assessment is sufficiently refuted by the general diffidence of ODM in its relations with the Kenya government, and by its tendency to respond to requests rather than to take the initiative in project proposals, for fear of being thought to push projects in the British interest. It is also refuted by the occasional differences that have arisen between the rather narrowly 'developmental' view that has been predominant in ODM and the less austere view of what projects should be supported in the interest of political goodwill to Britain in Kenya.

Another proposition about the allocation of aid – that aid is too often given to 'bad' governments – is somewhat at odds with the compliance theory. Of course, it is not at odds if it is believed that the donor is also 'bad'. But from a less demon-ridden point of view it is sometimes suggested that donors do not sufficiently refrain from aiding countries of whose governments they disapprove. There are many tests by which a government may be thought 'bad' and unqualified to receive aid. It may be externally aggressive, internally oppressive and lacking in popular support; its policies may frustrate development or foster the growth of inequality and the impoverishment of sections of the population; its administration may be so ineffective or venal that it cannot properly administer the aid it receives or prevent its misappropriation. We do not think that the Kenya government would score anything like zero in all these tests of unworthiness, but nor do we believe that its score of black marks would be notably high, as compared with that of many countries.

It may in any case be questioned whether it necessarily follows that a donor should refuse aid to a government of whose policies it disapproves. If it did so the donor could adopt a high moral tone, but it might worsen the lot of the people in the country deprived of aid. Should a donor exert its influence to improve the policies of the recipient government? 'Leverage' by donors is commonly condemned; it is often thought of as being exerted where a recipient government is not naturally compliant, but can be levered into compliance. Aid is then a cog in the machinery of domination. The condemnation of leverage could derive from a belief in the virtues of independence, even if it meant going your own way to perdition, but more commonly it derives from the hidden assumption that leverage is always exerted against the interests of the recipient country. But if the donor is 'good' and the recipient government is 'bad', leverage could be exerted with beneficial effects. In fact, of course, this approach to leverage is entirely too simple-minded. The uncertainties surrounding development policies are such that serious differences of view could exist between a donor and a recipient, when the concern of both was with development and economic improvement. Leverage is often about means rather than ends, and an attempt by a donor to exert leverage does not imply that either the donor or the recipient must necessarily be characterised as 'bad'.

In practice, on the occasions when ODM has tried to exert leverage on Kenya, it has generally been in the interest of development rather than in Britain's more direct commercial or political interest. Sometimes the leverage has been ineffective, and sometimes unnecessary. The simple stereotype of the reluctant but weak recipient being levered into pursuing policies in the interest of the powerful donor is far from the reality of the aid relationship between Britain and Kenya.

The policy on land transfer and the inclusion in the Kenya Constitution of rules protecting investors could be seen as the consequence of leverage exerted by the outgoing colonial power. But the official attitude towards private property in independent Kenya suggests that in these respects Britain may have been levering an already open door. Since independence Britain may be detected exerting leverage to resist an application for aid for the development of television in Mombasa, to accelerate the reduction in the numbers of OSAS personnel, to prevent an extension of the Land Transfer Programme through redefinition of 'mixed farm', and for a greater emphasis on rural development by indicating preference for projects concerned with this. In none of these cases can the leverage be seen as outstandingly successful. The lever was either too weak, was not pressed hard enough, or was superfluous. Funds were eventually given for Mombasa television; the number of OSAS personnel is falling at a slower rate than the British aid authorities think desirable; it would not be surprising if Britain relented in its determination not to extend the Land Transfer Programme. In the case of a greater emphasis on rural development, the Kenya government would claim that this was its own policy, and that no leverage was needed.

In none of these instances – successful or unsuccessful, necessary or not – can the attempt at leverage be seen as being made in an anti-developmental cause. Nor does it necessarily follow from this fact that the policies against which leverage was exerted were themselves anti-developmental or pursued for non-developmental motives. There can be a sufficient diversity of judgement on the effects of a slower rundown in OSAS staff and of an extension of land transfer for opposite policies to be supportable on developmental grounds. Aid policies and motives have been judged too much in terms of absolutes, of good and bad, and too little in terms of the balance of judgements.

In any case, these are pretty anaemic examples of leverage. It is only a negative kind of leverage to refuse funds for one kind of project and to express a preference for another kind. The same may be said of several other decisions: the refusal of aid for Phase II of the expansion of Kenyatta National Hospital, because it was judged that other forms of expansion of health services would be more beneficial; the unwillingness to supply funds for grain storage in the absence of an explicit policy on storage. It could be argued that Britain should have exerted more positive leverage to improve Kenya policies – for more egalitarian policies on land tenure and settlement, for example. In fact, there is an instance of leverage being used in this way. The settlement programme included the provision of so-called 'Z plots', which would be larger than was usual under the High-Density Scheme and which included the farm house of the old European farm. It was suggested by the settlement planners that the occupants of 'Z plots' would act as community leaders and would set an example to their neighbours of good agricultural practice. The judgement of the British aid authorities was that this form of settlement would not yield the suggested benefits, that the plots would often be taken by absentees, and that they would add to the inequality in the distribution of wealth. The provision of further funds for land transfer was made conditional on the abandonment of the 'Z plots' scheme, and the settlement authorities did, in fact, abandon them. This was direct leverage to change Kenya policy by exerting the influence of an aid donor. It should not be presumed, however, that such leverage by a single donor would always be effective. The characteristic of this example is that there was no other aid donor which would take on land transfer if Britain refused further funds. The existence of several potential donors for most projects makes land transfer a very special case. After 1966 Britain used leverage to resist extensive subdivision of transferred land, a policy with disinterested intentions but inegalitarian effects. The rarity of cases like the Z-plots does suggest that an over-nice regard for the autonomy of the Kenyan government in such fields of policy could have been a fault on Britain's part, but the end of subdivision shows the dangers of an eagerness to lever Kenyan policy in the direction that Britain thinks it should go.

Leverage of a kind, of course, may be exerted by the simple decision of a donor to support one project and not another. Unless there is full fungibility, the pattern of investment in the recipient will be affected by the decisions of the donor in giving project aid. Projects will then be undertaken as a result of project aid that would not be undertaken if the recipient were carrying out the same total expenditure on development from its own funds, or with the support of programme aid. Our view is that some British aid, probably most, has been shunted, but some has not. For some projects the funds were fungible. These include the Mumias sugar scheme and the improvement of the Mombasa road, which would almost certainly have been carried out in the absence of British aid, or even of aid funds from any source. Some British aid funds were not fungible. Funds for land transfer were not fungible, because in the absence of British aid the farmers would not have been bought out in the same way and on the same terms. They were not fungible, we suspect, for SRDP, because the absence of British funds would most likely have meant that one area would have been omitted from the scheme. Because of limitations in the capacity of the Kenya administration to administer and execute projects, the acceptance of aid for projects may sometimes have precluded or postponed the execution of some other projects. Aid as a whole, of which British project aid is a part, is therefore open to the comment that:

> the donors are able to pre-empt domestic resources and alter the entire investment programme, thereby substituting their preferences for those of the recipient government.[4]

It is not clear that such a change in priorities must inevitably be anti-developmental. Why should it be assumed that the donor always knows worse? What if the preference of the recipient is for Mercedes for ministers? But in fact there may not be wide differences between the preferences of Britain and Kenya. Britain selects projects from the list offered by Kenya, and it is not certain that Kenya has strong priorities within the list, and there are always other donors. Hence the leverage nominally exerted through project aid may not be effective, and if it is effective our examination of the projects selected for British support from among those offered them by the Kenyans does not suggest that it should be condemned.

But leverage can be more subtle and insidious than that exerted as overt pressure by the donor on the policies of the recipient or by the selection of projects under project aid. It is possible to consider as leverage the introduction of the various distortions in the economy and society of the recipient which have been alleged to be the consequence of the acceptance of aid on a large scale. 'External doles', it has been claimed: 'tend to bias the development process in directions based on external prototypes which are often inappropriate and therefore damaging.'[5] A similar thought is contained in the suggestion that 'aid may have retarded development . . . by distorting the composition of investment'.[6] These effects of aid might be thought of as 'implicit leverage'.

One alleged effect of implicit leverage is on the centralisation of power. It has been said that 'foreign aid augments the resources of the recipient governments compared to those of the private sector, thereby promoting concentration of power in the recipient countries'.[7] There has certainly been some increase in the relative size of the public sector of the Kenya economy since independence.[8] Aid is a direct addition to the resources of the government, so that it is to be expected that aid should increase the size of the public sector and the economic role of the government. However, if the inflow of aid and the facilities provided by aid encourage an inflow of private capital and an increase in domestically financed private investment, it is not inevitable that the relative size of the public sector should increase. Nationalisation of existing enterprises would increase the relative size of the public sector, and this has had some part to play in Kenya. Although the Kenya government has adopted a pragmatic and not an ideological attitude to nationalisation, it has taken some enterprises into public ownership – the Power and Lighting Company and the oil refinery, for example – and there is no evidence from Kenya for the belief that 'aid agencies . . . tend to discourage government ownership'.[9] But neither is it true that there is a simple connection between aid and the concentration of power.

If the centralisation of the economy and the concentration of power are to be deplored – if, so to say, small is beautiful – it would be an error to attribute the fault solely to the increase in government economic activity fostered by aid. However objectionable 'the insolence of office', the concentration of power in private corporations should not be forgotten. The argument for decentralisation against centralisation, for small against large, is not a matter of private versus public enterprise, but concerns the nature of economic development, whether the agents of development are public authorities or private enterprises. Aid must take its share of the blame for the fact that Kenyan development has not emphasised the small and decentralised. It does not follow that, if there had been no aid, the pattern of development would have been better; it is more likely that there would have been just less development. A development process of a different character would have required a firm policy decision to go for the small and decentralised and the will to enforce it. It would also have required a knowledge – not to be presumed to exist – of how to develop in this different way. Far from inhibiting the possibilities of such development, aid for investigation of alternative patterns of development and alternative techniques could facilitate it. Donors could also in their selection of projects favour the small against the large.

Although the change in British practice away from a willingness to pick up the 'odds and ends' left by other donors towards a liking for larger projects is, on these grounds, to be regretted, the policy of favouring projects which benefit agriculture and the poorer sections of the population does go in the right direction. There is, in practice, no visible connection between aid and the concentration of power.

The danger of distortions being introduced by aid has particular application to technical assistance. The supply of personnel can be a powerful instrument for introducing the attitudes and techniques of the donor country into the different economic and social circumstances of the recipient, for which they are inappropriate. One writer asks rhetorically:

> Will it ever be possible to evaluate the cost of the wastage and of the ill-conceived decisions due to technical assistance based on the application of inappropriate techniques prompted . . . by the unimaginative transplantation of western experience into vastly different sociological surroundings . . .?[10]

Although, as we remarked in Chapter Six, these strictures do not by any means apply to all technical assistance personnel in Kenya, such adverse effects of technical assistance are not unknown. After all, the quality of technical assistance personnel varies from the highly competent to the barely employable, and it would be surprising if technical assistance had always worked well. But the difficulty with a general condemnation of technical assistance on the grounds that it introduces inappropriate techniques, is the implicit assumption that appropriate techniques are available. The argument reflects the inverted arrogance that the donors inevitably know less than the recipients. If the recipient countries did without technical assistance, the argument implies, they would do things the right way. In reality, many instances of 'inappropriate' technical assistance – as of inappropriate technology in general – are cases where what is 'appropriate' is known only in principle and not in practice. In such instances, doubtless there is a better way of doing things – methods more appropriate to the factor endowment, products more appropriate to consumer needs – but no one has yet made it concrete. The argument for 'appropriateness' is, therefore, often an argument for more investigation and research, backed by the necessary resources and political will, rather than an argument against aid and technical assistance, which necessarily operate within the constraints of existing knowledge. There may, indeed, be circumstances in which an investment in 'inappropriate' technology would pre-empt future opportunities when a more appropriate technology is available. It must rarely be wise, however, to forgo a beneficial investment in favour of a better one that may (or may not) become available in the future.

Aid for education – an important sphere of British aid to Kenya – has come in for particular criticism for introducing inappropriate ideas. Again there are the rhetorical questions:

> . . . do these teachers . . . dispense the kind of education the host country really needs? Teaching little Africans . . . the history and geography of their former colonizers may be a long term investment on behalf of the donors, but how much does it contribute to local development? How can it be determined to what extent the teaching of metropolitan curricula has contributed to progress, or has rather helped to maintain or even broaden the cleavage between the intellectually expatriate ruling groups and the majorities . . .?[11]

This statement no more describes the reality of British educational aid to Kenya than the novels of Dickens describe life in modern Britain. There are, of course, immensely important issues about the appropriate structure of education and curricula in a country like Kenya. Education can be socially divisive. It can detract from a willingness to accept the life of the traditional society. It can produce half-educated, unemployed school-leavers. But a serious consideration of educational issues is not helped by the suggestion that what is wrong is that the schools teach the history and geography of the former colonial power (which, in fact, they do not in Kenya).

Britain's educational aid to Kenya is not, of course, above criticism (see Chapter Six) but it would be absurd to believe that the responsibility for the major faults in the Kenya educational system and in the curricula can be laid at the door of British aid. It would be quite mistaken to assume that if there had been no aid for education, even though the quantity of education provided might have been reduced, its quality and relevance would have been greater. The enormous political pressure for educational expansion would have made it difficult to keep down the numbers at school, though fees might have been higher and the children of the poorest kept out in consequence. But the effect of the removal of educational aid would have primarily been a decline in quality within the same conceptual framework. Some expatriate teachers might have been funded by the Kenya government itself, but there would inevitably have been far fewer, and for a considerable period there would have been insufficient equally qualified Kenyan teachers to replace them. The total number of teachers would have been smaller, and on average they would have been less well qualified. The precise pattern must be conjectural, but what is certain in our judgement is that the absence of expatriate teachers would not have resulted in an educational system more relevant to Kenya's needs. It would not have been different and better, but the same, only worse.

However inappropriate the curricula of the Kenya schools may still be, it is not because there is a powerful lobby of expatriate teachers hindering reform. Much effort has been, and continues to be, devoted to curriculum development. There is no simple explanation of remaining inadequacies; pressures and vested interests have their place, but they are not created by aid. More Kenyans than Englishmen have intellectual capital invested in the existing system, and the existence of a neo-colonial conspiracy is not necessary to explain conservatism. The pressure from the consumers for the maintenance of international comparability of the content and standards of education should not be underestimated. As a result it is difficult for changes to be introduced by expatriates. Too easily is 'different' interpreted as 'inferior', and if the structure of education is a colonial heritage, it is one from which it is equally difficult for Kenyans and expatriates to break away. And there is another important reason for the survival of 'inappropriate' curricula: there is no universally accepted answer to the question 'What is an "appropriate" curriculum?' It is not because of the baleful influence of the outmoded ideas of expatriate teachers that Kenya continues to produce unemployable – or at least unemployed – school-leavers. It is because this is a problem to which no one has yet found a solution, in Kenya or elsewhere. Certainly, many of the suggestions of foreign reformers have been too general to be useful. Technical assistance has improved the quality of teaching within a framework it was impotent to change. The fact that the framework was established in the colonial era, and is protected by attitudes that are influenced by colonial experience, does not mean that it either benefits the ex-colonialists now, or that they can do anything about it.

Aid has been accused of fostering corruption, and though the accusation might seem to be more plausibly made against foreign investors and businesses, which are competing for opportunities, than against aid agencies, it is obvious that the availability of aid funds makes their misappropriation possible. It cannot be denied that there is corruption in Kenya: it is widely discussed in the press, and in 1975 a Select Committee of the Legislature was set up to investigate the matter. It would be surprising if some British aid funds had not been corruptly diverted from their intended purpose, though the administration of aid, with tying to projects and payment in arrears for expenditures incurred, makes the more blatant forms of misappropriation difficult, if not impossible. In principle, the involvement of government in the expenditure of large funds widens the scope for corruption, but in practice it does not seem likely – except to the extent that the government has more money – that the availability of aid has led to significantly greater corruption than would otherwise have existed.

There is, however, a wider and less literal sense in which it is argued that aid corrupts. Aid corrupts morally: it establishes dependency, destroys self-reliance, and enervates government and society. On this view: 'there seems to be no short cut consistent with dignity which bypasses frugality today as a necessary condition for self-reliance and real progress tomorrow.'[12]

For this school of economic analysis, strength can come only through suffering. It can indeed happen that 'pre-occupation with aid diverts attention from the basic causes of poverty and the possibilities of acting on them',[13] and that aid 'enables those in power to evade and avoid fundamental reforms'[14] (why mend the bone when the broken leg can be cut off?). But it is not inevitable that aid should on balance be detrimental by distracting a government from its development task, rather than beneficial by increasing the resources of the recipient country. Although, as was concluded in Chapter Six, the receipt of aid has probably reduced resource mobilisation by the Kenya government, it does not follow that this has been detrimental to development. Even if reduced resource mobilisation had resulted in increased consumption, that would not necessarily have been a reason for condemning aid.

The developmental effect of aid is in part determined by the extent to which there is increased investment as a result of aid. Even though aid is given nominally for particular investment projects, this does not mean that total investment will necessarily be greater by the amount of the aid. The receipt of aid could be accompanied by a lower level of domestic saving brought about, for example, by a relaxation in the revenue-collecting efforts of the government. It is only in the extreme case that investment will rise by the full amount of the aid, just as the other extreme is approached when 'aid is essentially a substitute for savings and . . . a large fraction of foreign capital is used to increase consumption rather than investment'.[15]

More commonly, it would be expected that the increase in available resources resulting from the provision of aid would be partly consumed and partly invested. The developmental effect of the aid would probably be the greater, up to a point, the greater the rise in investment. An increase in consumption, on the other hand, might have a greater effect on welfare, and there may be important developmental benefits from a rise in what is classed as consumption. Aid is not necessarily wasted, therefore, if it increases consumption rather than investment.

It was pointed out in Chapter Six that although the lower level of resource mobilisation by government than might have occurred if aid had been smaller had released resources to the private sector, the resources could have gone into investment rather than into consumption. Some attempts at a statistical demonstration of the effect of aid on consumption and investment have been vitiated by a failure to disentangle the effect of aid from that of non-aid capital inflows. No judgement about aid can properly follow from such an analysis of changes in consumption and investment.[16] The effect of all inflows, aid and commercial, might be judged from changes in the distribution between consumption and investment of total available resources. A rising proportion of consumption would suggest that the situation was nearer to the extreme in which the inflows were a substitute for domestic saving; an increasing proportion of investment would suggest that the situation was nearer to the other extreme, and that the effect of the inflows on investment predominated.

The statistics for Kenya indicate a rising proportion of total resources being devoted to investment, and a declining proportion to private consumption (see Table 19). Such figures are not conclusive, because it cannot be known what would have happened if the inflows had been smaller. Nevertheless, in the light of them we find it impossible not to conclude that the inflows benefited investment rather than consumption.

Table 19: Use of resources available in the monetary economy

(percentages)

	1964	*1969*	*1970*	*1971*	*1972*	*1973*	*1974*
Investment	16	23	25	27	26	29	29
Public consumption	20	21	20	21	22	20	16
Private consumption	64	56	55	52	53	51	55

Sources: Economic Survey 1974, Table 1.6 and *Economic Survey 1975,* Table 2.5.

Indeed, it was argued in Chapter Six that the procedures and requirements of aid donors have resulted in a diversion of Kenya government funds to an undesirable extent away from recurrent expenditures into investment. Another undesirable effect of the administration of aid was identified in the same chapter. It was concluded that aid had had unfortunate effects on economic administration by undermining central control of operational ministries. But these arguments deal with the details of aid administration and cannot be used as ammunition for a general attack on aid. They do not carry the implication that Kenya would have been better off either without aid, or with less aid. They are concerned with practicalities and are far removed from the concerns of those who condemn aid because it makes possible the avoidance of 'fundamental reforms'.

Kenya can perhaps be criticised for being in some respects one of those recipients which 'pursue courses of action which patently reduce the level of income or retard its increase'.[17] Aid recipients do this, it has been argued, in various ways: 'For instance, they expel the most productive groups of the population from their countries, or restrict the inflow and the deployment of private capital'.[18]

Kenya has been criticised, however, for giving too much, not too little, encouragement to private capital. Nor can it be supposed that the attitude to the commercial activities of non-citizen Asians would have been less discouraging if aid had been less abundant; on the contrary, donor leverage has perhaps achieved a slower exodus of non-citizen Asians than would otherwise have been permitted.

There is, indeed, one field in which the availability of aid does appear to have encouraged, or at least permitted, a laxity of effort on the part of the Kenya government. It was explained in Chapter Six that the Kenya government has seemed unwilling to reduce its use of technical assistance staff under OSAS at as fast a rate as the British government thinks desirable. But it would be fatuous to generalise from this instance and to conclude that Kenya's development effort would have been greater and better directed in the absence of aid.

Another argument against aid, the persuasiveness of which is diminished by its failure to distinguish aid from foreign private investment, is that 'aid may have retarded development . . . by frustrating the emergence of an indigenous entrepreneurial class'.[19] This effect is, of course, even more difficult to identify than the effect of aid on savings, and it is not obvious that the development of entrepreneurial skills is inevitably frustrated by competition more than it is stimulated by example. Be that as it may, it is difficult to believe that foreign enterprise, let alone aid, has been a major barrier to the development of Kenyan entrepreneurship. In fact, the situation in Kenya is too complex to be analysed in simple terms of foreign enterprise *versus* indigenous entrepreneurs. If the emergence of an African entrepreneurial class has been frustrated it has been by Asian entrepreneurs, citizen and non-citizen, rather than by aid and foreign investment. The policy under which non-citizen Asians are being removed from business activity (for which aid and foreign investment can attract neither credit nor blame) is likely to protect African entrepreneurship much more than aid and foreign investment are likely to frustrate its emergence. In fact, foreign business, operating as it does under rules for Africanisation (even though to some extent these are satisfied by the employment of 'front men'), stimulates rather than frustrates the emergence of an African entrepreneurial, or at any rate a managerial, class. We have characterised Kenya government policy as aiming to foster the entrepreneurial society, and we do not believe that the inflow of aid and foreign investment has hindered the achievement of that aim.

That aid promotes such inequality in income and wealth between individuals and regions within the recipient country is a plank in the platform of the critics of aid. There are many possible links between aid and inequality. Aid funds may be corruptly diverted into the pockets of those who are already rich, and as a result powerful and influential, to make them still richer. Aid may provide services which benefit the rich, and not the poor – aid for improving a road along which the rich will drive, but not for roads which lead to the villages of the poor. Aid for education may help produce recruits for the rich from the ranks of the children of the rich, as when a university education guarantees employment at a 'European' level of pay, and when entry to a university requires an earlier education which few but the better-off can afford to buy their children. Aid may foster inequality by providing economic opportunities which only some are able to grasp. In fact, the concern of donors with the 'efficiency' of aid will encourage this effect by leading to a concentration of aid on projects and in places where people are able to grasp the opportunities created.

It is widely believed that inequality in the distribution of income and wealth has increased in Kenya since independence. Although no definitive statistical demonstration of a growth in inequality is available, we do not wish to argue that it has not occurred. Indeed, the conclusion was reached in Chapter Six that aid has indirectly contributed to the growth of inequality, at any rate before donors' recent emphasis on rural development. The question that remains to be considered is whether the growth of inequality is wholly to be deprecated, and aid criticised for contributing to it. Is the increased inequality resulting from aid to be seen, at best, as the price to be paid for the benefits of aid? Could not, alternatively, the growth of inequality be positively welcomed as a reflection of the fact that some people – in fact many people – are becoming better-off? It would be better still if all were becoming better-off, equally fast. But is not improvement, though unevenly spread, to be preferred to an equality of poverty? The emphasis on equality *versus* inequality is in danger of leading to a neglect of absolute changes in income and consumption. A growth of inequality can take very different forms. Inequality increases when a few get very rich while the absolute position of the majority remains unchanged or deteriorates. Inequality also increases when a large number, perhaps the great majority of the population, becomes absolutely better-off, though some become better-off faster than others, and a very few become very rich. Although undoubtedly some Kenyans have become worse-off with the disruption of traditional ways by economic development, the growth of inequality in Kenya conforms more closely to the second than to the first of these patterns.

Our conclusion, therefore, is that responsibility for the growth of inequality in Kenya cannot be laid at the door of aid in any crude or direct sense, though to the extent that aid has contributed to political stability and economic growth, it has contributed to the growth of inequality. Moreover, though there are features of the growth of inequality in Kenya which we – making our own value judgement – deplore, the conspicuous inequality – the stark contrast in Nairobi of *Mbenzi*[20] and beggar – is a more superficial, less fundamental feature of the situation, of post-independence developments, than the widely varying but for very large numbers significant improvement in the standard of life. Nor do we think that because some have become substantially better-off (we do not refer to the very rich) while others remain at little above the standard of life provided in the subsistence economy, this is a condemnation of the process of development, though it should be taken as a guide to policy, including the policy of aid donors, to focus on improving the position of the poorest of the poor. Inevitably, some will benefit more than others – the benefits will be unevenly spread – if only because resources are insufficient to benefit all equally at the same time, and because of differences in the ability and willingness of different individuals and the people of different areas to take advantage of opportunities for improvement. Inequality is increased, for example, when water supplies are introduced into one area, but not yet to another. The aim of policy should be, it appears to us, not to endeavour to prevent the growth of inequalities of this kind, but to see that there is no tendency for the cumulative favouring of particular areas or individuals. It appears to us that Britain and other aid donors, and the Kenya government, are aware of the possibility that policies will foster the cumulative growth of inequality beyond that which we see as a 'natural' and inevitable characteristic of the process of development. It remains to be seen whether understanding is, or can be, adequately translated into achievement.

Notes

1. Determined believers in the Machiavellian view will see this reason for the toleration of foreign capital as confirmation of the compliance theory. In fact, a more obvious reason for favouring foreign private capital is that it brings in foreign private capital rather than because it brings in aid.
2. K. B. Griffin, 'Foreign Capital, Domestic Savings and Economic Development: A Reply', *Bulletin* (Oxford University Institute of Economics and Statistics), Vol. 33, No. 2, May 1971, p. 157.
3. K. B. Griffin and J. L. Enos, 'Foreign Assistance: Objectives and Consequences', *Economic Development and Cultural Change*, Vol. 18, No. 3, March 1970, pp. 315-16.
4. Griffin, 1971, op. cit., p. 160. But compare the view that aid is fully fungible, so that it always finances the marginal expenditure, including consumption (K. B. Griffin, 'Foreign Capital, Domestic Savings and Economic Development', *Bulletin*, Vol. 32, No. 2, May 1970, p. 103) which is compatible only on the particular assumptions of excess capital and an administrative constraint. See Chapter Six.
5. P. T. Bauer, *Dissent on Development*, London, Weidenfeld and Nicolson, 1971, p. 103.
6. Griffin and Enos, op. cit., p. 326.
7. Bauer, op. cit., p. 104. The further contention that because of its effect on the concentration of power aid 'tends to favour and strengthen governments which lean towards the Soviet bloc' (p. 128) cannot with respect to Kenya be taken seriously.
8. The increase, according to the statistics (see Chapter Two), has been more modest than is often believed, and it has been large only in investment expenditure.
9. T. Mende, *From Aid to Re-Colonization*, London, George G. Harrap, 1973, p. 156.
10. Ibid., p. 51.
11. Ibid., p. 52.

12. Ibid., p. 158.
13. Bauer, op. cit., p. 101.
14. Griffin and Enos, op. cit.
15. Ibid.
16. It really will not do, as a way out of the difficulty, to say that 'public and private capital flows to the underdeveloped countries are often linked through the practice of aid-giving agencies of making their assistance contingent upon the willingness of the recipient countries to encourage foreign private investment' so that 'the effects of aid upon development cannot, in practice, be separated from the effects of private foreign capital on development'. (Griffin and Enos, op. cit., p. 324.) Even if their effects cannot be separated, it does not mean that the differences between them can be ignored, or that judgements about aid can be based on the effects of total inflows.
17. Bauer, op. cit., p. 101.
18. Ibid.
19. Griffin and Enos, op. cit., p. 326.
20. *Mbenzi*, the man who drives in a Mercedes Benz.

INDEX

For Product Safety Concerns and Information please contact our EU representative GPSR@taylorandfrancis.com
Taylor & Francis Verlag GmbH, Kaufingerstraße 24, 80331 München, Germany

www.ingramcontent.com/pod-product-compliance
Ingram Content Group UK Ltd.
Pitfield, Milton Keynes, MK11 3LW, UK
UKHW020011200926
475702UK00014B/1832
* 9 7 8 0 4 1 5 8 4 5 9 8 4 *